VALUE ECONOMICS

VALUE ECONOMICS

THE STUDY OF IDENTITY

SAM LACROSSE

Hardcover ISBN: 978-1-5445-2943-1
Paperback ISBN: 978-1-5445-2942-4
Ebook ISBN: 978-1-5445-2944-8
Audiobook ISBN: 978-1-5445-3210-3

To those that tell the truth.

"A change in values—that means a change in the creators of values.
He who has to be a creator always has to destroy."
—FRIEDRICH NIETZSCHE

"I know I'm gon' get got.
But I'm gon' get mine more than I get got doe."
—MARSHAWN LYNCH

CONTENTS

WHAT CAME BEFORE

"Alright, how's everybody? Good, good, good! Now, as your father prob-ably told you, my name is Matt Foley, and I am a motivational speaker! Now, let's get started by me giving you a little bit of a scenario of what MY LIFE is all about! First off, I am thirty-five years old, I am divorced, and I live IN A VAN DOWN BY THE RIVER!"[1]

FOR THOSE UNAWARE, THOSE LINES WERE SPOKEN BY THE funniest man to ever walk the stage of *Saturday Night Live*, Chris Farley, in his introduction to the funniest sketch that has aired during the show's near-forty-five-year history: "Matt Foley the Motivational Speaker." There are three reasons I chose to open with that quote.

The first reason is that it's fucking hilarious. It's my book; I do what I want.

The second reason is that it's the absolute perfect example of an in-troduction for any circumstance. Matt Foley shows you exactly who he is in that thirty-six-second carpet bomb of yelling. He doesn't give a single one of his ex-wife's shits what you think of it. This is who he is. He is here. He is Matt Foley. And there ain't a damn thing you can do about it.

It's a shame we don't do that anymore. We don't want to declare anything. We don't know who we are.

Let's expand on that point for a little bit. Each generation has something that I like to call a "Fatal Flaw." Something so obscenely backward about their version of society that we now condemn it because we now know it is, indeed, obscenely backward. Four generations of my family have lived in America, including myself, and I think I have a pretty good idea of what their respective Fatal Flaws are.

For my great-grandfather's generation, it was an intolerance of anyone who simply was not them. My great-grandfather was a straight-off-the-boat, Ellis-Island Italian. The guy who stamped his papers changed his last name from "LaCrucci" to "LaCrosse" because LaCrucci "sounded too Italian." I might change it back depending on how badly people flame this book on the internet.

Italians associated with Italians. Germans associated with Germans. Irish associated with Irish. That's how things like the Five Families of New York[2] and the boroughs of downtown Cleveland, where I'm from, came about. It's why there are Chinatowns and a street where you can find bomb Italian food in almost every major city in America. There wasn't really any crossing those boundaries back then. I think anybody fortunate enough to have living grandparents can attest to that reality.

For his son's, my grandpa's, generation, the Fatal Flaw was interethnic intolerance. My grandpa, an Italian, married my grandma, who was Czechoslovakian. My grandpa's dad made his living through manufacturing, my grandma's dad through farming. That really didn't matter much to my grandparents, although I assume it sure as shit mattered to my great-grandparents. However, my grandparents' generational tolerance to people with different cultural backgrounds went completely out the window when people who weren't white got involved in the picture (save for the few Mexican workers my grandma's family hired as seasonal farm hands, and take from that what you will). Anybody black, brown, or Asian was automatically in a "don't-go-there" zone.

White people associated with white people. Black people associated with black people. Hispanic people associated with Hispanic people. Asian people associated with Asian people. The list goes on. Until the Civil Rights Movement came about, there was hardly any disruption in this system.[3] And even then, a lot of people in my grandparents' generation didn't like the ensuing changes.

For my grandpa's son's, my dad's, generation, the Fatal Flaw can be seen through the Pride movement. Within my parents' generation, there was still some lingering bias from parental influence toward folks of other ethnicities, but it wasn't nearly as prominent as the upheaval caused by the struggle for gay rights in that era. Throw that pot roast of cultural change seasoned with a combination of the AIDS epidemic, Elton John, Freddie Mercury, and Magic Johnson into the oven at 350 for about twenty years, and you're gonna have people in my parents' generation a little spooked.

Straight people associated with straight people. Gay people associated with gay people. The list goes on.

For my dad's son's generation, my generation, Gen Z, the young people today, it is...?

That's the thing. The younger generation doesn't have the cognitive functionality to know what the fuck we're getting wrong about society. We can all mostly agree that the preceding generations were right about their Fatal Flaws. By almost all metrics (by most, not all, accounts, I should note), we are the most accepting, generous, and tolerant generation that has walked the earth. Frankly, it's not even close.

So, what now? What does a warrior do when there is no war to fight? No enemy at the gate? No dragon to slay?

The warrior turns inward and finds something he doesn't want to see. His own Fatal Flaw embedded deep within himself. He searches his identity for the answer then stumbles upon it in all its horror.

He has none.

That is our generation's Fatal Flaw. We have no identity. We've been so scarred by both the pains of our past and our own modern society that we refuse to acknowledge what we truly believe. We're too afraid to do so. It might get us in trouble with a friend or relative. It might cause some discomfort at work. It might cause us to fight with our significant other.

We've already talked about the sins of our past. But what of the problems of the present? Social media displays a highlight reel of nearly everyone in our generation that can be seen by anyone with an internet connection.[4] It showcases the extremes of human nature, the incredibly breathtaking and the atrociously horrible, in five-minute compilations not unlike the ones we'd find on Pornhub.[5] This has caused us to adopt a paralyzing fear of disconformity. We don't want to seem out of the loop and out of place. We're so afraid of taking a stance that we take no stances. We're so anxious about our choices that we make no choices. We're so petrified by the consequences of our actions that we take no actions. We'd rather be a purposeless ball of bleh. That's more comfortable. That's easier.

This might seem odd to some. We're more technologically advanced than ever before. Our healthcare, no matter what you think of the distribution system, is light-years ahead of where it was even ten years ago.[6] We have these things called "vaccines" now. An astronomically lower number of women die in childbirth.[7] An overwhelming number of children that survive childhood don't die until they're a ripe, old age.[8] We're more educated by a long shot.[9] Most of us can read and speak properly.[10] We're less racist, sexist, and any other -ist or -ism you can think of than ever before.[11] These are all very good things.

But, paradoxically, we're a lot worse off in a lot of areas. The rates of mental illness, specifically anxiety and depression and even more specifically for young women and girls, have skyrocketed.[12] We're more doped up and medicated than ever before.[13] We'd rather numb our emotions than feel them. Everybody seems to hate each other. A new calamity drops a nuke on our lives every day via our Facebook feeds. Automation is threatening to take a scythe to the innocent wheat field of truck drivers[14] and call-center workers,[15] two of the largest labor pools in America. And, despite all our advances in healthcare, male life expectancy has gone *down*.[16] The reason? A perfectly blended cocktail of drug overdoses and suicides. A recent report suggests the overall life expectancy in America has shed more than a year because of the toll of the COVID-19 pandemic.[17] In short? More and more people are thinking this whole "America" thing doesn't work for them anymore.[18]

Back to previous generations. We don't want to shit on them too much, just like we don't want our grandchildren to shit on us too much for being purposeless balls of bleh. What did these folks have that we don't? What bonded them together? What created that harmony inside groups before we fucked it all up?

Their values.

Say what you want about the actions or intentions of any of the above communities, but they all had an incredible sense of what was important to them. Most of them still do. The black community is strong when it sticks together. As is the Hispanic community, and the Jewish community, and the Italian community, and all the rest.

They had a culture, one defined by a set of principles that created a unilateral purpose for them to strive toward together. Tremendous accomplishments have been made because of these principles—look no further than the aforementioned Civil Rights and Pride movements for proof. But there's one problem: this approach is outdated.

Because now, all those barriers are broken down. As we've progressed further into our culture, we've come to accept that identity is malleable. It is not defined solely by a group of any kind but rather by who we are at the individual level. Group identity, as we've come to discover, is incredibly dangerous when it is the only thing we can rely on to define who we are. What does it mean to be a black person? A lesbian? A transgender man? We know what these identities are by their base definitions, but it is strictly impossible to know what they are in actuality.

Because in the end, a group is defined, in aggregate, by a series of individuals. And the thing that separates the individual from the group is what comprises that specific individual. That cannot be defined by stereotyping it against a group. That is a cheat against individual sovereignty, a robbery of the highest order of the thing we should all hold dearly above all else. Our individuality is sacred, something bestowed upon us to shape what we believe to be true about ourselves by ourselves.

Any attempt to weaponize the group to define the individual is not an act of "solidarity" or "unity." It is an act of totalitarianism and indoctrination. It is an act that should not be tolerated. While a group of individuals, as above referenced, can make miraculous strides to improve the lives of the group as a whole, it serves no purpose at the individual level other than to conform the individual to whatever the collective group (most likely a mob) would like that individual to conform to.

So what must we do when those barriers are broken down? When those silos have all converged? When we really don't give a shit about shit that didn't mean shit to begin with?

We must redefine our own values for our own purposes.

We have no identity because we've never been at this point before. For the vast majority of history, we had to deal with crises of the material. But now, when we have all the material things we could ever want and more, we have to search for something greater—meaning. The problem has flipped, and we don't know how to adjust. We have no identity because we've neglected looking inward at what we believe as *individuals* as opposed to what was opposing the *collective*. We have no identity because we have finally realized that the hardest war for the warrior to win is the one within himself.

We must fight this internal war. We must find our identities. We must be proud of them. We must accept others and be proud of them for fighting the good fight. But to do that, the fight itself must be good.

Which leads me to my third reason for starting this book with Matt Foley and his van down by the river. Chris Farley, other than being the funniest person to ever walk the earth, is also one of the most tragic people you'll ever read about. Chris Farley was a good person, a genuine Gold Soul. He was incredibly generous, kind, and loyal.

But Chris Farley had our generation's same Fatal Flaw. He had no identity.

The reason Chris Farley had no identity was because what he thought was his identity was not his identity at all. It was a mirage, one hastily propped up by shitty values. I don't want to put too much blame on Farley. But, at the end of the day, he was an adult. He had opportunities and a responsibility to fix his life. He didn't take advantage of those opportunities and unfortunately paid the ultimate price for it much sooner than any of us would have liked.

The main value that drove Farley was a massive need for outside validation. This was something baked into the Farley family cake and centered around the one person whose validation meant the most, especially for a young boy growing up in the Midwest: his dad.

Mr. Farley was an incredibly nice guy. He owned an asphalt contracting company and made good money. The Farleys were not poor by any means. But growing up with three brothers and a sister, Farley had to find a way to stand out. That way was comedy.

Farley intensely studied the greats, most notably (and ironically) John Belushi of the original *Saturday Night Live* cast. He became a living caricature, the guy who could make anyone laugh at any scenario at any time. But he eventually left his old personality behind entirely. The caricature consumed the man. Chris Farley no longer existed—only his desired projection of Chris Farley did.

After scraping through college, Farley briefly worked for his father before auditioning with a friend for The Second City, the legendary improv club in Chicago. He was a hit right from the go.

When Farley got to The Second City, the manager and owner, Del Close, gave him both the most important and most devastating piece of advice of his entire life: "Attack the stage like a bull."[19] And attack it he did. Farley's stage presence became something of legend. No one had ever seen anything like it. I personally don't think we've seen something like it since. He had the incredibly unique ability of getting so amped up for everything that nothing else mattered to the audience but him. He was electric.

However, that advice didn't stop at comedy. Farley had already been a shithead, like most early-twenty-year-olds, when it came to things like alcohol and weed. He began attacking those like a bull, too, and in greater quantities. It wasn't long before he was on cocaine and heroin. His apartment was a consistent mess. He never had to be responsible for anything—his parents were funding his entire living situation from back home in Wisconsin.

Farley was so unbelievably excellent so unbelievably fast that he soon catapulted himself onto *Saturday Night Live* during one of the show's greatest runs, becoming great friends with legends like David Spade, Adam Sandler, Chris Rock, Tim Meadows, Dana Carvey, Mike Myers, and Rob Schneider. Farley was the best out of them all. They all willingly admit it too.

But there were some issues right off the bat, most notably the immortal "Chippendales" skit, where Farley was forced to dance shirtless next to the lion-haired heartthrob of the 1980s, Patrick Swayze. It was only his fourth sketch on the show. That one act would define him as the "fat-funny" guy and haunt him for the rest of his days. His friend Chris Rock saw trouble immediately:[20]

> "Chippendales" was a weird sketch. I always hated it. The joke of it is basically, "We can't hire you because you're fat." I mean, he's a fat guy, and you're going to ask him to dance with no shirt on. Okay. That's enough. You're gonna get that laugh. But when he stops dancing you have to turn it in his favor. There's no turn there. There's no comic twist to it. It's just fucking mean. A more mentally together Chris Farley wouldn't have done it, but Chris wanted so much to be liked…
>
> That was a weird moment in Chris' life. As funny as the sketch was, and as many accolades as he got for it, it's one of the things that killed him. It really is. Something happened right then.

The bigger the star, the bigger the validation and the harder Farley went. His addictions soon began to follow him to work. He would regularly show up drunk and stoned. He did hard drugs in the office he shared with David Spade to keep his high. His weight ballooned. He was threatened with termination by Lorne Michaels, the creator of *Saturday Night Live*, three times. He swore to get his act together. He never did.

Farley was on a downward spiral fueled by alcohol, drugs, obesity, and validation. Fatty can only fall down so many times. Finally, on December 18, 1997, after seventeen stints in rehab, a couple of hit movies, and a truly valiant effort to kick his demons, Farley fell down for the last time.[21] He overdosed on a speedball of cocaine and morphine while with a $300-per-hour call girl in a hotel room in Chicago. After Farley begged for help and passed out, the call girl robbed him of his watch and left him spread eagle on the floor wearing only pajama bottoms. He was thirty-three years old.

But that wasn't the saddest part. According to police testimony from the woman, Farley didn't call her for sexual favors: he called her because he didn't want to do drugs alone.[22] Or worse, in front of his friends, where the shame would cast him into darkness once again. He just didn't want to be by himself when his own personal darkness inevitably came to claim his soul once again.

Chris Farley did not deserve that fate nor the humiliation that came with it. Yet, that's exactly what he got. You see, you don't get what you deserve. You don't get what you want. You get whatever the fuck the world decides to spit at you. What you do with that is up to you.

The focus of this book will be on the "up to you" part. In order to handle the storms of life, we must reclaim our identities through our values. However, we must use our values wisely. Chris Farley had some great values: he was kind, volunteered at children's hospitals, went to church every Sunday, and treated people with respect. The problem was that they dominated a very small portion of his value pie chart. The bad consumed the good, which ended up consuming him. Therefore, we must fill our value pie chart with (wait for it) good values.

But, as the ever-wise DMX once said, "Talk is cheap mothafucka!"[23]

There are many "self-help" con artists out there who use cheap nonsense like "love yourself" and "treat others the way you want to be treated" to make a lot of easy money from emotionally and mentally weak people. But you know what those platitudes are? Weak. They're simply words that anyone with an internet domain can pull out of their ass and throw onto a Microsoft Word document in order to make people "feel better."

This book's goal is not to make you feel better. Well, at least not in the way we're used to. If you're looking for a book that will tell you you're amazing, and you just need to find yourself and pull said words out of your ass, put this down and get you and your ass back to the self-help section. We're going into uncharted territory.

And that's where the title of this book comes in. In this day and age, it's not enough to just have values anymore. No. It's about our ability to use them to their greatest effect that will prove the difference.

According to the dictionary, the definition for the word "value" is "relative worth, utility, or importance."[24] The definition for the word "economics" is "a social science concerned chiefly with description and analysis of the production, distribution, and consumption of goods and services."[25] That last definition is a bit boring and stiff. Basically, think of economics as how we use our resources, which can be anything depending on the context of the conversation.

However, we still have a problem. Seeing as our identity groups are all but disintegrating in front of our very eyes, it is not useful to define individual value hierarchies in the form of a group identity—that defeats the whole purpose. Thus, we must create our own values from an individual level while simultaneously making sure they do not get in the way of anyone else pursuing the same goal.

Therefore, I define "Value Economics" as this: "how well one uses their values, and how those values intertwine with other factors in their life in order to navigate life itself without harming or infringing on anyone else's right to do the same."

A lot of you are probably about to blow chunks at the very mention of the word "economics." I get it. It's not sexy. It's not going to get you a bunch of likes on your photo-sharing social media site of choice. But that's exactly the point. You see, the best things in life are usually mundane. Boring, even. They don't get a lot of attention in mainstream media or Twitter algorithms.

You probably don't feel like your genitals are connected to a lightning rod when you kiss your spouse before you go to catch the subway every single morning. You probably don't feel like Leonardo DiCaprio's Jordan Belfort when you email a spreadsheet to your boss. You probably don't feel like the fake Jordan Belfort's wife, Margot Robbie, when you throw on a little bit of eyeliner and mascara, scarf down an English muffin coated with non-organic peanut butter, and drop your kids off before work in a used 2017 Honda Civic.

But yet, we still do these things.

We do these things because they provide a stable source of value in our lives. Surprises once in a while can be fun. Don't get me wrong. It's fun to go a little wild with your spouse during your "special alone time." It's fun to land a giant-ass sale and high-five Bob from accounting in a three-coffees-deep euphoria of emotion. It's fun to find out your son tripped and impaled his arm on a fork that was sticking upward in the dishwasher fifteen minutes after it happened when he calmly walked up to you and pointed at it. My brother did it once. He'll back me up.

But these cannot be relied on. These temporary highs are not fulfilling in the long run. Nothing gold can stay. If it could, we'd have cracked the magic code with the cocaine era of the 1980s. We'd just do a shit ton of blow all the time, and our problems would disappear. But blow has bad effects too. You go crazy. You crash your car. You smash mirrors. You do more blow. And then you pass out in a puddle of your own urine. This is not good.

We need something real to back up our values. This is why economics is so important. Economics, other than the definition above, has another definition, at least in my world: "How many fucking graphs can you draw?"

The answer? A *whole lot*. Economics has lasted so long as an academic study because we've realized over time that we can rely on a few of those whole lot to make sense of that particular field. They have never betrayed us and most likely never will. Anomalies happen, just like surprises in our lives, but they are few and far between.

Our values are the same way. We must know how to use our values in the proper way to navigate life. Only then can we have even a slight chance of getting what we deserve or want. Gone are the days of abstract statements and well-meaning words. Good riddance. You're a Value Economist now, baby.

Value Economics is meant to keep you on track. To qualitatively and quantitatively reassure you whenever you question yourself. To let you know when you're fucking up and how. To help you understand what caused a certain thing to happen and how to make sure it doesn't happen again. To keep a system for doing the most important thing: deploying your value resources. They are the most precious resources. They can't be wasted. And hey, if you miraculously end up learning about economics, that's great too.

But, most importantly, I believe this is the crucial step for reclaiming our identities as individuals. In the Western world, what made us so different from the East we left was that our culture was not focused on groups but on individuals. Based on great things and thinkers like the ancient Stoics and Enlightenment philosophy, our founders crafted a society in which individual responsibility and values were to reign supreme over the tyrannical collective.[26] And they were right to do so.

Because a non-tyrannical collective must start with a non-tyrannical self. The warrior must first master himself before he can assume the responsibility of doing his part in the war. Only when we establish our own identity can we contribute to something greater than that identity. That is the highest virtue. That is what purpose is. That is what identity is.

This book is set up in a specific way. The chapters are meant to be read in sequential order and accomplish two things. First, they will serve as an introduction to Value Economics, showing you how to qualitatively and quantitatively define and implement your own set of personal values. Second, they will show you how to take those defined and implemented values and use them to successfully interact with the world. The steps described in this book must be done in the order in which they are laid out, or the system cannot be implemented. The order is essential.

One last thing before you dive in. To put you all at ease, let me belt out my own Matt Foley-esque introduction to show you exactly what my identity is:

Alright, how's everybody? Good, good, good! Now, as nobody on the face of this fucking earth probably told you, my name is Sam LaCrosse, and I am a nobody, wannabe internet blogger who wanted to try his hand at becoming a nobody, wannabe author! Now, let's get started by me giving you a little bit of a scenario about what MY LIFE is all about. First off, I am a twenty-four-year-old recent college grad working an entry-level job, I've never had a romantic relationship that's lasted more than eight months, and I GOT THE LOWEST POSSIBLE SCORE ON MY AP ECONOMICS EXAM IN HIGH SCHOOL!

I want to come clean from the jump. I'm young. I don't have a lot of wisdom about "the way things work around here." I've been paying bills with non-parental money only for a little over eighteen months. I haven't been in a long-term relationship or a marriage. I don't have kids. I don't know what it's like to have the responsibility of owning a home or a business. I'm not that smart. I certainly am not that smart when it comes to economics. I'm just a young kid, trying to make his way in the world, who decided to start a low-traffic internet blog and then write a book on some of the stuff he posted on it. A lot of you are probably skeptical about what I can teach you about anything. Those foundations are warranted, and I accept my lack of life experience for what it is.

But I do know a thing or two about values. I don't think it takes much life experience to know what those are, to be honest. As Forrest Gump once said, "I'm not a smart man, but I know what love is."[27]

Additionally, in these times that change by the second, I think we need a nuanced approach. Something more agile and nimble to guide us through the turmoil of life. You can't help yourself without knowing what's important to you.

My aim with this book is to use the study of Value Economics to teach you how to find what that "important" is for you. What guides you through life and gets you through the darkness. What provides the rock upon which to build your proverbial church. What gives you your identity.

If there's one thing that's gotten me through life so far, it's the effective use of my values and learning from the people that taught them to me. I hope this knowledge can provide the same solace to you as it has to me. Let's get started.

"*Awesome!*" (Farley voice)[28]

CHAPTER ONE

THE FACTORS OF
VALUE PRODUCTION

"The fault, dear Brutus, is not in our stars,
But in ourselves, that we are underlings."
–CASSIUS, AS WRITTEN BY WILLIAM SHAKESPEARE (*JULIUS CAESAR*, 1599)

WORTH FROM THE WORTHLESS

I FEEL LIKE TWENTY-SOMETHING ANGST IS A GOOD PLACE to start when it comes to Value Economics. And I can't think of a more fitting example than the Most Angsty Twenty-Something Ever, Billie Joe Armstrong.

In early 1990s, Billie Joe Armstrong was the lead singer of a small band from the San Francisco Bay Area. The band had put out two albums on a smaller scale[29] and was searching for their big single that would help them go mainstream. One day, with his friend and bandmate Mike Dirnt, inspiration finally struck.

The story goes something like this. The two friends get really fucking high on LSD. Dirnt writes the iconic baseline for a song while orbiting somewhere around Jupiter. The two then pass out, wake up the next morning, scribble down what they could remember from their adventure, and ship it out as their big debut single as a band. The song is called "Longview," which acts as the first single from their then-little-known band Green Day.[30] Dirnt recalled the memory vividly in an interview with *Rolling Stone*:[31]

> "When Billie gave me a shuffle beat for 'Longview,' I was frying on acid so hard. I was laying up against the wall with my bass lying on my lap. It just came to me. I said, 'Billie, check this out. Isn't this the wackiest thing you've ever heard?' Later, it took me a long time to be able to play it, but it made sense when I was on drugs."

It apparently made sense to others as well. The song was an absolute smash hit.

Green Day went on later that year to be nominated for four Grammy awards, including Best Hard Rock Performance for "Longview," and to win one for Best Alternative Music Performance for the accompanying album, *Dookie*.[32] The song was rated by *Rolling Stone* as the third-best single of 1994,[33] an astounding feat for a small punk band competing with the titans of the '90s grunge movement, like Nirvana, Pearl Jam, The Smashing Pumpkins, Soundgarden, and Stone Temple Pilots.

So what made the song so good? What about it sent Green Day into the stratosphere?

I'll tell you. The song, quite simply, is about nothing. Nothing at all. Throughout the lyrics of the song (a whopping 244 words in total strung out over more than four minutes, a good portion of them repeated), Armstrong sings about being bored out of his fucking mind.[34] He sits on his ass, watches TV, shits on his mom, jerks off a lot, waits for someone to call him (no one does), and smokes weed. Armstrong recalled his inspiration from his expedition to Jupiter in an interview with VH1:[35]

"I was just in a creative rut. I was in-between houses sleeping on people's couches. It's a song trying not to feel pathetic and lonely…I was coming from a lonely guy's perspective: no girlfriend, no life, complete loser."

I was floored when I heard this. "Bite my lip and close my eyes, take me away to paradise" was about him tenderizing his man meat? Not about something meaningful or philosophical? As a hardcore fan back in the elementary school days, I was peeved.

It took me another decade to discover why the song had the impact it did. But when the epiphany materialized, it all made sense: everything is worthless.

Everything. We spend every waking moment of our lives making up ideas and stories based on no empirical evidence whatsoever. These are the stories we tell ourselves. We're purposeless balls of bleh, remember? Who is to say that everything else isn't the same?

* * *

IN 1953, THE WORLD WAS introduced to perhaps the finest Western of all time: *Shane*.[36] The titular character is a rogue drifter who wanders into a Plains town sometime after the Civil War. During his journey, he comes upon a small farm run by a family of three: a father named Joe, a mother named Marian, and a young boy named Joey. Shane agrees to stay at the farm in exchange for his labor.

As the film rolls along, Shane discovers the rest of the town is pinned under the thumb of a cattle rancher named Ryker, who is not relinquishing land the other settlers have claimed under the Homestead Acts.[37] Shane and Joe get into a fight with Ryker's men, who vow revenge.

Shane is a skilled gunfighter. He's also grown attached to Joey. Knowing that trouble is coming for the whole family, Shane teaches Joey how to shoot. The young man is thrilled. *Finally*, someone who sticks up for himself! *Finally*, someone who can fight back! *Finally*, someone who isn't afraid.

Joey's mother is appalled when she finds out. She sends Joey away, telling Shane that guns will not be a part of Joey's life. Shane replies, "A gun is a tool, Marian, no better or no worse than any other tool: an axe, a shovel, or anything. A gun is as good or as bad as the man using it."[38]

Marian isn't convinced. She retorts, "We'd all be much better off if there wasn't a single gun left in this valley—including yours."[39]

Shane's point is eerily reminiscent of Armstrong's. Shane doesn't believe in the worth of guns. He only believes in the worth of the person wielding them. A man who doesn't know how to swing an axe can't chop down a tree. A shovel can't dig a hole if the person using the shovel doesn't know how to dig.

Without purpose, everything *is* worthless. Without something to derive that purpose from, we are adrift, set to fend for ourselves in an endless sea of nothingness.

But we are not without tools. They're all around us. They create ways for us to carve meaning out of nothing. They give us abilities beyond what we could have ever imagined before we knew of their existence.

However, these tools must be used constructively. The same cavemen that used stones to strike sparks and create fire also used them to bash other cavemen's heads in. The same scalpel a surgeon uses to save someone in emergency surgery can be used by a depressed teenager, whose parents are going through a divorce, to slit his wrists. A religion that gives inspiration and light to so many can also be used as a manifesto of death and suffering for so many others.

Because, ultimately, it is what we do with these tools that determines our fate. Prior generations knew what these tools were. They used them to build cities, defend our country, and lift billions out of poverty. But they also used them to discriminate, segregate, and terrorize.

There is good and bad in all of us. You and I are no different. It's true that we as a species are more accepting and tolerant in general now than we were further back in our genealogy. But it's also true that we're the most tolerant with whom we're supposed to be the most intolerant when it comes to slipping down the slope to aimlessness: ourselves.

Only you can derive worth from the worthless for yourself. Our values are the way we do this. Remember the definition of value: "relative worth, utility, and importance." Tools are meant to be utilized, so we can utilize our values as personal tools to create meaning.

Billie Joe Armstrong understood this. He used the tools of twenty-something angst and malaise toward the world and created one of the greatest punk-rock songs in the history of music. He created something of incredible meaning for so many people from the maw of arguably the most meaningless things on Earth. Ask any guy who has jerked off as much as he does in that song. And yes, it does start to hurt when you do it that many times in a day.

However, values are something that people get wrong all the time. The self-help industry is the worst offender. "Anyone can have it all!" "You're special; you just need to manifest that specialness!" "Work hard, be positive, and you can accomplish your dreams!"

It all sounds nice. It makes people feel good. It probably would look good on a laminated poster in the lobby of your local insurance agency.

But those, my friends, are lies. Not everyone can have it all. Not everyone is special. Working hard and staying positive will *not* ensure everyone achieves their dreams. Some can and will have "it all," whatever that means. Some are special. Working hard and staying positive are admirable qualities in some cases. But not all.

Only when you have the proper values in place that work for you can you even stand a chance against life. This is how we combat our generation's Fatal Flaw. We must use our values to derive meaning and then translate those values to define meaning on a personal level. An efficient use of values will allow us to formulate our beliefs about the world and operate in it with purpose. Value Economics is the study of how to do this.

But we must be conscious of their permanence, of the double-edged sword that comes with having defined values. We must be self-aware. We must know what can happen through the inefficient use of our values. We must always be cognizant. We must always test and reexamine our values, or they will destroy rather than enrich our lives.

THE FACTORS OF PRODUCTION

Before we can practice economics, we need to form an economy. We need tools. In economics, these tools are known as the "Factors of Production."

According to the Federal Reserve Bank of St. Louis (SLF), one of the largest government observers of various economies, the Factors of Production are "resources that are the building blocks of the economy; what people use to produce goods and services."[40] Simply put, these factors allow an economy to function. Without specific inputs to produce goods and services, there cannot be a system involved with these goods and services. There must be a genesis, a beginning.

According to the SLF, there are four factors of production it considers inputs: land, labor, capital, and entrepreneurship. Let's go over these in turn.

"Land," as defined by the SLF, is "any natural resource used to produce goods and services. This includes not just land, but anything that comes from the land." Land can be the ground you walk on, minerals like copper or iron ore, or food like apples, barley, and wheat. They act as the raw supplies in the production process, the proverbial clay that will be molded to serve a designated function desired by the market.

"Labor" is defined as "the effort that people contribute to the production of goods and services." This is the waitress who brings you your burger and fries, the factory worker who runs the CNC machine at the hydraulic valve plant, or the adult film star of your preference. They all work for "wages," which are the main support for the income of most people in America.[41] Labor transforms the land into the goods and services that fulfill a function desired by the market.

"Capital" is left somewhat ambiguous by the SLF. What I define capital as is simply one thing: technology—technology leveraged by labor to better and more efficiently transform the land into goods and services. Some of the examples named by the SLF include buildings, machinery, and tools.

However, "technology" is a very broad term. This is where the "better and more efficiently transform" part of my definition comes in. Anything that makes the job of the labor to transform the land better and more efficient and specifically resides in the function of the job should be defined as capital, in my opinion. This can be an algorithm that a Silicon Valley startup uses to deliver better results to consumers. A thermometer that a pediatrician uses to take the temperature of a young child. A new position that the aforementioned adult film star uses to spice up the film. Capital serves as the leverage point for the labor to better and more efficiently transform the land into the goods and services desired by the market.

An "entrepreneur" is defined by the SLF as "a person who combines the other factors of production—land, labor, and capital—to earn a profit. The most successful entrepreneurs are innovators who find new ways to produce goods and services or who develop new goods and services to bring to market." Simply put, the entrepreneur is the catalyst that sparks the other factors to life.

Think of Bill Gates when he founded Microsoft.[42] In order to succeed, he needed the other three Factors of Production—land, labor, and capital. Gates' "land" was the materials used to make the discs the software was coded on, which were then sold to companies as technology that would help run their businesses. The "labor" was that of Gates, his co-founder Paul Allen, and the initial employees of the company like Andrea Lewis and Bob O'Rear (look up the OG photo of Microsoft's original team if you want a laugh).[43] The capital was the computers, office space, ink, microprocessors, and other things that expedited the labor of Gates, Allen, Lewis, O'Rear, and the rest. Combined together by Gates, these factors built Microsoft into one of the greatest business entities the world has ever seen.

You need all four factors to function properly in an economy. You cannot skimp on any one of them, or it will cost you. And, granted, you don't need to become a company like Microsoft in order to "function properly." There are plenty of small businesses and mom-and-pop shops that do this incredibly effectively as well. We cannot have economic concentration at either the big or small end of the company-size scale. That creates imbalance, which creates further societal pain that makes us all suffer. We're on a trend toward that now in areas such as finance, pharmaceuticals, and technology, where the markets are dominated by large companies such as JPMorgan Chase, Pfizer, and our friends at Microsoft.[44]

For an example of a company that is without effective land, take Silicon Valley giant Uber. Uber needs four things in order to function properly as a business: drivers, riders, cars, and an application to connect drivers to riders and process payments. The drivers act as the labor, the application and cars act as the capital, and Travis Kalanick (now ousted) and Garrett Camp provided the entrepreneurship.[45]

But what of the land? Where exactly does Uber extract its value from? Well, from the second thing I named in that list of Uber's needs—the riders. Without riders, the people who ride in the cars, Uber is worthless. Its stock goes to zero. A private equity executive loses out on her life savings and cries in her Bentley.

Investors are slowly realizing this. Uber was lauded pre-IPO as one of the greatest companies in the history of Silicon Valley.[46] An IPO, or initial public offering, is what happens when a company offers common outside investors the chance to invest in a company.[47] It also monetizes the company, shooting cash into its veins like a 0.300+ slugger from 1990s baseball.

But Uber's IPO did not go well.[48] Uber's valuation was inflated by its founders to raise expectations of a company worth as high as $120 billion,[49] an absolutely outrageous number even by Silicon Valley standards. At the time, Uber enjoyed a stronghold on the market, controlling 69 percent of the ride-sharing market, a feat potentially even more astounding than the valuation.[50] Uber eventually priced its shares at $45 a piece (totaling a valuation of around $82 billion, which was conservative at the time)[51] and hauled in an astounding $8.1 billion from outside investors. It was one of the top-ten largest IPOs ever in terms of valuation.[52]

But that didn't matter. The $82 billion debut valuation was 32 percent less than the $120 billion investors were expecting. That was $38 billion lopped right off the top, and $38 billion isn't small potatoes to any investor. Then came the decline. Realizing that Uber derived its value from nothing (like literally, nothing), the shares hit a low price of $26 per share, a 58 percent plunge from the IPO price and a whopping 78 percent less than what investors had originally pegged the company to be worth.[53]

The jury is still out on Uber. But in my estimation, it can expect a bumpy road ahead. For being worth all that money, Uber has yet to make a single cent of profit in its existence. Like, not even a penny. People keep shoveling money into a wood chipper, and Uber keeps throwing it out for the cows to shit all over it. It turns out when you have no real "land," it's hard to exist as a company. Especially one where the former CEO, Mr. Kalanick, turns out to be a pretty fucking terrible guy. Just ask the toxic workplace culture and sex scandals; they'll tell you.[54]

For an example of a company that is without effective labor, look at U.S. Steel.[55] Popularized by industrialist and "robber-baron" Andrew

Carnegie in 1901, U.S. Steel was one of the pillars of the US economy in the first half of the twentieth century, not unlike entities such as Apple and Goldman Sachs today. It seemed unstoppable.

Carnegie is potentially the richest American to have ever lived—his net worth was estimated to be $480 million in 1901, which was a whopping $372 billion in 2014 dollars.[56] That's $100 billion more than Elon Musk, the current richest person in the world at the time of this writing,[57] if you really get aroused by that type of thing.

But things have changed since Andrew Carnegie's reign. Due to factors such as the destruction of unionized labor and the rise of the North American Free Trade Agreement (NAFTA), manufacturing has fled the United States in droves.[58] Why? Because companies can simply get cheaper labor elsewhere in the world. Why pay a factory worker in the US $18 an hour with an attached medical plan and pension if you can pay someone in a country like Bangladesh $2 an hour with no attached benefits? It's simple math.

However, it turns out that U.S. Steel workers don't like it when you take that $18 an hour, medical plan, and pension away from them. They tend to like those things. But it was too little, too late. The blows had been struck. The United States manufacturing industry has taken a nosedive, with the manufacturing companies left to pay the price. U.S. Steel's stock as of this writing is currently trading somewhere around $22.99.[59] It was trading at $182.79 on June 20, 2008—you know, the year the entire world economy almost imploded.[60] U.S. Steel's 87 percent decline in price since that time shows that without "labor," you cannot have a functioning company.

For a company without capital, look to Blockbuster.[61] Blockbuster was once a titan in the film-rental industry. I'm old enough to remember when renting films was popular. It was a mammoth business. Renting films was cheap, convenient, and efficient for almost all consumers.

But then this thing called Netflix happened.[62] Netflix pioneered a then-little-known technology called "streaming." In perhaps the biggest business blunder of my lifetime, Netflix offered to be bought out by Blockbuster for a paltry $50 million.[63] Blockbuster said thanks, but no thanks. "That will never work" were the exact words used.

That spurning of capital would prove to be a Mike Tyson-esque uppercut to the future of Blockbuster. It turns out streaming does work and better than anyone expected. Netflix is now worth over $166 *billion*.[64] The last Blockbuster store in existence, located in Bend, Oregon, is a tourist attraction. It also rents out space as an Airbnb.[65] Without "capital," you cannot adapt.

And finally, a lack of entrepreneurship. A great example of this is the company WeWork, founded by Adam Neumann.[66] Neumann, a serial entrepreneur who was born in Israel, launched WeWork as an office-sharing space marketed to businesses as an alternative to renting dedicated offices of their own. Rent is among the most expensive fixed costs a company incurs.[67] WeWork looked to fix that by buying up rental properties and selling access to them in blocks of time so businesses could avoid rent and other overhead costs. It was a tremendous idea. Silicon Valley valued it at over $47 billion.[68]

But, much like Travis Kalanick, Adam Neumann turned out to be a Grade-A Jagoff. He wanted to do bizarre things like live forever, become "King of the World," and be the world's first trillionaire.[69] He was caught with a cereal box (not joking) full of weed on an overseas flight. When going through the IPO process, investors were shocked to learn he had stocked his company's board with family members, including his wife. Claims of drug use by company executives (see aforementioned cereal box), pregnancy discrimination, and sexual harassment ran rampant.[70]

Seeing enough, private equity firm Softbank (which was the majority investor in the company) forced Neumann out, gutted the rest of his staff, and did another steroid-shot of outside funding to try to save the company.[71] The valuation of WeWork fell from $47 billion to under $5 billion, more than an 80 percent drop in value.[72] It was one of the greatest pre-IPO implosions in the history of American business.

It turns out that when you have an incompetent entrepreneur at the helm, you cannot organize the other factors of production properly to get (wait for it) a competent company.

These factors are the genesis of any functioning economic entity. You need raw materials in order to transform them into goods and services. You need labor to produce that transformation. You need capital to facilitate the transformation and make it efficient and productive. And you need entrepreneurship to effectively organize and deploy the other three factors. Any lack of those four factors (throw in a cereal box full of weed for good measure) and an economic entity does not stand a chance of getting started.

THE FACTORS OF VALUE PRODUCTION

A lot of you are probably bored out of your fucking minds by now. Maybe some of you have returned the book already. I understand. That was a lot of tedious information, except potentially the part about the cereal box.

However, I do believe it is important to understand what makes up an economic entity. Why? Because in order to create a Value Economy, we need to understand what makes an economy productive. The same Factors of Production methodology that applies to all economies applies to Value Economies. There are still four factors. They still function with the same purposes. And they are all incredibly important—self-awareness the most so, which we will get to later. A lack in one of them will cause a failure in the Value Economy as a whole.

In a normal economic entity, land acts as the raw materials and supplies that make up goods and services. Labor acts as the action that transforms those raw materials and supplies into those goods and services. Capital acts as an expediter of that labor, making it more efficient. Entrepreneurship acts as the catalyst and deployer of the other factors to make the economic engine run properly.

The "Factors of Value Production" act in the same fashion. You need a raw source to draw from. You need something or someone to transform that raw source into a finished product. You need something to make that process of transformation efficient and continuously improve upon it. And you need something or someone to organize all the other factors in order to properly make a Value Economy.

When the Factors of Value Production are used properly, the finished product is a value. Something that can be created out of the ether, out of the meaninglessness of life, and deployed into the world to potentially give life meaning. But what is the genesis of our values? What are these Factors of Value Production?

In Value Economics, "land" represents our experiences. They are the raw sources of material from which we draw all meaning in our lives. They are the beginning point of Value Economics. Without experience, we cannot perceive anything. When we cannot perceive anything, we cannot derive anything from it, and most definitely not meaning.

Our experiences do not have to just be the gigantic moments in our lives. Life does not boil down to the moments that stand out most. In fact, it's quite the opposite. It is not one experience that defines our lives (although those definitely matter; more on this later) and therefore our values. No. It is the compounding of experiences over time that determines them. Those outstanding experiences, good or bad, are the exception, not the rule. It is patterns in life that we notice.

We are able to know what healthy relationships look like if we live our lives surrounded by healthy relationships. We know that neglect is not our parents leaving us at home by accident one time but rather by a pattern of inattentiveness and shunning. We know that efficiently working for something worthwhile for one day is not at all close to putting in the same efficient work for five days.

Those outlier experiences can be inflection points, certainly. They can provide a much-needed wake-up call. They can provide context. They can create a sense of fulfillment. These are things like marriages, acts of extreme violence, or mysterious, named-after-beer viruses that come from China to ravage the entire world on all fronts. We will examine these inflection points in Chapter Eight. These turning points are the most important drivers of change we will see in our lives.

But they are not what define us. Isolated acts of extreme behavior throughout the world do not define a complex system. A Middle Eastern Islamic terrorist suicide bombing an embassy does not mean that all Middle Eastern Islamic folks are terrorist suicide bombers. A frustrated, twenty-something white guy from Appalachia deciding to beat up his girlfriend out of frustration does not mean that all frustrated, twenty-something white guys from Appalachia are naturally inclined to commit acts of domestic violence. A young black kid from a lower-income housing community who grew up without a father joining a gang does not mean that all young black men without fathers are destined to join gangs. Correlation does not necessarily equal causation. Do not pretend it does.

But there are trends that can lead to these outlier events. The suicide bomber that lit up an embassy might have been fed a shit-ton of nonsense about how killing people that don't believe what he does is a righteous act that will get him in good with Allah in the next life. So why not commit violence on innocent people? The white guy that abuses his girlfriend might have been told all his life that he and his struggles aren't real, that he is in some way "privileged" because of the color of his skin. So why not beat up the one person who he feels he may have power over? The young black kid might have been told that there was no way to escape his situation, that everything was rigged against him. So why not join the only group of people that would accept and mentor him?

Experiences build, and experiences last. They are the bedrock upon which we form our perceptions, which then automatically translate into our value hierarchy. These raw materials of our experiences are not the finished product but merely the input from which the finished product will be formed. Their importance to the construction of our value system cannot be overstated.

"Labor" in Value Economics represents our actions. They are the transformation of that raw material (our experiences) into a finished product (our values). This is the potential energy of our experiences being transformed into the kinetic energy that leads us toward our values. Without action, our experiences are meaningless. When we take no action, we cannot create anything that can even come close to value.

Like our experiences, our actions do not have to be big. They do not have to be gaudy goals that you write on a whiteboard like something out of *The Wolf of Wall Street*. I would not urge you to throw midgets at the wall either—they probably wouldn't like that all too much.[73]

In fact, I'm actually going to do something that isn't popular in our culture. I'm going to *discourage* you from having goals. Goals are meaningless without constructive, habitual behaviors that reinforce them.[74] They're just a metric, a number written down in some Excel spreadsheet buried under your fifty other get-rich-quick schemes. Goals are a target. They're not how you get there. The means through which you achieve that end matter, as does the intent that drives those means. Don't pretend they don't.

A teenage girl can lose weight by talking to her doctor about eating healthy and her volleyball coach about exercise regimens. Or that same teenage girl can starve herself and force her finger down her throat every night before bed. They're both effective, and they both work. Humans have an innate preference to default to the path of least resistance.[75] Eating healthy and exercising on a consistent basis are hard things to do. Starving yourself and forcing yourself to throw up also aren't easy, but they're less hard than the alternative. The choice is hers.

Our actions start early, usually stemming from good (or at least not-totally-garbage) parenting. We're told to brush our teeth for a decent amount of time twice a day. We're told to share and respect whatever authority figure is in the room. We're told when to eat, sleep, and shit.

We are told these things because they are foundational actions drawn from experience. Our parents and other mentors know how things work (or at least pretend to). They know if you don't brush your teeth, they'll eventually fall out. If you don't share, Johnny is going to whack you upside the head for not giving up the block with the number three on it. If you don't eat and at the proper times, you will starve and be miserable. If you don't sleep enough and at the proper times, your equilibrium and sense of existence will be all fucked up. If you don't know when to shit, all of the shit that stays inside of your body will eventually accumulate and cause you to explode. I don't know which one of the named scenarios is the most horrifying.

These habits, these actions we repeat in order to form the physical patterns reinforced by the mental patterns of our experiences, form the skeleton of our existence, of our Value Economy. We know they must be done repeatedly to have a chance at a meaningful existence. If we shun these patterns, these repeated, reinforced, physical behaviors derived from repeated, reinforced, mental experiences, bad things happen.

This is the suicide bomber bombing the building, the guy from Appalachia abusing his girlfriend, or the kid from the ghetto joining a gang. You see, when you don't have a constructive set of actions to build toward your goal, the goal becomes the only thing you focus on. You want to get it by any means necessary. The means, therefore, become worthless.

The suicide bomber knows only that he will go to heaven if he bombs that embassy. He does not care that he will kill people, destroy a building, and cause immeasurable devastation to the families and friends of the people he destroys. White Appalachia guy cares only about taking out his pain. He doesn't care that he will inflict that pain tenfold on his girlfriend, her family and friends, and any children who might look up to him. The kid who joins the gang cares only about a sense of acceptance, belonging, and kinship. He doesn't care about the ramifications of his potentially nefarious actions down the road.

Actions are the realization of our experiences into what we want to project into our world. They show others that this is what we are, and this is who we are. When we transform the raw source of our experiences into actions, we show the world what we value. This can be either a good or a bad thing depending on how we deploy those experiences to best serve our actions.

Which is where capital comes into Value Economics. "Capital" represents our self-awareness. Self-awareness is what we use to make the process of transforming (our actions) the raw materials (our experiences) efficient, as we continuously examine and improve upon it. It is one thing to just transform something from simple raw materials to a finished product. It is another thing entirely to refine our process of doing so and improve upon it to become better and more constructive in our everyday lives.

Think of this in terms of what capital is in the normal economy: technology. Would the world be better off if we were still traveling in steam engines, throwing sticks of lit dynamite at each other in coal mines, and sawing each other's limbs off with no anesthesia or sterilized instruments? The answer is an emphatic fuck no, we would not.

Technology is the means by which we improve our lives. It's much better that we have cars, precision engineering, and modern medicine than the tools that came before. It makes our work easier, less harmful, and more productive to society. Just ask those coal miners. Oh wait, you can't. They're dead. Probably from getting a stick of lit dynamite accidentally chucked at their nads when they weren't looking.

Our self-awareness acts as technology for our values. It is our efficiency optimizer and vessel of continuous improvement. It allows us to course-correct when we don't exercise good habits of action. It allows us to accelerate those actions into other actions.

This is the suicide bomber deciding, "Hey, maybe Allah will love me if I, in fact, don't kill and maim all of these people." The guy from Appalachia realizing his girlfriend didn't do anything wrong and instead initiating a constructive conversation about his problems. The kid from the ghetto seeking kinship in the form of a community center, religious leader, or other figure of authority who has made it out of his situation. These are not easy decisions to make, but they are undisputedly better than the alternatives.

But we must be careful with our self-awareness. Because whenever we pivot from our self-awareness, whenever we create a new technological innovation that can accelerate our actions, it can wreak as much destruction as construction. It can affirm our previously held beliefs if we do not challenge ourselves enough on them.

Maybe the suicide bomber decides to plant another bomb somewhere else before he bombs the embassy. More chances he gets into the Promised Land. Maybe Appalachia guy decides to threaten his girlfriend with a knife instead of his fists. Better chance to inflict more pain. Maybe the kid from the ghetto goes all in and engages in all sorts of nefarious activities. More ways to achieve acceptance from a group of peers.

Self-awareness is what we use to accelerate our habitual actions derived from our bedrock of experiences. It is the confirmation in what we believe about our perceptions. When that certainty sinks in, there is little we can do to stop it. A person who has been strongly reinforced with an innumerable amount of experiences, a set of defined habitual actions, and a self-aware perception of those actions is difficult to stop indeed.

And finally, entrepreneurship. "Entrepreneurship" in Value Economics represents discipline. Discipline is the organization of the raw source, the process of transforming that raw source, and the efficiency and continuous monitoring of that process. It is the glue that holds the other three factors together and the catalyst that galvanizes all the other factors to properly make a Value Economy. It is the gatekeeper to the finished product and ultimate goal: a value.

Entrepreneurship/discipline must be ubiquitous. There cannot be an off switch. It must filter into everything you do, especially in regard to your values. You cannot decide to use it sometimes but not others. Your values must always be on, or they are not your values.

I want to use this opportunity to drop a nuke on another sickening trend in today's culture: the myth of motivation. In a lot of circles, we're taught that motivation is the key to success in life. With only the proper motivation, with only the desire to do something, we can achieve something worthwhile.

Hey, see that paragraph up there? The one I just wrote? *Fuck* that paragraph, okay? It's dead to you. Take it out behind the barn and shoot it. Piss on its grave, if you even have the decency to bury it. I wouldn't.

You don't "sometimes" love your husband. You don't "sometimes" want your daughter to have a great education. You don't "sometimes" want to be yourself. Motivation is just a giant excuse for when you come up short at doing something you know you should do. It's a shortage of discipline, not an abundance of it. It is the canary in the coal mine for when you know bad shit is going to happen. Because if you only "sometimes" value something (probably only when it suits your short-sighted and selfish aims), you don't value it at all. Stop being fake. Don't pretend that you value it. You don't.

Discipline is the antidote to motivation. Author, thought leader, and former Navy SEAL Jocko Willink knows a thing or two about discipline. Probably more than a thing or two since he's based his entire adult life on the principle. Here's an excerpt from his book *Discipline Equals Freedom: Field Manual*:[76]

> Don't worry about motivation. Motivation is fickle. It comes and goes. It is unreliable and when you are counting on motivation to get your goals accomplished—you will likely fall short. So. Don't expect to be motivated every day to get out there and make things happen. You won't be. Don't count on motivation. Count on Discipline. You know what you have to do. So: MAKE YOURSELF DO IT. You do that with Discipline.

Sound harsh? Good, it's supposed to. That's exactly the way you should approach the organization and evaluation of your Factors of Value Production. You must be merciless with how you observe and derive meaning from them. Anything less than that, and you could potentially slip down a slope that is incredibly difficult to climb out of.

Discipline is what we use to effectively enforce the acceleration of our habitual actions derived from our bedrock of experiences. It is our character, and it is how we conduct ourselves. It is the presentation of all that we are made up of from a cognitive sense. That is why it is the most important quality to have. Without discipline, things can go off the rails. You could lose control of one of the incredibly few things you have control over. It's important to maintain that control—it is too precious to let it fall by the wayside.

GOOD VERSUS BAD

But the Factors of Value Production are only that—factors. They are not the finished product. Our values are. And like any factors that make up a process, they can make things that are good and things that are bad.

Before you accuse me of being a hypocrite and going against what I said earlier, allow me to explain. Most things *do* fall into the category of being a tool, values being one of them. The utility of those tools/ values is in the usage of those tools/values. That is true. However, there are things within the factors and the process that can create inherently bad outcomes. I can think of no place where this takes place more insidiously than in the creation of values. People adopt bad values all the time, formed from corrupted and tainted factors and processes.

Think of a person who is blatantly unhealthy. He can go to the gym and lift all the damn weight he pleases. She can run ten miles a day for a month. That is all fine and good. But it doesn't mean a fucking thing if that guy goes home and slams chocolate cake every day after work, and she goes home and emulates Chunk from *The Goonies* by dumping an entire aerosol can of whipped cream in her mouth.[77]

The inputs matter much more than the outputs. What we put in is what we get out. It does not work in reverse. If you build a house with shitty labor and materials, the finished good (the house) is going to be just that—shitty. The same thing works for hydraulic valves, mobile applications, and sex toys. It is the same deal with everything. It is the universal constant of creation. You must derive finished goods from high-quality sources, or the finished product will not be high quality.

Our values work the same way. We must optimize our Factors of Value Production to derive inherently good values from them. If we derive them from shitty sources, we get shitty values. 2 + 2 = 4.

So the question remains: what differentiates a good value from a bad one? There are a lot of things that fall into both buckets. However, I believe when you strip all those factors down to the studs, there are three things that make up a good value and their three opposites that make up a bad value.

Good values are constructive, habitual, and controllable. Shitty values are destructive, sporadic, and uncontrollable. Let's visit each of these in turn to figure out why.

The definition for the word "constructive" is "promoting improvement or development."[78] Think about it. You don't adopt something new because you think it will make your life worse, right? There might be some growing pains, like if you decide to stop doing heroin or to start working out for the first time in your life, but the long-term gain is optimistic. You get better from adopting something that is constructive.

The definition for the word "destructive" is "designed or tending to hurt or destroy."[79] Shit, even the definition sounds like it hurts. This should be pretty self-explanatory. You shouldn't want to willingly adopt things that are designed to hurt and destroy you. That does nothing for you or your identity. They act conversely to constructive values—they don't hurt that much in the short run, but they feel horrific in the long term. Your first hit of meth probably feels amazing. Your five hundredth probably feels like hell.

A good example of a constructive value would be forgiveness. Forgiveness is *hard*. Especially when something or someone really hurts you. Forgiving that entity probably is going to suck for a while after you initially do it. But, with time, the pain subsides, and you become at peace with yourself. You give yourself permission to move on. It directly correlates with promoting your improvement and development if you clear that nonsense and negativity from your brain.

The inverse of the constructive value of forgiveness would be the destructive value of vengeance. The act of taking revenge and holding grudges fits the "designed or tending to hurt or destroy" definition quite nicely. It might give you validation immediately if you act out of spite. You might even enjoy it for a while. But if you keep holding onto that dead weight, if you keep letting someone else own your brain's real estate, it will begin to poison you. Pessimism will fill your head and corrupt it. You will create nothing of value, only a conduit for devastation.

The definition for the word "habitual" is "regularly or repeatedly doing or practicing something or acting in some manner."[80] This correlates directly to your labor and actions within the Factors of Value Production. Your values must be something you can depend on, something you can live and practice regularly. If they are not used much, or at all, they are not values. They are simply something that happens to you. You are not acting them out for the sake of acting them out.

The definition for the word "sporadic" is "occurring occasionally, singly, or in irregular or random instances."[81] These are just things that happen to you or that you do once in a while. They are motivated not by honest living but by impulse and deeper, tribal tendencies. You cannot depend on these things over the long haul because they are things that cannot last. You are doing them only because you "feel like it." Nothing gold can stay.[82]

Intimacy is a good example of a habitual thing of value. The most intimate of intimate things, I would argue, is sexual intimacy in a committed relationship. If you and your spouse have good-natured sex on the regular, that is a good thing. Evidence proves this.[83] It binds two people in a committed relationship together. It is what sets that relationship apart from all the other relationships in your life. It is something you can depend on, live through, and practice regularly. However, you don't have to go full Jenna Jameson and Manuel Ferrara on each other every night for three rounds in order to value sexual intimacy. More on this later. (Not Jenna Jameson and Manuel Ferrara, but the whole "doing lots of things lots of times" thing.)

But let's say your wife offers you a threesome. Your mind explodes. Your dick follows shortly after. You have the threesome, and it's just as you pictured. It's amazing. Your fantasies are fulfilled. You can't wait to tell Bob from accounting the next morning (hint: do not tell Bob from accounting the next morning).

A couple days later, your wife wants to have sex again, but no threesome. Just boring, plain sex. You throw a bitch fit. Kind of like a two-year-old. You start yelling at your wife to GET A COT-DAMN SECOND WOMAN IN HERE STAT. Your wife is confused, hurt. Isn't sex with just her good anymore? Isn't she desirable to you?

If you value the sporadic thing (the threesome) over the habitual thing (the constant, regular sex), your sex life *isn't* good anymore. Your wife isn't desirable to you. But this is a shitty thing to value. Your wife loves you. She's the mother of your two kids. She cooks great meals and pops off a "you can do it, babe" text a couple times a week. She's loving and supportive. But you don't care because you've adopted the shitty value of the temporary over the permanent. You've chosen a thing that *feels* good over a thing that is good. You've traded the intimate for the aloof. You've taken a sledgehammer to the knee of one of the cornerstones of your life. Congrats, asshole.

The definition for the word "controllable" is "to exercise restraining or directing influence over."[84] This factor is the single most important one mostly because it feeds all the others. Your values are one of the few things you have direct choice and control over. It's remarkable how little we have command over in this life. Do not surrender that limited control under any circumstances. Anything that takes that control away from you is something you should not value. Anything externally motivated is something you should not value.

The definition for the word "uncontrollable" is "incapable of being controlled; ungovernable."[85] If you cannot control something, it is not yours. Remember, these are *your* values. You have possession. You have control. Anything that can hijack your brain and take your values away from you, steer clear of.

Things you can directly control (when used appropriately) can unlock great happiness. Things that are externally motivated and controlled by others can unlock incredible suffering.

This segues into a division I would like to highlight: Primary versus Secondary Values. Primary Values are things that are not derivatives of anything else. They are baseline and largely inarguable because they are pure in and of themselves. Secondary Values are the things that are derivatives of other things, specifically of Primary Values.

It's hard to argue with Primary Values, such as being part of a community or being honest. The purity of them gets rid of any scrutiny simply because of the logic packed into the definitions of those words. That is why you should desire to control only the controllable and let the uncontrollable simply fall by the wayside.

The uncontrollable is anything commanded by external factors. Your sexual orientation should *not* be something you value at the center of your being. Why? Because it's controlled by the outside validation of other people. You cannot decide what they believe defines your Secondary Value, positive or negative. Your partner, whoever that may be, cannot be controlled by you, unless you're some sort of sadistic fuck who likes manipulating other people like puppets. This is true whether you're straight, homosexual, bisexual, whatever. You should be proud of embracing who you are. But making something so uncontrollable by you the center of your identity is a very precarious thing to do. Your sense of being should *only* pertain to you. Whenever something goes wrong in a relationship, you have no opportunity to fix it simply because you do not have control over that person.

Your political affiliation should *not* be something you value at the center of your being. Why? Because you get one vote. That's it. You are lower than pond scum. The political party you affiliate with, whatever that may be, is not controlled by you. A democratic republic (which the United States is) is physically incapable of being controlled by one man or woman. A president does not open their to-do list and say, "Hmmm, let's see, I'm just gonna take a massive shit all over Sam LaCrosse's life today." You're not that important, trust me. You're nothing. By placing the control of another person (probably many other people) at the center of your being, your identity will be destroyed every time adversity hits.

That's why identity politics is such a dangerous game to play.[86] To base an opinion on a certain person or group just on the narrow specifics of a Secondary (uncontrollable) Value is ludicrous on its face. You beholden yourself to the preconceived notions and shallow judgments of other people, and you may beholden other people to your own. This assumes that because someone is black, a lesbian, or a woman, for example, they must behave a certain way because of their identity.

This is, of course, completely erroneous. What if that person has a different opinion than you about being black or a lesbian or a woman? What the fuck does that even mean? Well, it could mean a lot of things. People are very different, as we'll discuss in Chapter Nine. This is a very slippery slope to ride down. If you base your Value Hierarchy on Secondary Values, anything that threatens them (being black, lesbian, or a woman) will throw you into immediate defense. This is not good.

You know something that *is* controllable? Being nice. It takes little to no effort to hold a door for an elderly woman walking into a Michael's.

Additionally, it is completely in your control to hold that door. A two-for-one. You don't *have* to do it. You could just as easily let that door swing back, sweep the walker out from under the old lady, and watch her break her hip on the sidewalk. That's completely in your control, too, and doesn't take much effort. But the first alternative is much better than the second one.

Just as there are shitty factors that make up shitty finished products, there are shitty Value Factors that make up shitty values. It is our knowledge of the bases of the good factors that will provide the foundation of Value Economics. But that selection of values comes with a price.

NO MORE GUNS

If I had to sum up this entire chapter, it would be with one word: choice. You *choose* to define what your values are. You *choose* to either follow good or shitty values based on their corresponding good and shitty inputs. Every one of these things is up to you. It is an awesome responsibility. If you avoid responsibility, you avoid choice. If you avoid choice, you avoid consequences.

But this is a paradox. You are *always* choosing. You always accept the consequences. I know that writing this book is going to take a shit ton of time. I have accepted the consequence of that loss of time because I think this book is important. Your values are the biggest choices you can make in your life as they define your identity.

There is something you must know, a warning you must hear, before you progress further. Once you define your values, you must know that something is coming. Something that will immediately happen once you adopt your values and live honestly through them. It is the core consequence. It is what my generation is avoiding like the plague. It is why we have no collective and very few individual identities. However, it is the key to living a meaningful life: polarization.

Get this through your thick skulls right now. If you don't, the rest of this book will be meaningless (and maybe even offensive) to you. When you adopt your values and live honestly through them, you will alienate a lot of people. A lot of people will not want to be around you. They'll say things about how you've "changed" or "switched up." They'll talk shit about you. They'll stop liking your posts. They'll distance themselves from you and potentially flame you in group chats.

And this is perfectly natural.

Polarization shows you stand for something. It shows you're not going to conform into a purposeless ball of bleh. It shows you have an identity, and you can stick up for yourself and what you believe in. There is a reason entrepreneurs don't start a business that does everything (unless you're Jeff Bezos, and you are probably not Jeff Bezos; sorry to shit in your cornflakes).[87] You need to specialize, to find your niche. The rest of this book will be devoted to helping you find and live through that niche, starting with the process of value selection in the next chapter.

Billie Joe Armstrong knew he would piss people off when he wrote "Longview." Yet he did it anyway. Why? Because Billie Joe Armstrong and Green Day didn't give a flying fuck what other people thought of them. "Yeah, we're gonna write a song about jerking ourselves off on my mom's couch. Eat a dick, Establishment!" They decided something else was more important than the outside validation and approval of others. They lived through their value of sharing their outlook on life honestly from their perspectives.

This is a tough reality to accept. But with great responsibility comes great power, to quote the great Mark Manson.[88] It's a big task to step up to the plate and define who you are. You will hurt people and things when you do so, most importantly yourself. But you must take up the mantle. It is the only way forward.

SHANE UNDERSTOOD THIS. IN THE final scene of the film, Shane has dispatched the marauders who dominated the town. The citizens are freed from their oppression. But Shane has been shot. He's bleeding and bleeding badly. Just as he begins to do the whole "ride off into the sunset" thing, Joey shows up. He begs Shane to stay, but Shane says he cannot.

A brand sticks, he tells Joey. He knows perfectly well who he is. Shane is a skilled gunfighter and the savior of the town. But he's also a criminal and a murderer. His values are drawn in the same sand that he and the marauders' blood now seeps.

Joey doesn't understand. Not that any young boy would. He doesn't want to lose Shane, but Shane feels like he has to go. But before he does, Shane gives the young man some words of what he feels are encouragement. However, to Joey, they're more terrifying than any bullet fired that night.

"There are no more guns in the valley."[89]

CHAPTER TWO

LIVING AT YOUR
MEANS OF VALUE

"Every virtue carried to an extreme degenerates into folly or positive vice."

—UNKNOWN

EVIL INCARNATE

FEBRUARY 27, 2012 WAS, AT FIRST, A PRETTY NORMAL DAY. It was a Monday, and I was in the eighth grade, enrolled at my local middle school just outside Cleveland.

Little did I know that that day would give me my first glimpse of the purest evil this world has to offer. And little did I know that that evil would strike so close to where I lived.

At approximately 7:30 a.m., students gathered in the cafeteria at Chardon High School (located on the other side of Cleveland from my school) before they were released for class. Some bought breakfast and talked. Others waited to be bused to the local vocational school. All was calm.

Then the shooting started.[90]

Using a 0.22-caliber handgun, seventeen-year-old T. J. Lane stood up from his table and shot four male students. Three of them died within the next two days at the hospital. The one that survived was shot multiple times in the arm, back, cheek, and neck. He would later find out he would never walk again.

Lane fired another shot, grazing another student's ear. Lane tried to flee. He shot his last victim, a female student, during his flight. Both later recovered. Lane was chased out of the cafeteria by a football coach and apprehended by the police near his parked car outside Chardon High School.

T. J. Lane was, by all accounts, a normal kid. A friend interviewed on CNN after the incident said Lane always seemed sad but never spiteful.[91] Almost no one thought there was any way he could have done something like this. Lane's main target (and the first person he shot), Russell King Jr., had recently started dating Lane's ex-girlfriend. The two kids were going to fight. Lane had taken up weight lifting to prepare.[92]

T. J. Lane, despite being seventeen, was tried as an adult and sentenced to three life sentences, one for each of the teenage boys he slaughtered.[93] After a year spent in a juvenile center, Lane was sent back to court for his plea arrangement. He was expected to plead guilty. What was not expected was perhaps the most disturbing sequence of events of all.

Lane walked into the courtroom dressed formally. But about midway through the hearing, he took off his dress shirt to reveal a white undershirt. The word "KILLER" was written on it in magic marker; a smile from ear to ear painted his face. The smirk remained as his punishment was handed down. When the judge finished the sentence, he asked Lane if he had anything to say before they took him away.

Lane turned to the families of the victims, put up the middle finger on his right hand, and said into the microphone, "This hand that pulled the trigger that killed your sons now masturbates to the memory. Fuck all of you."[94]

Lane was then taken away. The families were left in tears, broken, their lives completely torn apart.

AN ECONOMY OF INTEREST RATES

Just over seven years and a month later, on Friday, March 29, 2019, Representative Alexandria Ocasio-Cortez (AOC) held a town hall with MSNBC news anchor Chris Hayes.[95] The topic of the town hall was climate change. It was held in partial response to the Green New Deal, the legislation she had helped pioneer in order to combat climate issues such as global warming.[96]

The Green New Deal was perhaps the boldest piece of legislation proposed in some time. The core of it called for a fundamental reconstruction and/or elimination of several large sectors of the American economy. The total cost of the program was estimated by some to be as high as $93 trillion.[97] It was widely criticized and/or lauded, largely depending on what side of the political aisle you were on. The town hall went on as planned and was widely distributed on the following Monday's new cycle due to the polarizing nature of both AOC and the legislation.

Tucker Carlson was eager to pounce.[98] The Fox News host spared no insult in his evisceration of the event. He absolutely lambasted AOC, calling her "a moron, nasty, and more self-righteous than any televangelist who ever preached a sermon on cable access." In his defense, AOC did bring up completely unrelated topics, such as "white supremacy" and "xenophobia," to describe the American economic system, speaking to the misplaced virtue held by most of society's ruling class. He compared Chris Hayes to Ellen DeGeneres (which, let's face it, is pretty damn hilarious). It was a fairly typical Carlson segment. He poked holes left and right in the argument he was against, gave that famed look of disbelief on camera, laughed his trademark laugh, and then went about his business.

But this is not meant to be a referendum on either Carlson or Ocasio-Cortez. That would be too easy. It would be a waste of your time and whatever you paid to buy this book. Something truly unbelievable happened that Monday night during airing of Tucker Carlson Tonight: the two of them agreed on something.

I was stunned. I couldn't believe it when I heard it. Even though I've long given up on cable news and its trademark I CAN SCREAM AND YELL LOUDER THAN YOU political discourse, it's no secret to me or anyone else who is even remotely tuned into these sorts of things that these two human beings absolutely fucking hate each other's guts. It's incredibly amusing. Ocasio-Cortez is a progressive social justice warrior who demonizes just about everything having to do with the other side of the political aisle in excoriating fashion. Carlson is an old-school conservative populist who constantly roasts nearly everything opposing his core beliefs, which includes verbally incinerating multiple people a week on his nightly show. There's no way they should be able to come to a middle ground on anything.

And that's what made what I'm about to cite so intriguing.

As his roast drew to a close, Carlson pulled up another clip from the town hall. In it, AOC talks about income inequality and the flaws she believes to be causing it:[99]

> We have runaway income inequality. We are at one of our most in-equal points, economically speaking, in American history. We are dealing with a crisis of how our economy is even made up. Our economy is increasingly financialized, which means we are making profits off of interest—off of leasing your phone, off of doing all of these things. But we aren't producing, and we aren't innovating in the way that we need to as an economy.

Carlson didn't just acknowledge some points that she made, he agreed with every single word she said. He agreed so much that he called out both political establishments: the Republican party for not wanting to be unpopular and the Democratic Party for being insatiably power-hungry. Here is his analysis:[100]

Neither party will say that our economy, at its core, is badly distorted. Any economy based on interest payments isn't really an economy; it's a scam.

Healthy countries innovate. They make things. They don't treat people like interchangeable widgets. They don't worship finance. In a healthy country, bankers aren't heroes...Nobody brags about working at a hedge fund. In America right now, we have the opposite, unfortunately.

Now, if two people who despise each other as much as Alexandria Ocasio-Cortez and Tucker Carlson can agree so strongly on an issue, it should immediately raise some eyebrows. It's clearly not a partisan issue. I don't think it's a very extreme issue either. AOC may be a radical leftist and Carlson may be a Trumpian right-winger, but this issue isn't inherently political—it's something much deeper than that.

For those who aren't as attuned to business or economics as I am (intellectual superiority complex, can you tell?), I can say that AOC and Carlson are exactly right. We don't make things, produce things, or innovate things as much anymore and not nearly to the degree we could be. Why?

Because America's economy is not built on production anymore.

A big reason for this is technology. As we talked about in Chapter One, technology has been the biggest catalyst in economic systems since the cavemen learned how to make things like fire and the wheel. It makes work easier and more efficient. However, when we rely on it too much, it can cause problems. We can lose focus on what the technology makes easier and only focus on the "making it easier" part.

For a lot of people, this is why things like automation and artificial intelligence (AI) are so daunting and scary. Pundits don't help by fear-mongering the shit out of those folks, but the concern is very much rooted in fact. So rooted, in fact, that Andrew Yang based his whole presidential campaign on it.[101]

Andrew Yang was born to Korean immigrants and went to college to become a lawyer. However, after about five months working at a corporate law firm, he basically pulled out the ole "fuck it" and went on to become a serial entrepreneur,[102] eventually selling an education company to the conglomerate that owned *The Washington Post* for a good chunk of change.[103] Afterward, he started a nonprofit called Venture for America, which helps "train" prospective entrepreneurs to start businesses in areas that aren't as sexy as New York City or Silicon Valley, such as Baltimore and St. Louis.[104]

Yang's basic argument is the same as AOC's and Carlson's: not enough people are building things. In fact, he wrote a whole book called (not making this up) *Smart People Should Build Things*.[105] Yang's opinion is that too many people are concerned with doing the "right thing" and going after the "right job," and the economic system is leading smart, young people astray into careers that may not bring them fulfillment. In his words:[106]

> If year after year we send our top people to financial services, management consulting, and law schools, we'll wind up with the pattern we're already seeing: layers of highly paid professionals working astride faltering companies and industries. But if we send them to startups, we'll get something else. Early-stage companies in energy, retail, biotech, consumer products, health care, transportation, software, media, education, and other industries would have a better chance of innovating and creating value. Even allowing for a certain amount of failure, we'd create hundreds of new companies and tens of thousands of new jobs over time. Our economy and our country would be better off. Our communities' tax bases would go up, shoring up our ability to pay for schools and long-term development. We'd restore our culture of achievement to include value creation, risk and reward, and

the common good. By solving this one problem, we solve many other problems at the same time.

Again, like AOC and Carlson, this sounds pretty common sense. But that's not what Yang based his presidential campaign on. At least, not solely. That statement was made about five years prior to his presidential run. The main focus of Yang's 2020 campaign wasn't nearly as optimistic. He ran on the notion that the American system had taken an insidious turn, and we were about to hit a point of irreparable economic catastrophe. So he did what any concerned candidate would do. When there's a giant, seismic shift in American culture, where does one go?

The Joe Rogan Experience, of course.[107]

Joe Rogan, the number one podcaster in the world at the time of the 2020 election,[108] had Yang on his podcast to talk about this issue. In the episode, Yang issued a very dark warning about the rapidly advancing technology that was infiltrating our society. He explained that this technology is encouraging anxiety, depression, overdoses, and suicides, especially among middle-American men who had lost unskilled labor jobs. He warned AI and automation would take a scythe to the biggest employers in the United States. He had a twelve-year countdown of how many jobs would be lost due to these trends. Hint: it was a fuck ton. A very uncomfortable fuck ton.

Yang may have cited AI and automation as two of the primary drivers of this decline, but I see a broader trend. One that permeates everything, not just business and economics. One that, if succumbed to, allows a slippery slope to emerge that can lead to utter catastrophe.

* * *

T. J. LANE REMAINS TO this day the most sickening individual I've ever been personally exposed to. My life changed that morning in eighth grade.

I was too young to remember 9/11. I wasn't born when Columbine happened. I did not grow up in an environment where I was exposed to abuse or violence. That was stuff that only happened in movies and on television. It couldn't happen to me.

But then it did. A mere forty-five minutes away from my house by a kid only four years older than me. Two plus two didn't equal four anymore. It didn't compute or make sense. How could a young man be not only so lost in his actions but so lost in his thoughts? How could he possibly rip the hearts out of those families not once but twice? And make the second time potentially more brutal than the first?

When analyzing the psychology of T. J. Lane and other horrific individuals like him, a lot of people point to nihilism. I alluded to it with our generation's Fatal Flaw. These people conclude T. J. Lane must be so lost within himself he had nothing to lose. That he had no identity. So why not pull a 0.22 out in the middle of a school cafeteria and kill a kid he was beefing with along with several others? It's a possible explanation. It's widely circulated. A lot of people believe it.

But it's wrong.

T. J. Lane knew exactly who he was. He drew it right in the middle of his shirt. He *wanted* to kill those kids. He *wanted* to cause as much devastation and horror as possible. *That* was his identity. If he had none, he would have apologized, feigned remorse, and flip-flopped to the stance that best served him. That's what nihilists do when they figure out that the area of nothing they chose to focus on didn't work for them. They simply pivot to another area of nothing.

But T. J. Lane didn't do that. That's why he didn't apologize to those families in the courtroom that day.

That's why he twisted the knife in deeper. He knew what he valued. He *wanted* to make it hurt.

T. J. Lane certainly did that. He had a concrete set of values and chose to act on them. The problem was that he chose shitty values, or at least shitty perceptions of them. He took them too far. He could have had a conversation with Russell King instead of bringing a gun to school. He could have just fought with him in the hallway or out in the parking lot. That may have solved the issue.

But he didn't.

There is a concept in economics called "opportunity cost." The definition for "opportunity cost" is "the money or other benefits lost when pursuing a particular course of action instead of a mutually-exclusive alternative."[109]

You are *always* choosing. You are *always* giving something up for the sake of something else. This is the polarization I talked about in the previous chapter and will expand on in Chapter Four. Whenever you value something, you are automatically giving up the opposite of that value.

The Factors of Value Production are a great starting point and should screen out most of the shitty values in the world, but they alone are not enough. There's an additional wrinkle we must talk about.

It is one thing if the values that lead to a shitty outcome are shitty themselves. But what if the values are good and the outcome is shitty?

It's very possible, almost indisputable, that T. J. Lane had good values as well as his super shitty ones. Sticking up for yourself would be a good thing to value. But T. J. Lane chose to shoot up a school instead of telling Russell King and the other victims that it was not okay with him that Russell was dating his ex and he wanted to talk about it.

Having good values is not enough. You must know that values have consequences, especially when left unchecked. That is what makes the collective point of Carlson, Ocasio-Cortez, and Yang so important.

A CULTURE OF EXCESS

America has a culture of excess. Excess, like all other tools, is inherently neutral. Its effect is all up to the wielder. Some excess is fine. But misuse of excess can dilute value. In most cases, it does. There is also an opposite effect. In this sense, too *little* excess is *also* a bad thing.

As I mentioned earlier, I grew up in a suburb of Cleveland, Ohio. It was a good place to grow up. As I alluded to earlier, I was not exposed to anything abhorrently horrible growing up, such as extreme poverty or violence (although opiates would later come into the picture). It was also interesting because in a sense, I feel like I grew up *with* the town.

When my family moved and settled there when I was four, my town really wasn't anything special. It was a lot of farmland and fields, a couple decent neighborhoods, cheap home prices, and good schools. It was typical Midwestern suburbia. It was just enough but not too much.

And that was exactly what my parents wanted. My parents were the first generation in each of their families to have a chance at making consistently stable incomes. My grandpa told my dad two things about money that he always carried with him: "Always live below your means, and always save money for a rainy day."

When broaching this subject one day with my dad, he shocked me when he revealed we actually *didn't* have a lot of money growing up. That's a typical Midwest thing too. Give kids a decent house in a good neighborhood with ample space to roam, and we feel like Kings of the Universe. Having a daughter with a disability didn't necessarily help the pocketbook either. My parents chose the path of modesty and sacrifice. That was the way in which we lived.

But I began to notice a change as I went through high school and college. The land got bought up and sold to corporations. Housing communities went up left and right. People flooded to my town for the same reasons my parents did all those years ago, chasing the same excess they had chased.

But it soon became too much. There's no room to breathe in my town anymore. Nature has gone away. Everything has become commercialized. The overpopulation and traffic are out of control. The property values have skyrocketed. Everyone is all up in everyone else's shit.

But these people chose this life, just as my parents chose theirs. My parents chose to have my mom work part-time while raising us and watching my sister, while my dad worked sixty-hour weeks and traveled a third of the year for work. Other parents chose to drive a Mercedes and live in McMansions while not being able to cover small emergencies and shackling their children with tens of thousands of dollars of student loan debt.

But my parents were always there. My dad, despite his rigorous travel and work schedule, made all but two of my high school sporting events. I don't think my mom ever missed one. They made all my brother's band concerts and plays and all my sister's cheerleading and Special Olympics events.

My parents lived at their Means of Value. They didn't go too overboard in one area or another. They were always balanced. They knew what they valued, but they didn't let it get to an extreme. I lived a better life than most people on earth because of it.

My parents valued their family. We were always a priority, as were the members of our extended family that we were closest with. My parents valued education. They pushed us harder than most in school, so we would have the best chances of success. My parents valued financial security. I had to pay for a good portion of my college (I took home a grand total of zero dollars and zero cents of the wages I earned every summer between high school and college) but graduated without any debt. My parents valued constructive goal setting. Every New Year's Day, my dad would sit me down by his desk with a pen and piece of stationery to record my resolutions for the next year.

But my parents didn't let any of this consume them. They let us live our own lives and be our own people. They didn't force us to go to college. I was allowed to buy something for myself every once in a while. They weren't mad if I failed in a goal as long as I had put my best foot forward.

My parents were balanced. They were disciplined but not rigid, to call back to Jocko Willink.[110] They were balanced in how they carried out what they valued. They didn't let one thing dwarf another. There were things that were more important, of course. But they didn't think anything was so important they needed to obsess over it.

T. J. Lane did not have this balance. His plot for revenge consumed him. He was so taken by his fetish of slaughter and vengeance that he spared no expense in enforcing his values. T. J. Lane knew his values, but he was not a Value Economist. No Value Economist would infringe on the rights and well-being of others to live their values. It's right there in the definition.

So to the people that say T. J. Lane was a nihilist, I would say you're wrong. T. J. Lane was something worse: a narcissist.

The definition of narcissism is "inordinate fascination with oneself; excessive self-love; vanity."[111] T. J. Lane did not give a single fuck about anyone other than himself. He murdered those children and ruined those families simply because he thought what he cared about was more important than what anyone else thought.

If you look closely enough, you can see examples of this throughout history. Hitler wanted to rebuild Germany after World War I, and the Treaty of Versailles tore his beloved country to shreds.[112] But he didn't need to commit the genocide of twelve million people and facilitate the killing of tens of millions more to do so.[113] Mao[114] and Stalin[115] could have turned China and Russia around in ways that didn't starve tens of millions of their citizens. Oh, and they did the whole genocide thing too. Each one was not a raging nihilist but a raging narcissist. They knew perfectly well what they valued. They just didn't care about anyone else as they were acting on them.

When you succumb to narcissism, when you start thinking your values are more important than anyone else's, you tread dangerous ground. You pave the way for your own slippery slope to manifest, for your own demise to be shown right before you.

But engaging in your own values and believing what you want to believe are good things, right? Not necessarily. Values, if they follow the framework laid out in Chapter One, are not inherently good or bad. Neither is excess. It's all in the usage. If either values or excess are corrupted, your life will follow suit. It will become a shell of what it could have been. You will have hollowed it out with your own selfishness and desire for something greater than you deserve.

T. J. Lane slid down the slippery slope when he committed the Chardon High School shooting. Tucker Carlson, Alexandria Ocasio-Cortez, and Andrew Yang all talked about the slope when discussing the corrosion of the United States economy. While my parents chose to live at their means, others around them succumbed to the slope by living within their own worlds instead of within their means, ignoring the greater picture.

All three parties have to live with the consequences of slipping down the slope of corrupt values and excess. T. J. Lane is serving three life sentences in prison. The victims are still dead. The families of those victims will never totally recover. Economic polarity in the US is sky-rocketing.[116] The people of my suburb are feeling the walls closing in.

We must be careful not to let our true values become distorted in the pursuit of greater value. In order to do this, we must build our own value for ourselves, not simply derive it from something already there. We need our values to keep their integrity and not be undone by our recklessness and unbalanced behavior.

THE THREE LEVELS OF EXCESS

Everything is defined by excess, at least to a certain degree. This is why we do things like work and desire money and sex. We all want some sort of excess, but we don't know how much or little we need to find that sweet spot. This is what I meant by the whole "living at your means" thing earlier when talking about my parents and grandparents.

Let's lay out a scenario. You're a parent with a full-time job. You have a wife and three kids. Your wife works part-time (say about twenty hours a week) so she can generate income while watching the kids. You need a place to live, so you settle on a decent-sized house in the suburbs that has three bedrooms and two bathrooms. It's a nice house. It provides what you need. You're living at or below your means. Everything is fine. Let's call this scenario living at your Means of Value.

This, to most people, wouldn't be considered excess. They would call it a simple necessity. You need a nice, safe environment to foster a family and give your children a good place to grow up. But the question remains: do you really need the house?

Let's look at another scenario. A mysterious beer virus strain from China spreads throughout the world and sucker punches the American economy.[117] You get laid off, and your wife gets furloughed because her employer can't afford to keep on part-time employees right now. You sell off the nice house and move into a two-bedroom apartment with only one bathroom. This is below your Means of Value. It costs less, but it devalues your quality of life. Your kids are cramped, you don't have enough space to do activities, and you all want to rip each other's throats out within a few weeks.

Let's say in about six months, the economy begins to recover. You get a new job, and your wife can start working part-time again. Everything is great except for one thing: the apartment. Your kids are openly trying to murder one another now. Johnny hits Susie in the head with his Lego Batmobile, and Molly swings off of the ceiling fan with a Jorge Masvidal-esque flying knee[118] to protect Susie from Johnny. It is clear they need space to run around, screaming and hitting things and/or each other until they inevitably fall over and sleep their off-the-charts kid energy away. You repurchase a similar house and leave the apartment behind.

But why? Why would you do this? Isn't that chasing excess? Well, in theory, it is. The apartment suits your needs. It puts a roof over your family's heads and keeps them safe. That's what a shelter is supposed to do. That is its core function.

But let's say you pull an Andrew Yang–style "fuck it" and tell your whole family you're going to be roughing it in a tent from now on. The world is your oyster. That's an option too. Tens of thousands of people are doing it in wildernesses and cities right now.

But is it the *right* option? I would, again, argue that it's not. Why? Because a decent amount of excess is good. We should want to be comfortable and aspire to live a comfortable and decent life, as long as we're not selling illegal barbiturates or killing people or something of the like to fund it. We are fortunate enough to live in the country with the most opportunities in the history of the world. If we do the right things and live at or below our means, we should indulge in the opportunity to provide a comfortable lifestyle for ourselves. It's the American Dream. It's why more people have immigrated here than any other country in the world. If you look at the statistics, it's not even close. To keep it confined to a simple term, let's call the apartment scenario *Insufficient* Excess.

Let's flip to the other side of the spectrum. The economy starts to recover, and you see nothing but sunshine and rainbows and a bunch of other shit you see when you combine rose-colored glasses with your preferred hallucinogenic drug. You pull yet another "fuck it," take out five mortgages, and purchase a mansion with fifteen bedrooms and ten and a half bathrooms. You know, just for shits.

When your family and friends ask you if you're on crack, you simply tell them you wanted more. It is the American Dream, after all, right? It may be a shitty excuse, but I guess they can't really debate it.

Or could they?

You bet your ass they could. Why? Because there's no way that model of doing things is sustainable. A working, middle-class family could not support the financial strain of five mortgages on a fifteen-bedroom/10.5-bathroom house outside of winning the lottery (or maybe Dad *sells* crack, not uses it). For the sake of our definitions, we will call this scenario *Excessive* Excess.

So, in review, you don't want Insufficient *or* Excessive Excess. You generally want to be somewhere in the middle, like most things. In other words, you want to live at your means. Preferably below them, if you ask me. You don't want a tent, but you don't want a fifteen-bed/10.5-bath home either. That would be betraying your means on either side of the spectrum.

However, that does not mean you cannot increase your means. You could bust your ass at work and get promoted. Your wife could become full-time instead of part-time. You could invest in a pump-and-dump penny-stock scheme. The possibilities are endless!

The point is that increasing your means is fine (we all chase excess, remember?) as long as you can be stable about using the means themselves.

THE MOST DANGEROUS LEVEL

I like to view excess like a rubber band. If it's not stretched at all or enough, the rubber band is useless. This is Insufficient Excess. If the rubber band is stretched just enough, it has a ton of utility. This is living at your Means of Value. However, if the rubber band is stretched too far, it either breaks or snaps back to cause a pretty fucking big sting. This is Excessive Excess. This is why Excessive Excess is the most dangerous of the three levels—more to come on that in Chapter Six.

If we do not make new things, we eventually run out of things to derive value from. That value eventually gets diluted. Excessive Excess is the embodiment of that dilution. For those who are getting confused, let's talk about this in two terms: real and derivative assets.

A real asset is something that possesses value because of its physical properties.[119] These are things like an algorithm, gold, and oil. They have value simply for the fact that they are an algorithm, gold, and oil. A derivative asset is something that possesses value because its value is derived from a real asset.[120] These are things like the App Store, currency, and stocks.

The further you get away from the real asset, the more strained the value of that asset becomes. Money is a good example. The dollar bill is the standard currency of America. But is it valuable by itself? The answer is no. When you break it down, money is paper that is painted green with a bunch of letters, numbers, and an old guy stamped on the front of it. A two-year-old with a crayon and a legal pad could draw something similar.

The reason money used to have value was because our government had a shit ton of precious metals, natural resources, and other commodities that backed up the currency buried in various places across the country.[121] It guarded them with barbed-wire fences and Special Operations soldiers. Those were real assets. They had intrinsic value because the items themselves are valuable. Money is a derivative of those real assets to use as a unit of account, a store of value, and a medium of exchange. Take away the underlying real assets, and that fancy green paper becomes as useless of a currency as toilet paper.

However, that is not the case anymore. In 1971, President Richard Nixon unpegged the United States dollar from the price of gold, allowing it to float freely to be measured only by other currencies.[122] There was no longer any real asset to back up the economy. It was now up to excess to do the job.[123] This has had disastrous consequences. America's debt has soared to astronomical proportions,[124] expedited by unchecked and unrivaled bipartisan spending. Carlson, Ocasio-Cortez, and Yang weren't making it up when they said our economy is made of nothing. They were saying our economy is made up because it is made out of nothing. Like, literally, nothing. It's all about trust in the system, you see.

This trend is unsustainable. The people who are making these decisions know this. In 2011, the United States debt ceiling was nearing its peak. This is a massive problem. When the government spends so much money it can no longer borrow more, aided by the fact that the international economy is largely built off what the US economy does, this can lead to massive international problems. And I'm talking "sinking the entire world economy in one fell swoop"–type problems. More on this later.

The solution to this, proposed by academic economist Brad Delong, was a concept called the "trillion-dollar coin."[125] Under this theory, the United States treasury would mint a platinum coin worth $1 trillion in order to raise the level of funds that could be borrowed to save our economy from literal implosion. Think about that for a second. This is something out of a fairy tale, out of a fantasy land. Yet it exists, and we did it because our Excessive Excess ran wild. The last time it was used was in the fall of 2021, when the debt ceiling was nearly reached again. The trend is likely to continue, to all our peril.

We cannot add money to the system without adding more real assets underneath it to back it up. If we simply print more money, like the United States has done for over fifty years, the value of that money will go down if we don't add more real assets underneath it or remove money from other areas of the economy. That is called inflation, and inflation sucks ass.

Venezuela's economy is in total shambles because the guy who ran their country is a dickwad.[126] He totally tanked it through incompetent decisions like the unchecked printing of money. Their inflation rate hit 42,000 percent in 2018. At one point, it cost 220,000 bolivars (Venezuelan currency) to buy a kilo of rice.[127]

In his book *Zero to One*, venture capitalist Peter Thiel describes his version of Excessive Excess as the "Indefinite Optimist" mindset, of which he believes the finance industry is the epitome. "Money is more valuable than anything you could possibly do with it," says Thiel.[128] It begs the question, how many people do we need in this field before Excessive Excess starts to kick in? How many hedge fund managers and investment bankers do we *really* need?

The answer? Probably less than there are right now. Probably a *lot* less. These people aren't actively creating value. They're simply distorting value from something that has already been distorted multiple times over. They're distributing, not creating. Firms on Wall Street are beginning to take notice of this trend as well—a quarter of them are planning to downsize their New York offices as we speak.

The Great Recession of 2008,[129] as chronicled in the book[130] and film[131] *The Big Short*, is an example of Excessive Excess and Thiel's Indefinite Optimist mindset at its most lethal. For those who aren't aware (probably no fault of your own—just a lot of people talking way above their own heads to prove how smart they think they are), a lot of things caused the 2008 financial crisis. But the main catalyst was the inflation bubble in the housing market leading up to the crash.

Put simply, a lot of people within the credit, finance, and real estate industries got greedy, propped up the housing market on bad loans that people couldn't pay, and inflated that same market by enormous proportions based on value that wasn't really there. They got enormously rich in the process.

But then the rubber band snapped. Suddenly, a shit ton of people couldn't pay back their mortgages. This caused them to default on those mortgages. Loans, like mortgages, make up a large portion of the financial incomes of banks around the world.[132] It's how they make their money—borrow short, lend long. This caused the value of these banks to free fall.

A lot of people don't realize how astronomical of a problem it is when banks and financial markets cease to function. Imagine that you run a business with a revolving line of credit that you use for payroll and other expenses. What happens when the bank can't lend you that money?

Hint: you go out of business. The value of your company goes to zero. Which leads to people getting laid off. Which leads to a spike in unemployment. Which leads to people not having enough money. Which leads to people not being able to pay their rent or provide basic necessities for their families. Which leads to more businesses going out of business and laying off more people. Which leads to widespread anarchy, crime, and unrest. Which leads to economic and societal collapse. We came pretty damn close to taking an irreparable shit on the entire world in 2008. A shit that could have been entirely avoided if people didn't clog their pipes with proverbial Excessive Excess.

This is why Excessive Excess is so dangerous. It does not create value. It simply derives secondary value from other things. When ratcheted up this high, anything can become dangerous. It is with our personal values where this phenomenon reaches its highest importance.

I WALK THE LINE

Good values are neutral things. When derived from the factors of experience, action, self-awareness, and discipline, values are the system's outputs. From there, it is our choice what we do with them.

Discipline is an important factor. The reason for this, other than the ones previously named, is that your discipline directly correlates to something that defines the whole of this chapter and affects the Excessive Excess that can arise if not properly restrained: ethics.

The definition of the word "ethics" is "the discipline dealing with what is good and bad and with moral duty and obligation."[133] Since values are inherently neutral, they cannot have good or bad within. The Factors of Value Production make sure of that. They squeeze it all out until neutral values are formed.

Therefore, it is up to *you* to own that moral duty and obligation. Values cannot do it by themselves. That is not what their role is. Your role as the wielder of values is to use them appropriately. Like Shane said, a gun is a tool. As is a value. It is up to the person who uses that tool to see what ends up becoming of it. When you get down to issues of ethics, it *always* comes down to your values.

In college, we talked about ethical dilemmas quite a bit. The one that sticks out most to me was when my professor asked us to envision a fork in a train track with a switch that could send a train down two paths. He then told us to imagine a train barreling toward us. We are the only ones that can flip the switch to send the train down either of the two paths. We cannot stop the train. We can only direct it.

But there was a catch. If we flip the switch to send the train to the left, the train will run over five old people and kill them. If we do nothing, the train will travel down the right-side track and run over two small children. Remember, we cannot stop the train. We can only choose which group is more worthy to live.

People diverged early and often on this issue. Some took the utilitarian approach—why save two lives when you could save five? Others took a more sympathetic attitude—the elderly folks have lived full lives, why should we rob two young children of theirs? Arguments pinged back and forth in the room like the Powerball. No conclusion was reached as to which one was right.

Because in reality, was either of them really inherently "right"? No. And that was the point. You had to make the best out of a bad situation. You had to choose the path of what you believed to be the most ethical amount of suffering you could impose on other people.

In real life, we generally will not have to make this horrific of a decision. But what we can choose is how we exercise our discipline to enforce our values in the real world. If we do not enforce them at all by choosing Insufficient Excess, we simply will be embodying our generation's current Fatal Flaw. We will have no stances toward anything and simply get moved around by the people that do have firm values. Make that decision at your own peril.

However, we can't choose the most dangerous of the three levels—Excessive Excess—either. Which brings us full circle back to T. J. Lane. T. J. Lane had values. He just used those values to such an extreme that he destroyed his own life and the lives of dozens of people. T. J. Lane having values was not the problem. It was the implementation of those values where he failed, which left a horrific mark on the world that a lot of people will never forget. Because of a lack of discipline, T. J. Lane shredded the lives of several families and an entire community of citizens.

We cannot live at either side of the extremes, especially when it comes to the foundation of our identity, our values. When our identity is put firmly on one side of the fence versus the other, we consciously pick to be dominated or to dominate. Neither is a good option.

What we should do instead is to walk atop the fence. We walk the line, as sung by the great Johnny Cash.[134] We defy the impulse of extremes in order to blaze our own trail based on our own values.

But it's hard to balance on top of a fence. It is a very precarious position. Most of us do not do it well and have not done it well traditionally. Our society's Fatal Flaws of both the past and present reflect either Insufficient Excess (the present) or Excessive Excess (the past), both of which have edged the scale of the well-being of our society toward a tipping point.

But when we choose to be balanced and forgo the extremes, we can find harmony. We can live at our Means of Value. We can see both sides of extremism for what they are. We know that we deserve to live out our values, but we do not deserve to exert them over anyone else. We simply know who we are, what our identity is, and which values compose our identity. Nothing else matters. Nothing else *should* matter.

Our identities are individual. They should be kept that way. No one should impose on your identity. But the same goes in reverse. You should not impose your identity on anyone else. We should strive for coexistence, for acceptance. But we also should not let our identities fall by the wayside. We have to use them, or they will get dull and stale and embody our generation's Fatal Flaw.

Smart people build things and live at their Means of Value. Narcissistic people destroy things and create an extreme version of excess. The choice, as always, is yours.

TOO CLOSE TO THE SUN

There's a tale in Greek mythology about a father and son named Daedalus and Icarus. Daedalus, a great inventor, was tasked by King Minos with constructing the Labyrinth, an epic maze, to imprison the Minotaur. The Minotaur, a half-man, half-bull creature born of Minos' wife and the Cretan bull, was meant to be imprisoned in the Labyrinth out of Minos' own guilt. But there was a problem. The great Theseus was tasked by the Gods with killing the Minotaur. Upon realizing this, Minos decided to throw him into the Labyrinth as well.

Minos' daughter Ariadne, being in love with Theseus, begged Daedalus for help. Daedalus gave Ariadne a ball of string that helped lead Theseus out of the Labyrinth and slay the Minotaur. Enraged by the betrayal, Minos threw Daedalus and Icarus into the Labyrinth to imprison them forever.

Daedalus, never one to give up, fashioned two pairs of wings out of feathers and wax for himself and Icarus to use to fly away and escape over a grand ocean. They succeeded.

Icarus, fond of his newfound abilities, decided to test his wings as they flew away. He began to soar high into the sky, rising far above his father. Overcome by his father's invention, he believed he could test the wings to their limit. He flew higher and higher. Soon, the wax holding the feathers together began to melt until he realized in horror that no more feathers were attached to his father's invention. With nothing left to support his flight, Icarus fell into the sea and drowned.

Icarus, once he discovered the power of his father's new invention, flew too close to the sun. He didn't know the limitations of what his father created. That overambition, that imposing of his own Excessive Excess, cost him his life and his father a son. The wings were only supposed to help them escape the prison. They were not supposed to keep them off the ground forever nor fly them into the heavens. They had a purpose, one that Icarus ignored at his own expense.

But was Icarus really at fault? Or was it Daedalus, the man who created the invention, who was to blame? Icarus directly caused his own death, but Daedalus did not explain what the wings were to be used for. Daedalus' lack of discipline toward the intention of his invention led to an ethical dilemma: do I stay imprisoned, or do I risk death by unleashing this power onto the world? The choice, as always, was his.

Neither Daedalus nor Icarus lived at their means. Human beings are not meant to fly. But, like so many others, they fell into the trap of living beyond their Means of Value. They simply stretched it too far. They did not see the consequences of their actions before it was too late.

But can we blame them? It is so easy, especially in these times in which we live, to lose our balance on top of the fence. To succumb to one side of the extreme or the other. Like T. J. Lane, the United States economy, my old hometown, the Great Recession, and Venezuela, it is easy to become unbalanced in our values. We must commit to what they are and not derive so much from them that we become disassociated from what the values themselves really mean.

Yet, like Icarus, our ambitions carry us. They carry us high into the sky, away from reality, toward what we feel is where we were always meant to be. Our values act as the baseline to our ambitions, showing us how we can go so high yet fall so far. This is why selection, explained in Chapter Three, is so important. When you establish discipline over your values, you can trim them down to find the ones that will best support what will be your identity. Only after you forge your identity should you dare traverse into the world.

Because the universal truth is this: we *all* chase excess. We don't want to live at our Means of Value. The ethical implications can be overwhelming. In most cases, they are. Like Icarus, one question can be too much: where is my Means of Value at?

Only you can determine your own answer to that question. Only you can determine your own fate. The awesome responsibility and precariousness of this concept cannot be overstated. Perhaps best described in the words of Oscar Wilde, this dichotomy, the *ultimate* dichotomy, is one that should always be considered:[135]

Never regret they fall,
O Icarus of the fearless flight
For the greatest tragedy of them all
Is to never feel the burning light.

CHAPTER THREE

ESSENTIAL DIVERSIFICATION

"It's not activity that disturbs people, but false conceptions of things that drive them mad."

—SENECA

THE TWO ES

SEVEN AND A HALF YEARS AFTER T. J. LANE COMMITTED the Chardon High School shooting, I walked into my first lecture for Investments, one of the classes required for a finance degree at my university. It was an important class. Many people I would be sharing that hour and twenty minutes with would soon become the premium pipeline of talent for some of the top consulting and financial services firms in the world.

But, at that point, I'd become slightly disillusioned with my major. I didn't think (and still, to a large degree, don't) finance created value for anyone in business. It was merely a transactional piece of the pie. I saw it as a manifestation of excess, the focus of Chapter Two. I had no interest in trading derivatives or snorting coke out of a hooker's ass or any other Jordan Belfort-esque behavior.[136]

When I sat down, I was expecting my professor to be of that same ilk: loud, obnoxious, way-too-expensive haircut, tell us five times minimum per class about how hot his wife is, brag about what type of shellfish he had for dinner last night, avoid talking about his penis size, etc.

What I got was quite the opposite. The man came in wearing a pink Tommy Hilfiger polo (he has seven of them, all bought for him in bulk at Sam's Club by his wife), light blue dad jeans, and a baseball cap. He was quiet but not meek. You could tell he was strong, wise, and a non-bullshitter. He was just as good of a listener as he was a talker. He kept it real. He didn't embellish. He was The Man.

The other thing that made this man The Man was how he taught. It was unorthodox to say the least. A lot of the "college experience" nonsense is drastically overrated. A lot of professors just puke the book up on students. It's not at all personalized. To quote Will Hunting, "You dropped a hundred and fifty grand on a fuckin' education you coulda got for a dollar fifty in late charges at the public library."[137]

That was not the case with his course at all. He didn't believe in theory as a practice. He believed in practice as a practice. He encouraged open discussion. It often led to disagreements. He kept it real.

This was, indeed, not a class on theory. It was a class on how to become a good investor. And, believe it or not, being a good investor and a good liver of life are more related than one might think. There are trade-offs that you must choose between in order to best position yourself for success. These are usually between risk and reward, from whether to take out a second mortgage on your house to whether you want to Arc Trainer yourself into hell to burn off a second piece of carrot cake. There are systems that have hierarchies. One must know how they work to navigate them with success.

The Man had two "Golden Rules" for successful investing, which he suggested (much like everything else in his class) could also be applied to successful life living. In The Man's view, they are the two things that get people in trouble while investing that, paradoxically, aren't related to investing at all: ego and emotion.

The proof of the power of ego and emotion is everywhere. It's an incredibly accurate assessment. They can be attributed to most outbursts stemming from microaggressions on Twitter and other social media. They are on full display when young men in group chats drag a girl through the mud for being "crazy." Or when a young woman spills every detail about a sexual encounter with a guy to the other women in her group chat, humiliating him and exposing him to people who can't keep their mouths shut. Ego and emotion are problems, but not because of their existence.

They're problems because we as humans fucking suck at controlling them.

ESSENTIAL DIVERSIFICATION

Around my junior year of high school, shit wasn't making sense to me. This was the inevitable, "So, they teach us how to do calc, but they don't teach us how to do our taxes?" common-sense period that every high schooler goes through.

However, I was thankful I had a class on financial literacy in high school that was taught by a great teacher. But that great teacher also had a great teacher, one whom he had a fetish-like obsession with: Dave Motherfuckin' Ramsey.

In what quickly became a spoken-word meme around my high school, my financial literacy teacher would show us Dave Ramsey videos in bunches, making sure we soaked up the wisdom of The Almighty. Dave Ramsey, for those who don't know, is a personal finance guru with a wildly popular podcast and radio show.[138] In it, he gives advice that will hopefully lead his listeners to financial freedom. He also has done a series of equally popular live gigs, where he does corny and/or funny shit like cutting up credit cards with giant scissors and the like.[139]

My personal favorite of said corny/funny shit was the "don't put all your eggs in one basket" act. Ramsey would simulate various financial securities with colored eggs, throw them all into a basket, and then throw the basket across the stage to crush them and simulate a wild economic event, such as a market crash or a mysterious overseas virus that sends the world into a frenzy. To show the other side of the scenario, he would put one egg into individual baskets and then do the same thing. One basket containing all your eggs is much worse than one basket containing one egg.

It makes sense in theory (and in a finance-related comedy bit). But here's the thing. A lot of things that work in theory *don't* actually work in practice.

* * *

IN 2014, AUTHOR AND SILICON Valley leadership consultant Greg McKeown released his magnum opus: *Essentialism.* [140] In his work, McKeown takes issue with the very theory of diversification that Ramsey has preached his whole life. However, he doesn't reject it completely. He just puts it in a different context.

The context of our lives.

While he argues that it's good to have skills, McKeown takes issue with the frantic diversification of our lives. Now more than ever, we find ourselves busy, frazzled, and overwhelmed. We're going a millimeter in a million directions. We're not getting to a place of meaning. But as long as we don't put all our eggs in one basket, we'll be fine, right?

Wrong.

Constant distraction and chasing lead us nowhere. And, deep down, I think we all know that. Yet we continue to do it in all facets of our lives. Why?

There are a lot of reasons. Cancel culture, cultural fragility, and safety-ism all certainly play a role to some degree. But I think it comes down to a big thing that flies under the radar: our obsession with choice.

There is a concept within finance called "portfolio theory."[141] Developed by Harry Markowitz, it shows how risk-averse investors can construct investment portfolios to maximize expected returns based on a given level of risk. It was a genius innovation. Markowitz won the Nobel Prize for it.[142]

However, there are two types of risk in finance. The first, systematic risk, is the risk that comes just from entering the market.[143] It is unavoidable. This is the risk of a market crash, like the Great Depression or the one caused by COVID-19. The second, unsystematic risk, *is* avoidable.[144] That point was proven by Markowitz when he developed portfolio theory. It's better to spread your investments out rather than to throw your life savings into Dogecoin and see what happens.

The reason this concept is important is because it is the theoretical genesis of diversification. The mathematical model of portfolio theory states that an investor needs to have around forty-five to fifty companies across eleven GICS sectors (the different sectors of the economy) in their investment portfolio in order to be properly diversified from unsystematic risk and avoid losing money.

Which brings us back to The Man. The Man, in his infinite wisdom, said the best formula for investing (an opinion we both share) is to invest in good companies that are in good businesses in good industries and that have good management. Sounds like a pretty bulletproof concept.

At least in theory.

Who sees a giant red flag with what I just wrote? I sure as hell do. There is no way you can possibly update the good company/business/industry/management strategy for forty-five to fifty companies constantly. It's impossible. It's why 99.9999999998 percent of day traders can't make money using mathematical financial software and online courses they bought for way too much from a college student at a local Grant Cardone seminar.[145]

But you still need to have diversification. Just not to the degree that the wack-ass financial academics say you do. That's the epitome of taking a shotgun to the S&P 500 and seeing how much of a dent you can make. While shotguns are cool in movies and against Nazi zombies, they're not the most accurate at getting the job done in real life. I'd much prefer a sniper rifle, as much for picking investments as shooting Nazi zombies.

So I slightly modified the theory. (Here's my obligatory cover-my-ass sentence: I AM NOT A REGISTERED FINANCIAL ADVISOR AND AM NOT RESPONSIBLE FOR ANY DAMAGE YOU TAKE).

So what I did with my investments is what I call Essential Diversification. I took a piece of the pie from both McKeown and The Almighty Ramsey. I applied my framework to one company in each GICS sector, heavily vetted it, stripped it down to its studs, and rarely changed it. Best of both worlds. I was satisfied once I stepped back. But then a thought occurred to me: the same could be done for our values and lives.

Remember, Value Economics is the study of how well we use our value resources. However, for this chapter, it's important to focus on one thing (hint: it's what I spent my entire last chapter talking about): excess.

Excess for the sake of excess is not good. Not for culture, bath salts, anything. The same goes for our values. We need to choose carefully what we value and, correspondingly, how we choose what enters our lives. Classic diversification is good for two demographics of people:

1. Saps
2. Finance majors on a hellish mix of ecstasy and Viagra

Essential Diversification is different. In order to achieve it, we need to build a framework by allocating values, selecting ones that really matter, and deploying your value capital by investing in them.

ALLOCATION

Any good philosophy starts off with building a framework. In Value Economics, the study of deploying our resources into our values, this is especially important because we need to send our focus and energy to the things that matter to us as individuals. Anything else is a distraction and waste.

For Essential Diversification, the way we build our framework is much like the way we build a portfolio of investments. We allocate the assets we want to hold and build on—our values. Our values, if used constructively and correctly, are the basis of everything we do. It's important to get them right. How you get them right is by creating this initial framework.

The assets/values we hold were already created by our usage of the Factors of Value Production. But, as we've discussed, even though the Factors of Value Production create values, values in and of themselves are neutral. A gun is a tool, remember?

I also think it's important to address the number of values you should hold or strive to hold. Values, unlike stocks or investments, are unlimited. They don't have GICS sectors. There isn't a specific number I can pin down. But, then again, I can't really tell you what to do at all. You can tell me to go fuck myself, and I can't do anything about it.

But if you *don't* tell me to go fuck myself, what I would recommend is you pick somewhere between three and seven values. This works out to an average of (wait for it) five. Short lists bring me great joy. I think five is the magic number, but anywhere within this range is fine. Just avoid Excessive Excess, and you should be okay.

The reason you shouldn't have more than seven values is because that's where I think your values start to overlap and/or get cheesy as fuck. For example, the company I currently work for has eleven. I have no fucking idea how that is possible. How could you possibly base the core of a large and complex living organization, such as a company, on eleven different values? How can you do extreme vetting? How could you make a big decision based on one value without inevitably betraying one of the other values that overlap?

Even if the number of values I recommend seems low, it doesn't mean they should come to you in five minutes. Choosing them should take you very long. Why? Because extreme vetting *should* take very long for the Essential Diversification of both stocks and values. It's important to get the very few things you base your life and/or financial well-being on correct. You want to make sure they fit, and you trust them to come through. You don't want to rush. If you aren't sure about something, look some more.

Because the reality is values can be deceiving and destructive if they aren't applied in the right context by the right people. Look at Enron, the company that committed arguably the biggest corporate crime of the modern era.[146] It crushed tens of thousands of people's livelihoods and imploded over $60 billion of shareholder value like it was nothing. This was abhorrent and begs the question: what were Enron's core values?

Respect, integrity, communication, and excellence.[147]

In other words: didn't do that, nope, for *sure* didn't do that, and fuck off.

Just because values look and sound good on paper doesn't mean they *are* good. You need to live and practice them. However, this leads to another big problem a lot of people (myself included) have with the allocation of values through Essential Diversification: values can be cliche and boring as fuck.

Think about it—how many company web pages have you looked at and seen words like "integrity," "teamwork," and "trust" and wanted to yak? The lack of originality always stuns me. When everyone has the same values, no one has those values. You need a source of differentiation to make values meaningful. All you need to do is look at Enron's values above to know that to be true. Nothing about the way it conducted business represented respect, integrity, communication, and excellence.

A lot of people look at allocating values as boring and mundane. It certainly can be. But it doesn't have to be. The thing that often gets lost in the shuffle is the fact that these are *your* values, not anyone else's. Why not personalize them? Make them cool? Use cultural references and inside jokes to make them funny and unique? They will hold meaning as well as those corny one-worders. But they will have more meaning because they are tailored to what you want from your version of Essential Diversification.

For example, there are a lot of things I disagree with about how modern companies run their businesses. However, one thing I fully support is the new way some of them are writing their values statements. I don't think any company epitomizes this dichotomy more than Zappos, the shoe company that was founded by the late Tony Hsieh and is currently owned by Amazon.

For the most part, I *hate* Zappos' culture. They're cheerful all the time. Everything is sunshine and rainbows. I'm pretty sure all of their employees have developed the ability to shit glitter. They practice a system called "holacracy,"[148] where apparently no one has a defined role or is in charge of anything. I have no fucking clue how this is supposed to work. As someone high in conscientiousness, I couldn't disagree with these philosophies more.

But one thing I absolutely love about Zappos is the way they phrase their values. They violate the "between three and seven" rule, but to their credit, their values aren't boring. They're fun phrases that make people think about the essence of their culture. Furthermore, they aren't so boring you want to channel your inner Eminem and stick nine-inch nails through each one of your eyelids.[149] The ten (at least it's less than eleven) values for Zappos are as follows:

1. Deliver WOW through Service.
2. Embrace and Drive Change.
3. Create Fun and a Little Weirdness.

4. Be Adventurous, Creative, and Open-Minded.
5. Pursue Growth and Learning.
6. Build Open and Honest Relationships with Communication.
7. Build a Positive Team and Family Spirit.
8. Do More with Less.
9. Be Passionate and Determined.
10. 10. Be Humble.[150]

While that much excessive positivity makes me queasy, there is no denying those are some kick-ass phrases. They describe, on a personal level, what Zappos is all about, and they do it in a way that reflects their brand and the personality of their workers. It's fantastic—except for the fact that they contradict each other at least once. That's the "average of five" rule in action. Regardless, they're doing incredibly well for a reason. There's no denying this allocation of values has helped them get there.

One last point before we move on. The biggest advantage to building your framework is not the benefit that comes with using those values. That comes later. The biggest advantage is screening out all the shit you don't need. You clean out your Value Closet, to drop another Eminem reference.

When you stop focusing on what doesn't matter, you automatically shift to what does matter. Your values act as a filter for what comes into your life. The values you allocate have to be in the right context for you. Just because a lot of other people value something doesn't mean you have to. Just make sure your values are formed by the Factors of Value Production and live within your Means of Value.

But allocation is not enough. You still need to do extreme vetting in order to get the right values that fit specifically to your framework.

I KNEW THIS BITCH NAMED BECKY (SELECTION) [151]

We all knew that goody-two shoes girl in school. Let's call her Becky. I don't know a fucking single good Becky. The closest thing was Lori Loughlin in Full House, which is now both so much more hilarious and worse.[152]

Becky is involved in *everything*. She's the captain of the cheerleading team who also runs the 50/50 raffle during halftime and is the place-kicker for the football team she cheers for. She volunteers for AIDS, breast cancer, down syndrome, hemorrhoids, *and* sexually transmitted diseases in the elderly. She hosts debates for local politicians on Facebook Live. She's in chess club for some fucking reason.

What does this tell you about Becky? The kinder among us might say that she's a doll and a great person. I, unfortunately for Becky, am not one of the kinder among us. I would say that Becky's problem was T. J. Lane's problem. She's a raging narcissist. She's so desperate for attention and validation she throws herself at anything that comes near just so she can get some sort of sick kick out of it. Kind of like a Middle Ages whore, only a Middle Ages whore didn't drive a used 2019 Honda CR-V.

Becky's choice to not choose specific skills to pursue is drastically holding her back. The best of the best buy in. This poor diversification of skills might seem nice on the surface, but it blinds her to the bigger picture. The thought of getting compared to someone else for *not* doing something far outweighs the cost of her losing out on potentially hitting it big at one thing.

Apply this thinking to anything worthwhile. Would you be a generalist when it comes to marriage? "Oh shit, this whole 'I do' thing with Karen isn't working out, let's go to Julia instead." Children? "You know what, Billy isn't working out—let's just chuck him in the dumpster and pop out another one to see if we could do better." Career? "You know, I went to college for four years to be an architect, but I woke up on the other side of the bed today and now want to sell my internal organs to the local hobo population for crack."

While I hope real-life examples would not be this extreme, this trend is dangerous. It leads to people going nowhere. When you only go a little bit in a lot of directions, as mentioned by McKeown, odds are a lot of those directions won't work out. They'll fall through the floor like Daniel Stern in the *Home Alone* movies.[153] And then you'll be left with nothing but a shit ton of failures and bullshit excuses. Put that in your pipe and smoke it, Becky.

When you succumb to unlimited choice, you cheat yourself of the ability to develop greatness at something or a few things. Don't do that to yourself. You're better than that. You should respect yourself more than that. Don't be a Becky. Remember, there are no good Beckys.

* * *

IN ORDER TO NOT BE a Becky, you must move from Value Allocation to the next step in Essential Diversification: Value Selection. Value Selection, which takes place after you build your framework, is when you select the values you put into your life that *fit* that framework. This step correlates to how you want to live your life and what type of relationships you want with people.

You need to identify if the values that you sift through fit the framework in order to move further along in the process. If a value doesn't fit, screen it out immediately. Forget about it. Remember, this is about what you *don't* want in your life as much as what you *do* want in your life.

To create your best version of Essential Diversification, you must select only the values that will directly fit the Factors of Value Production and your Means of Value. You need enough values to base the framework of your life on. But you can't go overboard, or they will start to overlap and contradict each other.

We'll get more into this in Chapter Eight, but let's visit one dichotomy briefly. In a normal society, equality and meritocracy can and should be balanced. However, as they pertain to your values (or the value of anything, really) equality needs to be thrown out the window. Think about it. You value something because you think of it more highly than something else. That's not equality. It's something that won out based on your Factors of Value Production.

Your values and the values that can potentially replace them should compete with each other. You need to constantly test your values against new ones. Complacency in this area is a poor strategy. Complacent values can cause you to become rigid. And, while you must be disciplined, as expressed by the Factors of Value Production, you cannot allow yourself to become rigid. Rigid values lead to a rigid life in a world that is ever-more defined by agility and flexibility, and that's not a good way to be.

Your values, if done right, are the bedrock of your life. It's important your life reflects your values, or else you're not being authentic. If your values are inauthentic, you will live an inauthentic life. That's no fun. If you're fake with others (which you will be if you're being fake about how you treat yourself and what your values are), you do *them* a disservice by giving them a false impression by presenting yourself as someone you aren't.

The one thing that can trip you up in any area of Essential Diversification, but especially in the process of Selection, is outside pressure. Peer pressure is a motherfucker. It's very hard to say no to things that don't fit into your Essential Diversification framework. Why?

Because human beings are social creatures, as we've found out in very hard fashion from the pandemic. We don't like turning people away. We want connection and interaction. It's understandable to see why so many people (particularly the young and impressionable) fall into the pattern of giving in to peer pressure.

But the thing that some people don't realize is, it's that turning away that can lead to the most meaning. When you Essentially Diversify and force yourself into a group of people with the same values you have, you will automatically have a community of support that will enrich your life in more ways than you can imagine. Constructive polarization isn't a bad thing. If you don't value outside noise and pressure (hint: you shouldn't, per the Factors), they shouldn't have any impact on your decisions.

INVESTMENT

So we've created our framework for Essential Diversification and allocated and selected our values defined by our framework. A lot of people think this is where they should stop, but that is incorrect. Like investing, you can't really reap the benefits of your Essential Diversification unless you, um, actually *invest* in those assets. With investing, it's money or some sort of capital. With values, it can be a multitude of things. But that's what it all comes down to—an *investment* in your values.

I'm an investor in people. I do deep dives. I don't have a very large circle of people I trust. I live a pretty lonely existence. But that's fine. I'm okay with my investments in those people because I think they do a great job at rewarding me for my investment in them. It hurts when those investments don't work out (I'm looking at *you*, women from Hinge!).[154] But in the end, I'm glad they don't. Investments are supposed to reward you for your investment. If they don't, cut them loose and move on.

Find things that reward you for your investment, especially people. Meet people where they are. That is the investment. That's the value capital you have to deploy. Ask them how they are. Ask them how they're feeling—and, you know, actually mean it. If you see them post on social media about something that is distressing them, reach out and offer encouragement or advice. Ask if they *want* encouragement or advice. In fact, ask them, "Hey, do you want me to help you with this?"

Just show people that you care, and ask how they would like to be cared for, so you can be there when they need you. The reciprocal goes for you. Tell the people you have relationships with how you would like to be cared for. Set boundaries and time. Do the little things. They matter.

However, throughout all of this, that outside-pressure gremlin is still lurking. Don't let it get to you. Stick to your guns. They're your guns, and you have the right to use them. If you really do the exercises into your values, you should know who you are and what you have to work with. Outside pressure shouldn't be a factor. If it is, make sure to learn about your support. Life is a team game, in the words of Joe Namath.[155] Don't try to play hero ball.

Like a proper investment portfolio, you must determine, allocate, and invest in your values in order to have a chance to reap their benefits. Only when a framework is compiled will you be able to screen the values that do and do not work for you and then apply them to get rewarded.

MY VALUES

Okay, so I just yelled at you for a couple chapters about how to form values. I figured I would pay you back by describing my values. These could change, as most values eventually do. But through my own personal lens of the Factors of Value Production (experiences, actions, self-awareness, and discipline), Means of Value, and Essential Diversification framework, these are the ones I currently have:

1) Self-Awareness

I believe self-awareness is the single most important trait a person can possess. Self-awareness is what gives you the ability to thoroughly examine your entire being to see what you value in the first place. Without self-awareness, you cannot see who you are. When you cannot see who you are, you can't possibly know your values. Without knowing your values, you can't possibly have an identity.

Additionally, you might remember the term "self-awareness" from the Factors of Value Production. Self-awareness is the "capital," which is the thing that transforms your experiences and actions into usable values when you are properly disciplined. It is the catalyst in value formation.

Your self-awareness is and should be the catalyst for anything transformative in your life. When you are self-aware, you open doors for that catalyst to come in and work its magic. You open the door for improvement of the most important things. You can expedite transformation within yourself to form a constantly evolving being, one that tests itself to keep proving it can always get better.

It is through self-awareness that all growth and value in life can be found. You know when you meet people that are self-aware. They tell you. They always tell you. Their ego does not get in the way of who they truly are. When you are self-aware, people can sense and are attracted to that vulnerability. You open the door for trust to be fostered and relationships to be built.

Additionally, and most importantly, you open the door to a great relationship with yourself. Only in being forthcoming and honest about yourself and your intentions can you inhabit a greater sense of internal vulnerability. When you can have honest and tough conversations with yourself, it will trickle into every aspect of your being. When self-awareness trickles into other aspects of your life, those other aspects of your life have the opportunity to yield growth and value.

2) Discipline

Discipline is a misunderstood but highly valuable trait. Motivation, as said earlier, is fickle. It comes and goes. It's unreliable when you really need it. Discipline, however, can stick with you throughout your life and keep you on track when motivation fails you.

The reason discipline so often gets confused is people usually associate it with punishment. It can be. People definitely refer to it as such. But, as we've seen with our entrepreneurship factor in the Factors of Value Production, it is simply the regimented style that holds up the construction of our values. You might not always feel like keeping to your values. Values are hard to stick by, particularly in trying situations. Which is why it's very important to choose values that are good for you.

Discipline, however, is different. Discipline does not care how you feel. It simply cares about doing what needs to be done. When the shit hits the fan, your motivation can waver. However, with a clear mind and purpose, you can power through with discipline. Only in a life constrained by discipline can meaning be found.

Discipline, as it does in the Factors of Value Production and your Means of Value, puts you on the path to find a plan of attack. In order to have values, they must consistently be reinforced. Discipline gives you the best shot at doing so.

3) Responsibility

If discipline forms the constraints that lead to meaning, then responsibility is the gateway to it. A meaningful burden in life is one of the best blessings you can have. Burdens demand you be responsible for them. Burdens, however, can be misunderstood too. Most people, when they hear the word, associate it negatively. That having a burden, something to carry, is always a bad thing.

This is far from true. A marriage is a burden. Children are a burden. True friends are a burden. In fact, I would argue that *every* healthy relationship is a burden. It is a burden to invest in other people, much like it is a burden to invest in good values. However, if it is a mutually beneficial relationship that can help you through life's trials, you must bear the responsibility of that burden for yourself and the other person.

When you value responsibility, you value elements of your life that are meaningful to you. Values, as we've discussed, trickle into all parts of your life. It is important your values make it to your meaningful burdens, so your values can be reflected in those burdens. Whether it's a relationship, a career, or a business, I always believe that, if it's important to you, you need to be responsible for taking care of it. That's what gives it meaning and, therefore, value.

4) Stability

I always think it's a good thing to be even-keeled and balanced. This is the point I was attempting to make in Chapter Two. It is never good, with any aspect of life, to be so one-sided toward something you lose your grip on reality. Excess (and its cousin, deprivation) in any form is not good.

This also pertains to your relationships with others. People that can keep a steady hand on the wheel of their own life are more likely to do the same inside of yours. Unhealthy relationships manifest themselves out of a failure of people to be internally balanced. Whether that's codependency, jealousy, narcissism, or anything else, it all stems from not having a stable and balanced mind.

When you do yourself the favor of valuing stability, you ease the burden of responsibility to where you don't feel you have to "fix" other people and their problems. Fixing people is something I've had to deal with a lot. However, fixing people is just another form of narcissism.

They're individuals, just like you. They have the capacity to fix themselves. This does not mean you should not attempt to guide or help the people you care about, but it *does* mean you have to leave it up to them to fix their own problems.

Keeping stable is making sure you're doing everything you can to keep the car of your life from careening off the road. You're not going too fast or slow. You're going at your pace, one that keeps up with your values and the identity forged from them. You keep yourself and your values in check.

5) Authenticity

While honesty is telling the truth, authenticity *is* the truth. When you embody truth, you don't have to tell it. You just are it. You don't just talk the talk; you walk the walk.

It's one thing for a person to be honest and tell the truth. It's another thing completely for a person to be honest and *live* the truth. This is "being yourself" phrased another way. Living authentically is one of the most liberating things you can do. You don't have to hide or put up a front with anyone. You can just be who you are.

However, naturally, this will polarize people. When you live your truth, some people may not like what that truth is. But that is an important part of this value. Like we talked about earlier with the Factors of Value Production, constructive polarization is necessary to attract what you want in life. A man who values everything values nothing.

Authenticity is the way to best express your other values, as it is living the truth about who you are as a person. This is not a call to be bold or brash (aka, a douchebag) about who you are by imposing it on other people. This is a call to free yourself from who you are not.

6) ....

I can't give away all my secrets, can I?

My sixth value is the most important one that anyone can hold. It is higher than self-awareness only because it is the first step to *getting* to your other values. The only reason I'm holding off on getting to it is I believe we need a whole chapter to go over its importance. I suggest you wait until that chapter (Chapter Ten) because it is the bow that ties the rest of the book together. If you really can't wait, go ahead and read ahead. But if you don't, I promise it will be worth it.

WHERE WE GO FROM HERE

Okay, so if you're still here, congratulations!

This is the part of the book where we begin the transition from the first goal I wanted to accomplish with this book to the second goal I described in "What Came Before." With the close of this chapter, we end the first part of the book—how to qualitatively and quantitatively define and implement your values. Now, we move to the more important part—taking those values and using them to interact with the world.

Economics is all about modeling. There are models that lay out general rules as to how an economy functions and how the people that study it make sense of their world. As Value Economists, there are also models that define rules for how to deploy our values into our lives and worlds. Proper knowledge and understanding those models and the rules we take from them will help ensure 1) our values work, and 2) they can be relied on consistently. If you find your values do not work or do not work consistently, reread Chapters One through Three and try to correct them.

The next chapter begins with the journey of understanding what I believe is the bedrock model and rule of Value Economics. And it starts with our favorite childhood pastime: trauma.

CHAPTER FOUR

THE VALUE/SACRIFICE TRADE-OFF

"The true mind can weather all the lies and illusions without being lost. The true heart can tough the poison of hatred without being harmed. Since beginningless time, darkness thrives in the void, but always yields to purifying light."

—THE LION TURTLE, "SOZIN'S COMET, PART 2: THE OLD MASTERS,"
AVATAR: THE LAST AIRBENDER

THE BEST TEACHER

THERE ARE MANY INSTANCES IN CHILDHOOD WHERE YOU learn what not to do. If you touch the hot stove, you'll get burned. If you Zaza Pachulia–kick your brother in the nuts, [156] he'll get hurt, and you'll get sent to your room. If you turn your head away when your mom is talking to you, you'll catch a backhand from Dad that will snap it right back in place.

These instances all have a commonality—pain. We learn very quickly as humans that pain hurts. We eventually interpret pain as a negative thing and try to run away from it. A lot of that is for good reason, as shown in the examples of touching a red-hot surface and castrating your brother. It's a hard lesson to teach humans that pain can be used for bad things.

But it is much harder to teach humans that pain can be used for good things.

* * *

TWO SPECIFIC INCIDENTS OF MY childhood stick out when it comes to teaching me the second lesson.

The first was when I was in the sixth grade. I had just started playing tackle football a year before and was attending a summer skills camp at the local Catholic school my grandpa had graduated from. The only problem was that I was not skilled at all. I was an unathletic, unco-ordinated, unanything, pudgy kid with a bowl haircut and Rec Specs who didn't offer anything of value to a football team except for being a living and breathing tackle dummy.

But, after encouragement from my parents, I went. Not only was I an unanything, pudgy kid, I was also among the youngest there. This specific camp was for middle schoolers ranging from the sixth to eighth grades, from kids who hadn't had their first pubes to kids who looked like they could rep 225 on the bench for ten. Additionally, the eighth graders were treating this as an audition for spots on the Catholic school's high school team. They wanted to impress the coaches by making a good first impression. A lot of those kids came off as typical middle school football jocks—like assholes.

But there was one kid who was a particularly vicious breed of ass-hole. He was an eighth grader with a mohawk, white cutoff shirt, and a voice so fake you knew he had to be making it up just to sound tough. But he was a really good athlete and had a lot of friends, so no one called him out on his asshole-ness.

One thing that not a lot of people know about Ohio weather (not that anyone outside of people from Ohio would ever want to know about Ohio weather) is that, being right by one of the biggest freshwater sources in the world (the Great Lakes), it gets *humid*.[157] Like, unbearably humid. Combine that with summer heat, and we're talking 100 to 120 degrees easily, particularly if you're playing on turf. Thankfully, we weren't, but as middle schoolers, it was still a challenge to keep up with the pace the coaches were setting. Water breaks were like gifts from the gods and cherished every time they let us have one.

My dad, who was a stellar high school football player, knew the tricks of the trade. Before every practice, he and my mom would fill my water jug up with 75 percent ice and 25 percent water to make sure it stayed cold. Most days, it did. But on the first day of the camp, the heat soared. My water got sickeningly warm. The coaches running the camp, however, had set up a trough where cold water flowed freely. So I did what I thought was the best thing to do—I dumped the warm water out and went to the spigot.

The Asshole pounced immediately. As soon as I got back from the spigot and walked to the sideline to wait for the coaches to whistle us back into drills, he pointed at me and yelled:

"This kid just dumped his water on the ground. He likes to kill animals!"

Everyone laughed at me. I felt the anvil of shame drop from a Wile E. Coyote height[158] right onto my head. I wasn't wasting water. I was simply watering the grass while at the same time trying to survive a hot day. I didn't want to kill animals. I loved animals. I tried to muster up the words to have dialogue with The Asshole, but little did I know, The Asshole did not have brains. Being drowned out by embarrassment and laughter, I forced back tears and went through the rest of the drills.

The Asshole didn't stop there. Every time he came across me in the camp, he would say to his fellow assholes, "Guys, look! There's the kid that wastes water and kills animals!" People would laugh, and I would feel shame. I began to hate every second of that camp because I felt like I wasn't wanted there. People were only there to make fun of me, I thought.

On the last day of that three-day camp, I had had enough. The final whistle blew, and we were all dismissed to the parking lot for our parents to pick us up. I picked up my full, warm water jug and started my walk to the parking lot. I hadn't touched it all day. I had been saving it for something better.

I spotted The Asshole and his friends and began to tail them. When I was around five feet behind, I walked to the side of them and unscrewed my jug. The Asshole spotted me and got his trademark line in. But as soon as he finished, I threw the cap open and dumped my animal-killing water all over him. "What the fuck!" he shouted, his fake voice cracking with every word. I started laughing at him, his fraudulent machismo exposed.

However, that smile was quickly blown off my face when his closed right hand caved in the side of my head and sent me face first into the dirt. Laughing at my pain, The Asshole and his friends walked away.

A lot of people talk about getting punched. They say it makes you tough; it makes you a man. But I didn't feel like a man at all. I felt like a nerd who had made a stupid mistake by going after the bully only for him to end up rearranging my face. Tears in my eyes, I walked to my mom's minivan.

However, as I got in and lied about how awesome football camp was, a strange feeling came over me. Even though I had ended up with a bruised face, I smiled. I had won.

* * *

THE SECOND INCIDENT TOOK PLACE in the eighth grade, two years after the "caving in the side of my head" incident. I was more involved in football by this time, and even though I still was unanything and not very good, I was beginning to like it. I had friends and something to be involved in outside of school. I had also gotten involved in throwing discus and shot put in track and field when it was offered as a sport in the seventh grade. I loved that as well. It was something different, unique.

But it wasn't cool. At least, not as cool as other things. The cool kids in my school, in my and seemingly everyone else's opinion at the time, wrestled. Yeah, the basketball players were flashy (I was one of five kids out of forty-five tryouts that got cut), and the football jocks were the football jocks, but the wrestlers were different. They were tough guys. The "bad motherfucker" wallet owners.[159] And I wanted in.

Myself and three of my football buddies decided to join to have fun and become a part of the Tough Guy crowd. Little did we know the Tough Guy crowd wasn't filled only with tough guys. The wrestlers, as it turned out, were more like The Asshole. They weren't tough, even though they pretended to be. They were something truly tough people never are. They were bullies.

Unlike football, I was a starter, wrestling in the 170-pound weight class. But it wasn't for my ability to wrestle. In fact, I was *worse* at wrestling than I was at football. I was only there to fill a spot. We had no one else to wrestle 170, so I was the lucky guy that had to go and fill it.

Every single time I wrestled, I got thrown around in that duct-taped circle of hell like a rag doll. It wasn't for a lack of trying (no pubescent teenage boy wants to get their ass kicked in front of their family, other pubescent teenage boys, and, most importantly, pubescent teenage girls). I just wasn't as experienced or talented as the others. In total, forfeits included, I won four matches that entire season.

Normally, in a supportive team environment, teammates try to lift you up when they see you getting your ass whooped, especially in an arena that's as brutally difficult as wrestling. But this was not a supportive team environment, for the most part. The wrestlers mocked and made fun of us lesser individuals. The bullies, the ones who I thought were the Tough Guys, hounded us in packs and degraded us at every possible chance. Not only was I not good, but I wasn't even wanted there. Again.

But I had another outlet during the wrestling season. Throughout the entire year, I participated in a school club called Power of the Pen,[160] a writing organization tailored to middle-school students across my home state of Ohio. Over a course of three forty-minute, timed essays, students were given a prompt and several minutes to brainstorm and had to write a piece of creative writing on it that was then scored by judges. There was a district, regional, and state competition, and you could progress through the tournament as the months went on. I was good at it—I placed in the top forty-five out of eight thousand participants across the entire state my seventh-grade year. I was exhilarated. I loved every minute of it.

But there was a problem. Power of the Pen wasn't cool. Not nearly as cool as wrestling. The Tough Guys made fun of me for that too. "Going back to your gay club?" they would ask. "How are the Asperger's kids doing?" they would inquire. Humiliated and shamed, I would continue to live my duplicitous existence, just waiting for the season to be over.

Then it got worse. At one of our Power of the Pen practices, my coach announced the date of the regional competition, which I had advanced to. To my horror, it was the same day as my conference championship for wrestling, in which I was supposed to wrestle (aka, just survive long enough to place). It was a tight competition between us and another school that was excellent at wrestling, and I was needed to get points from forfeits. My heart sank. I knew what was coming if I went to the writing competition—more humiliation and shame. My heart sank further when I thought about missing the writing competition for wrestling. It was one pain versus another. Both choices were going to hurt.

But the look of disbelief and outrage on my wrestling teammates' faces when I said I was ditching them made it all worthwhile.

Our wrestling team ended up placing second to the other team by an incredibly small margin. Meanwhile, I bombed at the writing competition, scoring lower than I had in any competition prior. Apparently, the piece I wrote about some guy getting high on psychedelics and pulling a Stan[161] by driving his car off a bridge and into a river didn't sit too well with the middle-school English teachers who judged it. I failed to make it to State, and my team blamed me for their failure to win our wrestling championship. They called me names—faggot, gay, nerd. They roasted me on Facebook.

And I couldn't have been fucking happier.

THE VALUE/SACRIFICE TRADE-OFF

Remember when you were in high school and college, and you had to memorize a ton of shit? Like the scientific method? Renaissance art? The Pythagorean Theorem? God fucking forbid you FORGET THE FUCKING PYTHAGOREAN THEOREM.

In my economics classes in high school, the big thing you had to memorize was graphs. Lots of graphs. And, to the credit of my teachers, it was important that we did so. That's what economics is all about, really. It's basic cause and effect. One thing does X, another thing does Y, and vice versa. There are hundreds of these things. If you really want to get granular, there are an *infinite* number of these things. The people that research these things could get paid by someone (more than likely with your and my tax dollars) to research the economic correlation of various things, such as the amount of times dogs shit per week to the amount of residential fencing per square mile in Elyria, Ohio, if they so desired.

However, there is one graph that stands above the rest. One that these economic academics bow to like the immaculate combination of

Gandhi, Jesus Christ, and Tupac Shakur all rolled into one: the supply/demand graph.[162]

Supply and Demand

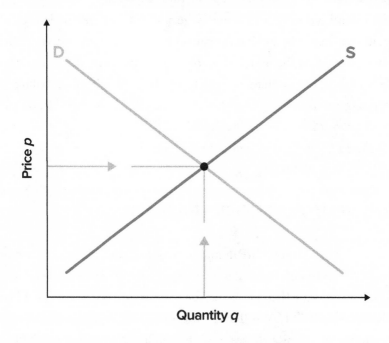

Basically, the supply/demand graph shows the relationship between how much of a thing is available versus how much consumers want that thing. This is a pretty big deal. It influences the entire world economy, from pricing to marketing to housing to college students' obsession with nostalgic vinyl records in order for them to feel ~individualistic~, all that jazz.

Take the supply of oranges in Florida for example. Suppose tomorrow, some guy who claims to be a medical dietetics expert goes on daytime television and proclaims that oranges cure 99.9 percent of all cancers. Based on data collected by the government from 2013–2015, approximately 38.4 percent of all people in America will get some form of cancer at some stage in their life.[163] Sorry for being such a ray of sunshine.

People want to avoid dying of cancer. To save themselves, they will therefore demand more oranges. This pushes demand for oranges up while the supply of oranges stays at the quantity it's at.

Now for the flip side. Suppose after the demand for oranges goes through the roof, the same closeted dumbass comes on TV and says (with "very solemn regret") that oranges actually *enhance* the growth of 99.9 percent of cancers. Pandemonium ensues. People start making picket signs. The state of Florida collapses into the ocean. Consequently, the demand for oranges goes to zero because of the aforementioned "people not wanting to die of cancer" thing. This massive shift pushes demand for oranges down while the supply of oranges stays at the quantity it's at.

It's remarkable how many people don't give a single fuck about this. Granted, it's pretty boring stuff, but some people think it's a big deal. And, to their credit, it kind of is. However, this is Value Economics, and there is new ground that must be broken and improved upon using this framework.

So I am here to revolutionize the world and present to you a new graph. Yes, a *new* graph. *Career academic economist's head explodes in the distance.* However, it does not deal with supply and demand, quantity and price, or anything like that. *Previously mentioned career academic economist's head rematerializes.* No, this graph is better. This graph is easier to understand. This graph can provide meaning to the noneconomists in the world, which I am assuming is most of you.

Before we dive in, there's one more thing we need to get straight. Economics, at its core, is a series of trade-offs.[164] This is what all the graphs included in this book, both regular and Value Economics–based, illustrate. Supply and demand, quantity and price, etc. If there is more demand for something, there will be less supply of that something. If there is less demand for something, there will be more supply of that something. If there is more quantity of something, the less the price will be. If there is less quantity of something, the more the price will be (all else being equal).

However, in terms of Value Economics, we're not going to be doing the typical trade-offs that the do-nothing academic economists do. The goal with Value Economics, and this chapter specifically, is to dive deeper into what our values are and how we can best use them. Whether that's building sewage systems for third-world countries or snorting gas station vodka with your buddies in the basement of a fraternity house, all of the answers can be found below in the graph to end all graphs: the value/sacrifice graph.

Value/Sacrifice Curve

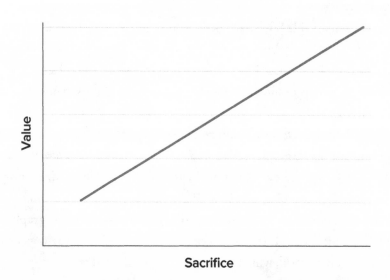

Now that your socks have been effectively knocked off, let's get into what this shit actually means.

Right off the bat, you should notice a big difference between this graph and the one before. This graph contains only one line, versus two on the other. This is because the relationship depicted in this graph is linear. Think y = mx+b or a simple line of regression.[165] (If this gave you PTSD, I don't apologize. Teddy Grahams and juice boxes will be conveniently not provided at the end of this chapter.)

With the supply-and-demand curve, you had two different forces working in opposite directions, which is why there were two lines. One of more means less of the other and vice versa. However, with the value/sacrifice graph, these two forces work in the *same* direction, meaning more of one means more of the other, and less of one means less of the other. And, since I did it with the other two terms (I have a weird interest in diction), let's explore what the definition of "sacrifice" is. According to the dictionary, the definition of sacrifice is the "destruction or surrender of something for the sake of something else."[166]

To indulge my inner emotional economic nerdergy, let's go back to the frat guy snorting gas station vodka example. Suppose he really loves doing this. Like, it's a problem. He goes full season-two *Blue Mountain State* and completely fries his brain and nerve endings at every chance he gets ("It's either this, or we funnel beer through our asses, I'll do either one!").[167] Frat Guy knows it's an incredibly dangerous and reckless thing to be doing. It can cause major health issues. He has a huge exam (economics, the irony) on Monday, and he hasn't studied yet because he's too busy doing this bizarre activity.

However, it makes him look cool. His Little thinks he's the dopest thing since either sliced bread or Snoop Dogg. His buddies take Snapchat videos of him. Sorority women oddly swoon over those Snapchat videos of him. They don't care about his physical well-being or his exam on Monday. Why would they? HE'S SNORTING SHITTY K UP HIS NOSE, if you haven't heard.

So Frat Guy keeps doing this ridiculous behavior. Or, to keep it in perspective, he finds value (relative merit, worth, or importance) in doing it. So after ripping ten shots through his nose and giving a few of his buddies content to get a couple of people to slide up on their stories, he passes out in a stupor, wakes up at five in the morning, throws up profusely, pops a couple of blood vessels in his eyes,[168] orders a pizza, smashes said pizza, and sleeps for the rest of the day after his body finally gives out on him.

Frat Guy then gets woken up by his alarm. It's 7:30 in the morning. His exam ("Fuck, that's today?") is at 8:00. He then throws clothes on, chugs a bottle of water, realizes the water is actually leftover vodka, pukes again, chugs an actual bottle of water, and runs out to take his exam, totally unprepared. He takes his exam and knows nothing. Afterward, he texts the buddies that took videos of him, saying things like, "Bro, that was *such* bullshit!" "How could they do us like that?" "But mannnnn, Erin was looking *fire* on Saturday. I couldn't study! The professors should know this, smfh."

The grades come in a few days later. Frat Guy pulls up his grade on his phone. Oof, a 23 percent. Oh well, the gas station vodka will still be there for him. Or, to keep it relative to the point, he has *sacrificed* (surrendered or given up and permitted injury to something for the sake of something else) his grades for the experience he had over the weekend (and the gas station vodka).

ONE CHOSEN, ONE TAKEN

So, in the grand scheme of this thing, what does this have to do with anything? Well, Mr./Ms. Skeptic, the point is the more you *value* something, the more you will *sacrifice* to get it. Frat Guy sacrificed getting a good grade on his exam in order to rip shots of gas station vodka with his friends because he found value in doing so. The more he values this activity, the more he is willing to sacrifice for it.

Sacrifices are made all the time. Some women sacrifice their careers when they have children due to the fact that they value spending time raising their children more than advancing in the job they have. Some workaholic fathers sacrifice time with their families because they value their careers and making money more than time with their kids or because working gives them the feeling of emotionally balancing out not being there by "doing it for the family" in the form of monetary compensation. The morbidly obese kid from *Willy Wonka and the Chocolate Factory* was willing to miss out on landing (you guessed it) the *whole fucking factory* because he placed too much value on gluttony.[169]

Now you're seeing the trend. Value goes up, sacrifice goes up. Value goes down, sacrifice goes down. Linear relationship, remember? Two plus two equals four. Earth rotates around the sun. Biggie Smalls was a good rapper. These are facts. They are part of human nature. And as we can see from the world we live in, molecular genetics, and *Jurassic Park*,[170] when we try to cheat it, humans *always* lose. Always.

Take the workaholic dad example. Suppose one day, he realizes he's missing out on spending time with the family. He goes to his boss, flips him off, and tells him to stick his head and 5 percent 401(k) match up his slightly loosened asshole. He is promptly fired on the spot, gives his receptionist an apple, and peels out of the parking lot blasting ignorant rap music, feeling more liberated than he has in years.

Former-workaholic dad then goes home and starts living blissfully in his new life. He and his kids do sidewalk chalk. They go to the park. Ice cream for breakfast. The whole nine yards. Everything is great.

Until it isn't.

It turns out, dad's six-figure income, insurance plan, retirement account, and benefits were key to the family's survival. Mom asks her company for more hours, but they are hesitant to give them to her because she's been part-time ever since dad got the promotion that led to him becoming a workaholic all those years ago. Why should they pay her benefits? Why should they give her a salary instead of keeping her on hourly pay?

So the once-blissful situation starts to turn grim. The house falls into disrepair. The family has to wonder if the heat will come on. Junior gets listeria from eating too much Jeni's Ice Cream.[171]

Why does this happen? Well, because it's the *reverse* of the effect I talked about earlier. When dad *stopped sacrificing* sidewalk-chalk time for all the benefits that came from working that job, the value of his and his family's life decreased tremendously. When sacrifice goes down, value goes down. When one wishes to have more value, one must make more sacrifices.

So what does this mean? Does it mean dad is doomed to be enslaved to work, never seeing his family and/or the light of day again?

Of course not. But does it mean dad can give up *everything* that causes stress either? No, because that leads to even more (and probably worse) problems.

The correct answer to this question? I don't know. I can't make that decision. That decision rests with every person individually. One cannot value everything, and one cannot value nothing. That much is certain. But I think I have an idea that could flip this phenomenon on its head. Maybe we should not value nothing but make a more concerted effort about *what* we value.

It's not about valuing things. It's about picking the *right things to value*. These values are different for everyone. So the best thing you can do to pick the right things to value is know yourself. To a tee. This is a very excruciating process for some, but it is absolutely worth it.

The most successful people in the world, for the most part, have nothing in common except for one thing: they are authentic and true to who they are. Regardless of their field of choice or personality type, they never deviate from it. If they did, it would be a cheat. They would immediately feel the repercussions. Think Adam Sandler when he tried to make a tame children's movie. Then you get *Jack and Jill*, and we all know how that turned out.[172]

Finding the right things to value is important for the exact reason you've seen in the graphs and examples. Finding the right things to value for *yourself* is directly correlated to discovering what you're willing to sacrifice.

I say these things not to make you feel bad but to give examples of how this shit actually works in real life. The word "sacrifice" might not have a lot of sex appeal because (guess what?) it *isn't* sexy. It's hard. It's uncomfortable. It can be downright miserable at times. However, the math works. The examples, graphs, and my lackluster sense of economic theory prove it.

THE WILL TO ACT

In the prior three chapters, we formed the basis for our own value hierarchies. We saw how the Factors of Value Production intertwine with our lives to form our values. We saw examples of how to figure out where your Means of Value lies. We then went through the process of value selection and investment to solidify which values really mean something to us, which ones we should hold the most dearly, and why. Remember, the non-tyrannical collective begins with the non-tyrannical self.

But it cannot stop there either.

It's not enough to simply know your values. It is not enough to simply exist in the world as a person who holds them. That certainly gets you somewhere, but it cannot forge your identity. Because whether you like to admit it or not, we live in a world that is defined by our interactions with one another. All that bullshit about not caring about how people think of you? It's not true. In fact, it's the antithesis of true.

You *should* care about what people think of you. If you don't, you have no way of telling if your values are really your values. Mark Manson defined this in his first book, *Models*, as the art of polarization.[173] A book about modern dating for men, Manson stated that the worst thing men do when approaching women is not being authentic. Not only is it boring, it's useless. It's unattractive to anyone, most certainly a potential partner, if you don't declare something about who you are.

Values work the same way. If you don't assert who you are, if you don't present your values, you blend into the mob. You become a purposeless ball of bleh, constantly adrift among your compatriots who also assert or stand for nothing. When you cannot stand as an individual, you can easily succumb to victimization by societal tribalism, as we've seen with the identity politics issue that played out in "What Came Before." Only truly robust individuals composed of robust individual values can afford to look away from the dogma to check themselves before they wreck themselves.

In the film *Batman Begins*, Ra's al Ghul attempts to bring this out of a shattered Bruce Wayne after the death of his parents.[174] Seeking enlightenment and justice, Wayne travels the world until he happens upon Ghul. Wayne becomes Ghul's protege. Ghul disciplines Wayne in the art of radical personal responsibility, convincing him the only way to ensure triumph is through swift and decisive action. A lot of people can train. A lot of people can think. A lot of people can believe. But very few are willing to act.

The hard truth people need to realize about identity is that it is not something you simply are. Your identity is the things you *do*. You need to impose your identity on the world through your actions and your will. The actions you take are reflective of your values. You would be hard pressed to find someone taking action, particularly intensive action, if that person did not value something. The will to act, like all emotions (as we covered in Chapter Two), must be driven by intense conviction and belief in something you hold dear. We are emotional creatures first and logical creatures second. Belief is a powerful emotion. It's the architect of perception, and one that should not be taken lightly. If perception is indeed reality, belief is necessary for that reality to manifest itself.

But belief in what?

That is the question, isn't it? What do we believe? As I stated in "What Came Before," I believe we (and especially Generation Z) believe in nothing. But not a universal nothing. We each believe in our own personal nothing. We all derive meaning from our own lives, as the Factors of Value Production prove. But where does the convergence come from? How do we get from disillusioned individuals to angry mobs? From promising potential to disastrous end results?

It is the will to act.

Since we refused to act on our individual values, we created a vacuum inside our culture. And, since nature abhors a vacuum, something must sweep in to take its place. And that something cannot be small. It must be something powerful, something that gives you a taste of what your identity could be but still provides enough of a hunger to keep you forever wanting more. This sensation drugs people. It creates inertia, so people are willing to forsake their individual identities for the sake of conformity.

Conformity is not just something we fall into, however. It is also something that empowers people. The will of the collective can overpower the will of the individual should the will of that individual be weak. And that's exactly what's happening. The indoctrination that we are currently dealing with cripples the identity of the individual by morphing it carelessly and insidiously within the context of a larger group.

The group cannot define an individual holistically. It's simply too broad of a categorization. A group of individuals define a group, one that encapsulates all the intricacies and shortcomings of everyone involved. Because what works for that identity group can also work against it. In the words of author and journalist Douglas Murray:[175]

If somebody has the competency to do something, and the desire to do something, then nothing about their race, sex or sexual orientation should hold them back. But minimizing difference is not the same as pretending difference does not exist. To assume that sex, sexuality and skin color mean nothing would be ridiculous. But to assume that they mean everything will be fatal.

We have chosen to fill our individual value vacuums with the identity not chosen by us but chosen *for* us. One where a larger group gets to decide who we are, not the individuals that make up the group.

But that is proven to be untrue.

The value/sacrifice curve proves it. A group's curve may look totally different than any one of the individuals that make it up. This is the crux of the difference. No one's values perfectly align because no one's sacrifices perfectly align. People end up in different places and with different people because they are willing to tolerate different types of pain (more on this in Chapter Eight) and sacrifice.

Because pain can be used for good things, remember? Pain is not just good for telling us to avoid harmful things. That is too simplistic a definition. Pain is also good, fortunately for us, at telling us where to go. It is the pain we are willing to sustain that will grant us our own individual level of providence. This cannot be determined from a larger group because the larger group cannot force you to undergo pain that you do not want to undergo (if they're a group worth belonging to, that is). Only you can muster the will to do that. Only you can evolve into that level of self-definition.

You are the one with your unique set of Factors of Value Production. You are the one that knows your Means of Value. You are the one that knows what values you want to select and invest in. That cannot be formed outside of your own consciousness. People can try to convince you, and even force you, to do otherwise. But deep down, you will know it to be wrong, and you will know it to be a lie.

IN ACTION

When I dumped my water bottle on The Asshole and gave the literary middle finger to my middle school wrestling team, all I could see through my narrow scope of vision was how fucked up a decision I had made. The crowd is a menace to you when you oppose it, and it is incredibly difficult to walk against it. It takes courage to willingly tolerate pain, to step up to the plate and know that you're going to get beaned in the ego with a fastball of people who are intolerant of your values.

So the question you must ask yourself when undertaking any decision of this magnitude is—is it worth it? Is it worth being smashed in the face by a football jock after a week of bullying? Is it worth being embarrassed and socially ostracized by the coolest kids in school to do something you deem more important?

Only the person getting smashed in the face, embarrassed, and socially ostracized can truly provide an answer. But perspective can provide a window. I didn't feel satisfied because I had dumped a jug of lukewarm water on The Asshole in front of his friends. I felt satisfied because I let him know through action that I wasn't going to sit back and eat his cock in front of his friends. It was satisfying in knowing that I could stand up for myself, even against a force that seemed so much bigger and badder than I.

Because when you enact your values in the world, you are directly communicating who you are. You put a stake in the ground and draw a line in the sand that tells everyone in your life you are what you act out. Your actions are the greatest form of sacrifice. When someone sees you doing something, they at least know you "are that" or "aren't that." They know something about you, whether that something is significant or not.

In action, you can learn to live with who you really are, not who you say you are. You can know yourself better than you ever thought possible because in order to know yourself, you must be yourself. In being yourself, you must act as yourself. Only then will true belief settle in. When belief settles in, your identity will begin to slowly but surely crystalize on top of your sacrifices, allowing your values to come springing to the surface for you and the whole world to see.

CHAPTER FIVE

THE LIFE-DEFINING PRINCIPLE

"For what shall it profit a man, if he shall gain the whole world, and lose his own soul?"

—MARK 8:36

WHAT'S AT THE CENTER OF YOUR UNIVERSE?

"NO, I DROPPED OUT OF COMMUNITY COLLEGE TO DO PERCOCET and sell subprime mortgages on Long Island, which I still believe is what I'll return to."[176]

The current state of American comedy is a sad one. There are very few people in the profession who are truly funny anymore—people that play the role of the playful anarchist, forcefully but gracefully pushing back the established order as a natural check to the current conditions of the popular culture.

Tim Dillon is one of that very few. Dillon and his large, Irish Catholic family grew up in Island Park, New York. His home life had its ups and downs. His parents divorced when he was growing up, and his mother was diagnosed with schizophrenia and institutionalized after she had a mental breakdown when he was twenty. To cope with his homelife and attempt to fit in, Dillon got into a life of debauchery. He started smoking cigarettes and marijuana and did cocaine, which later devolved into the aforementioned Percocet. In his own words, he "idolizes hucksters, thieves, cons, and cheats."[177]

After the whole "dropping out of community college and selling subprime mortgages" period of his life imploded with the 2008 financial crisis,[178] Dillon began to scrape together odd jobs to make ends meet. He worked on a cruise ship,[179] as a New York City tour guide,[180] and as an actor. But unfortunately, his big break in television had come much earlier when he successfully auditioned for *Sesame Street*.[181] As he told Joe Rogan on his podcast, "I was on *Sesame Street* twice. I did the polka with Snuffleupagus. Legitimately."[182]

Seeing that his life left a lot to be desired, Dillon decided to go all in on the one thing he found he was good at—making people laugh. He decided to stop hiding from what he wasn't and fully devote himself to what he was. He quit all his jobs and started blitzing the comedy scene, doing three shows a night to get his name out there. Dillon's second (non-*Sesame Street*) big break came at the Just for Laughs comedy festival, where *Rolling Stone* named him one of the "Ten Comedians You Need to Know."[183]

Dillon made the rounds on several podcasts, most notably seven times on Rogan's, which furthered his rise into the comedy stratosphere. His Instagram and YouTube channels became wildly popular, with his impersonations of Meghan McCain,[184] the QAnon Shaman,[185] and Jeffrey Epstein's temple[186] going viral. He currently hosts *The Tim Dillon Show* and is one of the most popular comedians in America.

There are many reasons people find others funny. We all like different types of humor and find different subjects funny, whether it be the mundane aspects of daily life or what color someone's shit is in the morning. But I believe the main reason people find others funny is there is honesty in how they present themselves. There is identity. You feel like you can trust them. Throughout history, comedians have been one of the most necessary groups in society simply because they act as the relief valve for the heaviness and tragedy of life. It's also why they are often so sad. We saw this earlier with Chris Farley.

The reason Tim Dillon is one of the last truly funny comedians in America is because he acknowledges this. Tim Dillon does not hide who he is. He's the one that told everyone his mother was a nutcase. He's the one that openly acknowledges he's fat. He's the one that admitted he had a problem with numerous substances. The difference between him and someone like Chris Farley is he is honest with himself about his problems. He does everything he can to avoid self-destruction.

Tim Dillon chose what he wanted his life to be and acted on it. He valued being a successful stand-up comedian. He knew what he had to sacrifice to become one. He understood the Value/Sacrifice Trade-Off. But he also saw the pitfalls some of his colleagues in comedy fell victim to. In an interview with Megyn Kelly, he laid out the state of the comedic landscape in one of his trademark rants:[187]

> People have Google. People can remember that Chelsea Handler made a living doing race material, and now Chelsea Handler does documentaries on white privilege. Jimmy Kimmel had a show called *The Man Show* where they did wet T-shirt contests, and now he's talking about health insurance. Stephen Colbert did a show where he was a very funny guy impersonating Bill O'Reilly and got away with saying a lot of crazy things because it was satire and it was very funny, and now a lot of these people act like satire doesn't exist. If you say something, you're dead serious about it. If you make a racial joke, you're a racist, or if it's a homophobic joke, you're a homophobe. If you make a joke about trans people, you're diminishing trans identity. All of these people are very Googleable. They've all had long careers. None of them felt this way years ago. And I mean, you don't have to go back ten years, you can go back right before

Trump got into the primaries…I have comedian friends that are tweeting about trade agreements all day, it's like, what are you doing here? Tweeting at Mayor Garcetti—these people have roommates, they're on drugs, and they're going, "What's the budget of L.A.? The cops better not be getting more than this percentage of the budget!" I'm like, "The budget? You can't afford a car!" It's a mind virus, truly it's a mind virus. And people like me being pretty well-received pointing it out and people are going "Yeah, man, that's the way I feel." They grew up watching these comics. These guys were very funny—Colbert, Kimmel—these guys were really funny people. But now I think they feel that for whatever reason that isn't their job.

A lot of people "want" to be something. A successful stand-up comedian, a good father, whatever. But do they really? Does the sacrifice they're making really reflect the value they're getting out of it? Is what they're saying is the most important thing to them really the most important thing?

A person who looks in front of a mirror every morning and tells themselves they're successful probably isn't. A person who writes in their journal every night that they love themselves probably doesn't. Like Chris Farley and Tim Dillon's portrayal in Jeffrey Epstein's temple, they're playing a character. They have no idea what's at the center of their universe because they have no idea how complex their universe is.

* * *

WHEN I WAS TEN YEARS old, my family bought a timeshare down in Orlando, Florida. This was during the prime "Disney World phase" of our family's life, and we were going to use the timeshare to whisk us away for a week. I was about to graduate into fifth grade, which meant more commitments for events and sports during the summer. To avoid potential conflicts, my family decided to go during spring break, right before Easter. However, on the Friday before we left, my fourth-grade teacher did the absolute unthinkable. Something so satanic that not even Lucifer himself could have dreamt a worse punishment:

She gave us homework. *Math* homework.

If either you or your kids have experienced this kind of teacher before, you know they are the absolute fucking worst. They're a disgusting, vile species of vermin who have nothing better to do on spring break, so they punish their students by making them share their suffering. It's abhorrent. Thankfully, my parents thought so too. We made a deal. As soon as we touched down, I would do the problems, my dad (the resident engineer) would check them over, and we would proceed with our plans.

As soon as we got everything settled in our hotel room, I immediately whipped out my folder and got to work. I was a reasonably smart student. The problems weren't difficult. They were order of operations questions that were more cumbersome in time than actual difficulty. Pulling my best Alan from *The Hangover*,[188] my mind turned into a mental computer, spitting out answers rapidly with my hand dutifully following. After half an hour, I finished and went over to my dad to have him check them.

I confidently handed the paper to my dad, who looked it over. Emotionless, my dad asked, "Where's your work?"

I didn't have an answer for him. I pointed out that the answers, all my teacher cared about, were underneath the problems on the sheet. I was pretty sure they all were right. I didn't ask my dad to check my work. I asked him to check if the answers were right so I could get a fucking Mickey Mouse ice cream bar. I was quite sure my dad wanted that as well. It was his vacation too.

Calmly, my dad asked me to bring him my pencil. Thinking I got an answer wrong, I went back to the coffee table where I had done my work, picked up my Number Two, and handed it to him. But my dad didn't cross anything out. He didn't point out which ones I had gotten wrong, if any at all.

He took the pencil, flipped it over, and erased my answer to every single problem.

My jaw dropped. Tears welled in my eyes. If I had known the word "fuck," I would have asked him what the fuck he was doing. There was no way I could remember the answers. I would have to start over.

My dad handed the sheet back. "If you're gonna do something, do it right. Do it again, write out every single step of your work, and have me check it." Fuming, I ripped the paper from his hands and sat on the couch. Fortunately, I had a decent memory and remembered most of the answers. I scribbled some work down to show I had done something different, walked over to him, and gave it back.

He took the sheet, checked it, and erased everything again. "You missed some steps. Do it again."

My shock turned to rage. I looked over at my mom and pleaded with my eyes to have my dad show mercy. My mom began to speak, but he waved her off. "Take Jackie and Jake down to the pool, Kris. We'll hit Animal Kingdom tomorrow. Sam and I will meet you when we're finished up here." It wasn't up for debate. My mom, with a twinge of pity in her eyes, took my siblings down to the pool. I was left in that wretched hotel room with a man who I was convinced wanted to make my life a living hell.

I had no choice. I took the paper back to that awful fucking coffee table and did it again. I finished in half an hour. "You missed some steps. Do it again." The paper started to wear through from all the eraser marks after the fourth time. "Write out *all* the steps. Again." My tear ducts stung with rage. "You're still missing a few. Do it again." The paper did wear through after the sixth time. No worries. My dad whipped out a spare piece from his folder and wrote the problems out for me.

Something strange happened after the seventh time. My anger subsided. My emotions numbed. I was nothing more than a math robot confined to a process repeated over and over again until perfection was achieved. Human error wasn't an option for me. I had to be perfect. At least, the process had to be.

That was what blew my mind as I moved toward Attempt Ten. If the answers were right, then what was the point of the work? Isn't that what anyone ever cared about? Sure, Superman raced trains[189] and Tommy Lee puked on strippers and twirled his drumsticks,[190] but all anyone cared about was that Superman saved the day, and Tommy Lee was able to spin in a cage in the air while he did his drum solo.

I forced my brain to slow down. I had been at this for hours. I had missed my first day of vacation doing math homework given to me by my Fallen Angel Fourth Grade Teacher. It then clicked. I might as well do it right. What could I lose? I already saw my mistakes. I knew the answers. Time to put it all together.

Like John Nash in *A Beautiful Mind*,[191] it all clicked. I saw both the beginning and end simultaneously. I saw the flow of the process, every little detail stretched out on a perfect continuum. It very well could have been delirium and nausea from the hours of nonstop math, but something definitely was happening.

I turned it over to my dad. He smiled. "Looks good Sammo, nice job." Too tired to give him a piece of my mind, I walked into my room and collapsed. My brain was fried. It had never worked that hard in its short life. But little did I know, those hours of math would change the way I looked at everything.

THE LIFE-DEFINING PRINCIPLE

Everyone's looking for a hack. A trick. A way to game the system. A methodology for looking up your boyfriend's activity on Instagram after the company took specific measures to dissuade that behavior.[192]

The effort people undergo to *not* do work always amazes me. In reality, all they're doing is wasting time doing other work to avoid doing actual work. They call that a paradox. (Frank Costello voice.)[193]

This happens across all walks of life. In fact, this is what civilization has been ever since man invented things like fire and the wheel. Every single piece of technology in and of itself is "a hack." Technology, no matter what the technology does, exists for one purpose—to make our lives easier. To avoid us spending energy on things that can be solved with that technology. To make us do less work. This is both the capital and self-awareness components of the economic production factors and the Value Factors of Production. The iPhone, Microsoft Office, and literally anything sold by the late, great Billy Mays are all examples of this.

However, most people look at this from the wrong lens. They see only the finished product, not what went into it. Take the three afore-mentioned examples. It took Apple five years to develop the first iPhone, which was so rudimentary the newest iPhone uses it to wipe its ass.[194] Microsoft didn't launch Office until fourteen years after it was founded.[195] Billy Mays built an unprecedented large meme culture over years of advertising various cleaning products on daytime television.[196] It didn't happen overnight.

The lens through which people look at greatness needs adjustment. It's inaccurate and misleading. The people that think you accomplish great things by doing less don't see the big picture. They think it's the hack that defines the finished product, when in reality, it's the opposite. Your life is explicitly defined by one thing: doing the things others are not willing to do. This is the Life-Defining Principle.

Opportunity is found by looking specifically where other people don't. However, very few do this. Why? For multiple reasons—comfort, conformity, being possessed by Satan, etc.

Don't believe me? Good, most people don't. That's why entrepreneurs have been profiting off this since capitalism was invented. Now, a lot of people that *didn't* realize this work for those people. This is not to dissuade the common man because we need those people way more than they're given credit for (more on this in Chapter Nine). But they didn't look for the opportunity, so that opportunity was not realized by them.

In most cases, to get more out of life, you just need to do more, not find a shortcut to do less. Not only is it wasted energy, but it is wasted potential on the path to something better. You set yourself apart not by finding the crack in the Matrix but by coding the Matrix itself, line by line.

Jocko Willink doesn't like hacks. At all. He states this in *Discipline Equals Freedom: Field Manual*:[197]

The shortcut is a lie. The hack doesn't get you there.

And if you want to take the easy road, it won't take you to where you want to be: Stronger. Smarter. Faster. Healthier. Better.

Free.

To reach goals and overcome obstacles and become the best version of you possible will not happen by itself. It will not happen by cutting corners, taking shortcuts, or looking for the easy way.

There is no easy way.

Now, before you club me to death with the "this dude is a Navy SEAL—what do you expect?" mantra, I think it's practical to understand what this principle *isn't* before we understand what it *is*. This principle is *not* going to tell you to bury yourself in the minutiae of life. This principle is *not* going to tell you to drive yourself nuts over every little detail. This principle is *not* meant to work you up so much you devolve into insanity like a coked-out Lorraine Bracco and Ray Liotta at the end of *Goodfellas.*[198]

Instead, this concept will actually get you to cut *down* on the nonsensical shit too many people get stuck in. Yes, you will have to do more. Kind of. But this principle is set to prove why doing more of the right things is better than doing less of the things that don't do anything for you. Those lesser things may string you along for a bit. But eventually, they will all lead to the same place: unpreparedness based on a false sense of getting ahead, which doesn't get you ahead at all.

This chapter is going to describe this phenomenon and how we can use it to better our lives and improve our value-oriented compasses. A culmination of doing the right little things leads to doing the right big things. A culmination of doing the wrong little things leads to doing the wrong big things. You can either get both right or both wrong. It's a binary equation. One explicitly leads to the other.

* * *

FIRST, WE NEED TO REVISIT our friend from the last chapter: the Value/Sacrifice Trade-Off. If you remember (you should, it was only one chapter ago), the Value/Sacrifice Trade-Off is the bedrock of Value Economics. The reason it's the bedrock of Value Economics is it explains the fundamental undercurrent of why we make decisions. The more value we put in something, the more we will sacrifice to obtain it. The less value we put in something, the less we will sacrifice to obtain it.

This is why the Life-Defining Principle is called what it is. Because it's true. The Life-Defining Principle is perfectly correlated with the value/sacrifice curve because by doing the things that others aren't willing to do to obtain something, you are intrinsically sacrificing more to get it. Free time, devotion to a religion, snorting horse tranquilizers off a linoleum countertop, you name it.

The reason the life-hack methodology is inherently wrong is because it's *reversely* correlated with the value/sacrifice graph. Instead of following what is proven (sacrificing more to get something of value), you try to game the system (sacrificing less to get something of value). You cheat your way forward to try to get something of value that can only be gotten by proven methods.

If you truly value being in shape, you will sacrifice more and do more of the right little things in order to be in shape. You'll sacrifice some sleep (but not an unhealthy amount)[199] to get up before the sun and work out. You'll get the right fluids in your body and eat the right things. You'll limit your alcohol and post-alcohol greasy food consumption so as not to compromise the hard work you've done.

If you truly value being in a relationship, you'll sacrifice some time to invest in your significant other and genuinely ask (and care, by the way) about how their day was. You'll listen to their problems. You'll be faithful to them and supportive of them. You won't let them compromise themselves with derogatory decisions. You'll hold them accountable for both their actions and inactions.

But within this inherently lies the whole "Lorraine Bracco and Ray Liotta on coke" problem. This does not mean you should become a Burrower. Burrowers invest *too* much into something to the point they lose context. There is such a thing as valuing something too much. It causes imbalance within your life and will thereby create a catastrophe if something were to happen to that thing you value too much.

Remember the whole "read the book in order" thing I alluded to in "What Came Before"? This is another example. If you can't control living within your Means of Value, you cannot possibly apply the Life-Defining Principle with success. You'll simply blow everything in the world out to beyond-optimal maximization (more on this in Chapter Six) and end up fucking everything up. There's a reason the chapter on excess came before we learned about Essential Diversification. Essential Diversification is the first check on excess. You can't have all your value eggs in one excessive basket.

You don't have to work out three times a day, drink a gallon of water every hour, and eat only chicken and rice for the rest of your life to prove you value your health. You're allowed to have a cheat day or meal once a week. You're allowed to rest, particularly if you feel something is so fucked up you could injure yourself. If you don't, that's not healthy. That's mental and physical imprisonment.

You don't have to alternate between texting, tweeting, Instagram-DMing, Snapchatting, and whatever the fuck else psychopathic relationship guys/girls do to prove you value your relationship. You should create boundaries, so you can still realize and be in touch with your individuality. You should respect if your significant other says they don't feel like talking or they tell you they don't want you to help solve their problems. If you don't, that's not healthy. That's being emotionally insensitive.

That is the balance. You have to be able to differentiate what value-added activities and sacrifices correlate to the things you value while not choking out anyone else trying to apply the Life-Defining Principle. In any team-oriented setting, whether it be a sales operations staff or a family of five, this is essential to realize. Everyone has a role to play, and they'd better play it well. If anyone over- or under-steps, if anyone doesn't have balance, everything can go to hell much quicker than people think.

CZ GET DEGREEZ

I majored in finance in college. I had a lot of ambitious people surrounding me, most of whom probably watched *Entourage* at least twice and jerked to a picture of Jordan Belfort every day. ("Gotta pump those numbers up, those are rookie numbers in this racket.")[200] Additionally, I worked for two years as a TA for the accounting department. I had touch points with all these ambitious jerkers constantly.

The classes I TAed for were very hard. They were considered the business college's "weed-out" classes. We had to take them to access the rest of the business college. So, naturally, we had a lot of people come into our tutor room to get help with their problems or help studying.

Unfortunately, like a lot of young people, they didn't listen all that well. Me and my coworkers had all taken the class. We knew what it took. We would tell them what to focus on, how hard to work, and how to implement that work and tune their focus to guarantee their success. My colleagues and I weren't the typical cockolas that withheld from our classmates. We had the key. They just needed to open the door.

But, in most cases, the kids chucked the key over the hedges, got out some spermicidal lube (probably the same bottle they used to help get off to The Wolf) and a toothpick, and tried to pick the lock. They already had everything they needed. Yet, they tried to work around that simple action to try to find another way into the door. I was baffled when I saw this in action, until I began to understand why.

Most of the students didn't want to go through the action of putting the key in the lock, turning it, and opening the door. For them, it was too traditional and robotic to sit down with a pencil and paper and work out accounting problems. It was simple in description but not easy in implementation. Students saw it as easier to attempt to go about it their own way. By trying to game the system by using a way other than the way specifically recommended by the people who ran the class.

You may be saying to yourself, "Sam, you're a fucking hypocrite. An asshole. A cockola in and of itself! Why are you judging? If you're in a position of authority, why wouldn't you be accommodating toward them and their specific methods? Isn't that what a good teacher and coach should do?"

The answer is yes, Dear Reader. A good teacher and coach should do those things. But only if it's the right approach. The reason I didn't do that method was because I knew personally that it didn't work.

The reason I knew was because I initially thought the exact same thing they did.

"These people don't know me," I thought. "How could they? I'm smarter than them because I know myself. I know how I work, how I study, how I get myself a good grade. I can do this my own way."

Well, I tried to do it my own way. And I nearly failed out of college because of it.

When I transferred to the main campus of The Ohio State University for my sophomore year of college (more on this in Chapter Eight), I was riding high. I had a 3.9 GPA. I had proven to myself that I belonged at the place I wanted to live my dream. I came in confident. It was time to show all these motherfuckers how they wronged me. I was going to go Goku Super Saiyan Mode.[201] I was set to destroy.

I walked into the course that I would eventually TA on the first day of classes and got the typical spiel that my professor (later boss) gave everyone. This class is hard. Very hard. A good portion of you will not make it through. However, there is a simple solution. All we had to do, according to my professor, was follow the study formula he recommended. Having done the job and taught the class for over twenty years, he had a system that worked with everyone who applied themselves to it.

The only problem was the system required one thing most public-university business majors don't possess in great quantities— commitment. For any system to work properly, the parts comprising that system must be completely in sync. In the system of a studying routine, the single biggest catalyst by far is the person who, you know, actually has to study. After the professor went over the routine, he asked if anyone had questions. Unsurprisingly, no one in that 280-person lecture hall raised their hand.

This class was laid out in the following format. There was no book. All the material came from the professor in the form of online lecture videos. There were homework assignments, but they weren't graded. They were only to be done for practice if we wanted to. Attendance at recitation was a smaller part of our grade. But the biggest part (again, unsurprisingly) was the three exams. There was no final but three exams that each covered a third of the class. They built upon one another as the semester went on. Added together, they came out to a whopping 82.5 percent of our grade. A misstep on one of those exams was a direct step onto the land mine that left your academic life bleeding out and crying for help.

But remember, I was confident. I "knew what I was doing." I didn't just completely ignore the professor; I did the complete opposite of what he said. I thought I knew what was best. I carved out a completely niche model of studying for myself, meticulously going over every detail up until the first exam. I was completely bulletproof according to the standards I set for myself. I went in confident. I had other fish to fry. I had two exams in other classes the following week, ones I thought would be much harder than this one.

A week after I took the exam, I was cramming for my second one I had to take for a statistics course. Exactly two hours before that exam, I got an email from my accounting professor. The grades had been posted. A smile broke open on my face. Before I knew how terribly this can flip on you, I opened up my grade portal and looked at the number that virtually painted my face: 48 percent.

I refreshed the screen, idiotically hoping it would somehow change the fact that I had bombed. To my dismay, it didn't. I went into panic mode. I scrolled down to the bottom of the page to see my overall grade: 52 percent. I was failing. I looked at the average grade, praying I wasn't the stupid one. I didn't get the 11 percent. That was the low, but I certainly didn't get the 82 percent class average either.

My entire world shattered. My entire perception of the student I thought I was collapsed in front of my eyes. All the confidence I had regarding academics was shot. I had finally gone to the big leagues, stepped up to the plate, and gotten hit in the dick with a 110 MPH fastball. I had fucked up. Badly.

Remember, I had another exam to take in less than two hours and another the next morning. Was I going to fail those too? I called my mom and broke the news, using the public shower in my dorm to cover my frequently cracking voice as I tried to keep it together. My mom, obviously, couldn't be of much help. It was my grades and my responsibility. She told me the typical advice—keep your head down, put it behind you, all that jazz. I thought it helped. I calmed down slightly and went to take the next exam.

To say I did better on those exams isn't saying much. I got a low D on the statistics exam and a C– on my other test. At the end of the carnage, my cumulative GPA stood at a 1.02. I was failing out of school.

I sat down in my dorm the night I did the worst math equation of my life (my GPA) and weighed my options. I felt so disheartened. I had done so much, worked so hard. I did so many things to ensure success. But I failed. Now the only thing that had sustained me for the last year, the potential of graduating, was being taken from me because of my own ignorance. After a long and hard talk with myself, I came to only one solution that could maybe fix my current predicament: I had to completely obliterate everything.

My professor had office hours the next day. I walked in and did the only thing I could think to show him I wanted to change. I begged for mercy. I knew I was beaten, that I hadn't listened, that I had deliberately disobeyed him. So I showed humility. I took ownership of the entire situation. Unlike most of my classmates who came in here, I knew the fault was not his, or the class', or the material's. It was mine. I was arrogant, cocky, and stupid, and I had come pleading to him to spare my academic life.

Thankfully, like Xerxes, he was a merciful god.[202] He had seen people like me before. People that thought they could do it without listening.

But there was a difference. They were too proud to admit their failure. They didn't heed the words of the great and powerful Marsellus Wallace—pride only hurts, it never helps.[203] My professor didn't just tell me I could pass. He told me, to my complete and utter shock, that I could end up doing quite well even after my self-induced carpet bombing. However, there was a caveat: I had to do even more work than before.

My professor laid out a daily routine, explaining what I had to do each and every day to improve in the class. It wasn't pretty. I had to do the optional weekly homework not only once but three times, including the ones I had completely ignored earlier in the semester. I had to watch all of the videos twice. I had to take both handwritten and typed notes. I had to be an active participant in a 280-person lecture hall, a scary task in and of itself. But, in the words of *The Mandalorian*, this was the way.[204] I left feeling more intimidated than I ever had in my life.

It all seemed so tedious. So annoying. So fucking stupid. No one else was doing this. No one else had to do what I did to get my grades to where I needed and wanted them to be. But then, something in my head clicked. What if that was the point? What if this was, indeed, the way?

My head immediately flashed back to that fateful day in Florida when my dad made me do those math problems ten times over. At the time, all I could feel was the intense hatred I had for math and my dad's actions. But now I looked back on the aftereffects of that day for the first time in my entire life. Never once after that day did I ever fail to write out my work to completion, even on my bombed exams. They may have been wrong, but at least I did everything possible to increase my chances of doing well.

It finally clicked. My dad's teaching, after more than eight years, finally made sense. It wasn't about doing them over and over again to make me suffer, although that certainly was part of it. It was about making sure I was doing every little thing possible (writing out every single step of my work numerous times over) to create the best chance of getting something of value (the correct answers to the problems). Did I *have* to write out my work? No. But did it increase the chance of me getting the right answer by really thinking and working through it? It absolutely did.

No little things could be skipped if I wanted to obtain what I valued. The same could be applied to my accounting regimen. The little things could not be skipped because, at the end of the day, they weren't little things to me. I wanted what was on the other end (not to flunk out of college) more than I wanted to not do the little things required to get to the other end. Whether other people did them or not was irrelevant. This was me and the right system against me and my other shittier system.

So I did a wild thing. I listened. I did exactly what he told me to do and more. I worked the program like nothing I've ever done before or since. If I thought doing one set of elementary school math problems ten times was difficult, twelve sets of complex accounting problems twenty times was the next level. I forcibly bashed them into my brain for weeks, mercilessly tearing my mind to shreds. I eventually was able to write out the work and correct answer for a specific problem without even looking at my handwriting.

But it wasn't just the routine. The Life-Defining Principle began to trickle into other things surrounding the course as well. I lived in the tutor room. I asked questions. I went to office hours every week, sometimes to talk about accounting but other times to talk about nothing at all. I gave up playing beer pong with Four Loko on Saturday nights in favor of both my basic brain health and rewatching the online modules. I began to apply the same rigorous work ethic to my other courses because I liked the momentum I was experiencing. I just wanted to know I was doing everything I could.

I went into the second exam in a state of Zen. I knew what I had to do. And I did it. I went up 40 percent on that next exam, improving my overall grade by 25 percent. The last exam, according to the TAs, was apparently the hardest he'd given in five years. Ironically, the class average was 48 percent. I scored forty points better than average and placed in the top 10 percent. If my professor hadn't given the most gracious curve of his tenure, only two hundred students out of the original 1,100 would've passed. Only about four hundred did, a 36 percent pass rate.

But the most amazing thing of all happened after that semester. I had done similarly well in my other course and kept in contact with my professor. I was one of the few students he recognized out of an absurd three thousand he had per semester. He was undergoing a massive internal transition. The infrastructure needed to maintain his massive course load included around fifty undergraduate teaching assistants. Half of them would be turning over due to graduation. I asked about applying for a position, and while he didn't guarantee anything, he invited me to a casual networking event the following week.

I walked into the lecture hall and was crestfallen. Among the generous spread of local pizza and two-liters of pop (it's not soda) was a 120-person mob of students who all did better than me. While I couldn't possibly know all of them personally, I knew one thing was true—I didn't belong. How could I? These were the best students in my class who were interviewing for the most coveted teaching assistant position in one of the biggest public business schools in the world. The people currently in those positions were the crème de la crème of the talent pipeline for Big Four accounting and financial institutions throughout the world. I, on the other hand, was a guy that had nearly flunked out. I highly doubted any of these classmates had gotten below a B in their lives, let alone in this specific course.

And I let them all know that.

Whether I liked it or not, that specific grade defined me. It was my identity. So in every breakout room we did, I made a point to let the TA running the discussion know I was a loser. I had done everything wrong. I fucked up. I was the dumbest person in the room. My classmates looked at me like I was batshit. They thought I was pissing all over my chances. And during that time, I thought I very well could be too. But, embodying Tim Dillon's point, I thought it better to tell the truth and use it to define me rather than sit back and pretend I was one of the 119 other people who didn't struggle at all.

My strategy worked. I was invited back for another interview, this time with my professor and two of his TAs. I smiled. I had won. I had done the things that no one had wanted to do. I had gone into the man's office and talked with him dozens of times. I was incredibly comfortable. To me, he was just a 5'9" accounting professor with a middle part. To most everyone else, he was a god. And I would have to imagine an interview with god would be a pretty damn intimidating one to prepare for.

The interview was a breeze, and I was offered the job a week afterward. I accepted. I was one of twenty-two people in that original class of 1,100 to get offered that position, which put me in the top 2 percent of all of my classmates. Not bad for a dude who eight months earlier masked his tears with a public shower when he admitted to his mom he was washing out of school.

This proves the theory of the Life-Defining Principle correct. Earlier, when I and the kids who thought they could take a shortcut implemented our hacks, we set ourselves up for failure. Later, when I and (some of) the other kids fixed our issues by doing the little things that most others in our classes were not willing to do, not only were we able to survive, we were able to thrive and be better than everyone else.

REVERSE HACKINEERING

Not only do these stories prove the Life-Defining Principle to be correct, but they also provide a four-step framework for how to get out of the destructive life-hack model. The four steps are as follows:

1. Honestly look at the results of the attempted life hack.
2. See why the results of the attempted life hack suck.
3. Accept that the process and results of the attempted life hack suck.
4. Embrace the reality of the Life-Defining Principle.

Like most things, the first step is always the hardest. It is very hard to put our ego to the side and admit when we're wrong. It's even harder to take ownership of the situation we're in and why we're in it. You need to be completely objective about the first step or you'll find yourself in a hellacious death spiral that will eventually crash you into the earth. When you stop the lies, you, by consequence, have to face the truth. When you see the truth that the life-hack methodology sucks and you need to do the things the people enslaved to that methodology don't do to escape, that is the point when you can move on.

My moment came when I got my exam back. That was my "holy fuck, I guess I'm really not hot shit after all" moment. I was able to honestly assess that the life-hack way of studying did me no good whatsoever. Therefore, I needed to change.

The second step is the second hardest because it typically involves going into the shit-mess that blew up all over your life when you tried to hack it. It involves going into the filth, seeing the line-by-line reason for why it's filth, and seeing why and how it doesn't work. This is a very hard step to come to terms with. A lot of people shy away from looking at how and why they fucked up, so they don't have to damage their ego. Checking your ego is very hard, but it is very necessary.

My second step was when I went and saw the results of my test. Originally, I thought there was a mistake—they used a wrong key to grade my test, the person who graded mine was on bath salts, etc. I had studied a combined thirty hours for the first exam. I didn't figure there was any way I could have done as poorly as I did. I was still in denial. I didn't want to believe my hack sucked.

I was dumbfounded when I went through the answer key for the exam and saw I had just laid a gigantic dump all over it. I hadn't just messed up. I wasn't even close. I looked painstakingly for errors made by the grader. I didn't find any. The only flaws were mine. I saw first-hand that the life hack I attempted sucked, and it didn't get me where I needed or wanted to be.

If you did steps one and two right, the third should be easy. If you looked honestly at the results and saw the details of what got you those results, you should know that something needs to change. All you need to do is accept it. Sometimes, if you're fortunate, someone will hit you with the truth, so you can hear it from an outside perspective. Most aren't. You need to come to terms with it yourself. The biggest obstacle to doing this is something I mentioned before—denial. People want to write this off as a one-off. That their hack can work if only applied in another fashion, another life hack. But this is just another form of avoidance. You cannot hide. Accept that you and this life hack suck, and move onto something that doesn't.

My third step was when I visited my professor. I knew I had put in the adequate amount of time studying, but now I needed to pivot my methodology, so I could do better. But I was silently hoping he would tell me what I wanted to hear. That it was just a one-off thing, and I could continue down my path of avoidance and not do the little things that mattered and still get the grade I wanted—something I valued.

Instead, he told me straight to my face that my grade sucked its own dick. My method of studying needed to change, or I would fail. It was a hard pill to swallow, but I'm glad he gave it to me. By going to an (actual) expert, I automatically made the situation objective and impersonal. I also got an honest answer from someone who honestly wanted to help. That is always a good thing too. That scenario helped me accept the results of my sucky life hack and that I needed to adapt a whole new method.

The fourth step is hard only for one reason—temptation. The Life-Defining Principle isn't sexy. It's not something that has a lot of flair to it. It's gritty, hard, and tough. It is the road less traveled. It is very easy to get lulled in by the siren's song of the life hack. To take the shortcut that will ultimately lead you to getting the same result as before. Or getting your face ripped off, if we're referencing Homer's work, *The Odyssey*. You need to ignore the temptation, make the proper adjustments that you should have made in the first place, and (wait for it) *do the work*. Sit down, and force yourself to do the work.

My fourth step came when my professor gave me a symbolic glass of water to wash down that pill—my routine. He said all I needed to do was better allocate my time. The results spoke for themselves.

The framework of adjusting from the life-hack methodology to the Life-Defining Principle is simple but not easy. Careful, measured steps are needed to bridge this gap to sacrifice more and create more value.

* * *

THE LIFE-DEFINING PRINCIPLE IS UBIQUITOUS and applicable to anything in our lives. If we embrace it, we'll find greater value. If we try to cheat, we'll probably catch a value-oriented flying knee to the face.

If you adopt the Life-Defining Principle, you will find yourself adopting the Value/Sacrifice Trade-Off, the bedrock of Value Economics. The Value/Sacrifice Trade-Off cannot be adopted if you don't Essentially Diversify, getting your values in order to get something from them. You can't Essentially Diversify if you don't realize where your Means of Value is. You cannot discover your Means of Value without first knowing what comprises them, which are the Factors of Value Production.

The key is to start small. There's no use trying to do something incredibly complicated with an insufficient amount of steps. That's what the life hackers do. You're better than them. Start small, and identify the little right things to use. In doing so, you'll find yourself orienting around the right things to value. Whether that's accounting, order of operations, stand-up comedy, or selling cleaning products to stay-at-home parents over television, it's a good thing if it aligns with the Life-Defining Principle.

However, our Means of Value tells us our values can go too far. The same can be said with Value Economics. For the next logical step in developing our values, we go to a tale of a beautiful princess.

CHAPTER SIX

DIMINISHING RETURNS
OF VALUE

"You either die a hero, or you live long enough to see yourself become the villain."

−HARVEY DENT, *THE DARK KNIGHT* (2008)

A MODERN-DAY FAIRY TALE

ONCE UPON A TIME IN A FARAWAY LAND CALLED WESTERN Pennsylvania, a young woman got a Golden Ticket to live her dreams, becoming a student-athlete in one of the biggest cities in America.[205] She had the time of her life, mingling with men who tickled her sexual fantasies. After, she started a podcast talking about all this with a self-ish girl she met at a festival while living off unemployment.[206] Both became famous.

However, a television executive with the face of an Easter Island head and the hair of Severus Snape got involved, broke up the pair, and ruined everything.[207] The head of the company the women were signed to used his huge balls to roast the women and Severus Easter Island Head Snape on their own podcast.[208] Our princess then realized her fault, came back, and ran off to talk about sex some more.[209] The End.

In case you haven't caught on by now, the situation I'm referencing is the now-infamous fallout of the original *Call Her Daddy* podcast. Our princess is Alex Cooper, the heroine of the story who is now one of the biggest independent media stars in the world. The selfish festival girl is Sofia Franklyn, her former co-host and current parents'-basement dweller. Severus Easter Island Head Snape is Peter Nelson, an executive for HBO Sports who broke an unwritten rule of the media business (and number one rule of the podcast, ironically enough) by getting involved where he shouldn't have. Huge Balls Guy is Dave Portnoy/ El Presidente, the founder of Barstool Sports, the company that signed Cooper and Franklyn.

As odd and unconventional as it may seem, *Call Her Daddy* is an amazingly unique story of business success. In a move that took some serious balls/ovaries of their own, Cooper and Franklyn dove head-first into completely uncharted territory: women talking about sex over a public forum. For the longest time in our culture, it was taboo for women to do this. It wasn't "ladylike," or something. But, like any good disruptive entrepreneurs, the two women saw an opportunity and capitalized on it. They created a blue ocean—an untapped market ripe for the taking.[210]

Being friends with a decent amount of women afforded me a sur-prise. Women love to talk about sex. And I mean *love* it. I was blown away when I first heard this. You mean, women aren't sweet and inno-cent until men corrupt them? They "do that stuff"? They do, as a matter of fact. Actually, from my experience, they're *more* lewd than men. I get uncomfortable within about five seconds of their conversations.

Cooper and Franklyn swung at this opportunity and were rewarded tremendously. They got the attention of Portnoy and were signed within a month. They soon became the most popular podcast on Barstool, catapulting them into the stratosphere. Their brand became a cult. It was lightning in a bottle. The two women had a complete monopoly over the market. No one could touch them. They seemed invincible.

But then, the money happened. "Always the dollars. Always the fuckin' dollars." (Nicky Santoro voice.)[211] Portnoy, seeing the incredible growth of the podcast, redid their contracts to keep them happy. Cooper, who did most of the behind-the-scenes work, asked Portnoy for additional money, which he gave her.

But it wasn't enough. Franklyn had gotten into a relationship with the aforementioned Peter Nelson, who began whispering in her ear (probably after enacting all of the moves they talk about for an hour EVERY FUCKING WEDNESDAY, BABY) that they were getting cheated by Barstool. That they were undervalued. That they were getting used and whored out while "The Man" cashed in on their success. Franklyn then took this information to Cooper, who initially backed her.

However, something began to happen. The money became the focal point of the conversation. Cooper cared deeply about building the business. She felt Franklyn cared only about the money.

Her fears soon proved true when Portnoy set up a meeting and gave them the offer of a lifetime: half a million dollars each (plus bonuses), 20 percent of all merchandise, and the intellectual property rights. Cooper's mouth fell open, and not for a Gluck Gluck 9000.[212] She, being the smart businesswoman that she is, knew it wasn't going to get any better than what Portnoy had offered. She knew when to cash in.

But Franklyn and Nelson didn't see it that way. They kept coming back to Portnoy with ludicrous demands. Cooper was essentially held hostage. Nothing was good enough. Cooper eventually confronted Franklyn about this, and the line was drawn. It was either *Call Her Daddy* or their friendship.

Cooper chose the former. She went back to Portnoy, took the deal, and got the show entirely rebranded around her. Franklyn, after a horribly attempted intervention by Scooter Braun,[213] a bizarre series of Instagram stories trying to explain how she didn't dick (wink wink) Cooper (she did, there was nothing to explain),[214] and an unprecedented amount of roasts from El Presidente,[215] was kicked to the curb.

So where are our two women now? In June of 2021, Alex Cooper took the IP rights to *Call Her Daddy* and inked a three-year, $60 million deal with Spotify.[216] This blew everyone away. Joe Rogan, the man who commands the greatest podcasting empire in history, made $100 million from his podcast deal with Spotify.[217] The difference? Cooper has been famous only for about a tenth of the time Rogan has.

Franklyn eventually emerged from the void/Phantom Zone and started *her* own solo podcast, *Sofia with an F*. It was initially a poor attempt to catch lightning in a bottle a second time, but she began to gain traction. She gained some sponsors back, repeatedly stated how she had been "wronged," and attempted to revitalize her career.[218] She was still very famous. Lots of people were on her side during the split.

Until May 19, 2021. On that fateful day, Franklyn went on a rant about a childhood birthday party (she was twenty-eight at the time) that her slightly older "best friend" did not invite her to. After some careful digging by her listeners, the friend was identified as Mollee Gray, a TikTok influencer and former Disney star. Not thinking it was immature to still be miffed, Franklyn went nuclear:[219]

> This fucking bitch opened up my message and didn't respond—what the fuck is she? She has a blue checkmark on Instagram, for what? She has a million followers on TikTok, but for what, like, what does she do?…She has an issue with me, that stupid fucking blonde disgusting chicklet gum mouth bitch. Give me a fucking response, like, she knows who I am…She's a fucking cunt. I think she's fucking stupid, and gross, and she wants to be Julianne Hough and she never will be because you look like an inbred and you have a Muppet mouth…I don't care if this segment pisses people off…I hope there's a Teen Beach Movie 3 because I think that's gonna be the end of your fucking career because you are such a big bitch.

Yikes. That's three of Carlin's seven dirty words,[220] not to mention "chicklet," "gum mouth," "inbred," and "Muppet mouth." And, contrary to her words, people *did* care. In one of the biggest twists of irony you'll ever read about, the e-counseling and mental health platform BetterHelp canceled their sponsorship immediately following the incident. Three others followed. Franklyn apologized, but who knows if anyone listened. One can cry wolf only so many times before those same wolves end up devouring you.

Do you see the difference? One is living the dream life of most young Americans; the other is talking shit about a childhood beef with a Disney star on her second-rate podcast.

Call Her Daddy is a once-in-a-lifetime idea. It's a completely untapped market with a rabid fanbase. If it were a mainstream business, every single venture capitalist in the world would be salivating over it. Alex Cooper went from food stamps to tens of millions of guaranteed dollars, a cult following, and untapped opportunity. Sofia Franklyn left her job in finance, fucked up because she violated the one rule that she and Cooper preached (handle your own shit), and is putzing in her mom's Utah basement talking shit about former Disney stars and losing thousands of dollars in sponsorship revenue.

Sofia Franklyn didn't know when to say when. She outplayed her hand. It cost her everything. She's a has-been, a wannabe.

Alex Cooper knew when to settle. She knew when she had been beaten. She's now one of the biggest up-and-coming media personalities in the world. Her upward ascension continues. Just as Portnoy had alluded to, she took all of her Gluck Glucks and rabid fans with her to the Promised Land.

* * *

UNFORTUNATELY, THE MINDSET OF SOFIA Franklyn gets pushed more in our society than the mindset of Alex Cooper.

Here's why. How many times have your parents told you to "never quit"? To never settle? To work your ass off until such things manifest themselves into being? To never bend a knee to anyone, no matter how powerful, so you can "achieve your dreams"?

Probably a lot. Which is a shame because it's completely and utterly wrong.

Not only is it wrong, but it's dangerous. Look no further than Sofia Franklyn. She knows better than anyone. What good is plowing ahead if you're plowing ahead for the wrong reasons? When you lose sight of the value that can potentially get you more value? When you abuse and stretch what you originally valued to fit something you didn't really value as much?

The answer is that it's no good. This is why people run businesses into the ground. Why people chase after former flings and broken relationships. Why people revolve their lives around fitness trends and makeup bloggers. Are these things valuable? They can be. It depends. But they immediately become invaluable as soon as you lose sight of the value itself and only focus on the gains reaped from it.

In the words of Kevin O'Leary, sometimes you have to take something behind the barn and shoot it.[221] Sometimes you have to settle. It's not a bad thing if it's for a good reason. Too often, we're told that mindless pursuit without a sense of internal value is good. It's not. To prove it, let's go back to The Man.

DIMINISHING RETURNS OF VALUE

Remember The Man? Shame on you if you don't—that was only, like, three chapters ago, or whatever. The Man was, indeed, The Man. My Investments professor in college, he was a twenty-five-year-old Wall

Street vet who managed billions of dollars in assets, wined and dined with the elite of America's business class (he was one of the people that heard Jeff Bezos' original Amazon pitch[222]), has run over one hundred marathons, has a wife and daughter, listened about five times as much as he talked, talked softly, and, most importantly, wasn't a Wall Street cock-ola. It was a breath of fresh air to say the least.

The Man, in his wisdom, taught us the Two Es—ego and emotion. The Two Es, if left unchecked, can wreak some serious havoc in both your investment portfolio and your life. According to The Man, if you could control those two things, you'd probably end up doing well in the long run both as an investor and a human being. He was full of gems like that. But what he said directly after that was just as fascinating.

When he was presenting on this topic, he flipped to the next slide (he had about one hundred per class, full of typos, lots of punctuation errors, and some with only memes and various pictures on them) that had a singular picture on it—a Wall Street guy being led out of a building in handcuffs.

The Man wasted no time in roasting him ("I actually knew this guy—he was a scumbag"). Wall Street Guy had been arrested for insider trading. Insider trading is when a person employed by a company (an insider) leaks confidential information to the world.[223] It's a big no-no. There are a lot of laws against it.[224] This guy did a big no-no—he went to the klink for twenty-five for it. The Man then let out another gem, one so simple but so often misused: "Don't be greedy."

He then switched to the next slide, probably to talk about P/E ratios or something. I don't even think The Man knew how much that one sentence resonated around the room, particularly when the dozens of wannabe Wall Street Guys saw how their lives could be ruined by their own potential profession. How applicable it was to all of us aspiring young businesspeople sitting in on the conversation.

Wall Street Guy made the same mistake as Franklyn. He got greedy. He chased value where there was none. He plowed so heavily and risked so much into nothing that he lost everything. Sofia Franklyn overplayed her hand, took her eye off the ball, and is now blacklisted. According to *KFC Radio*, Peter Nelson is now a laughingstock at HBO.[225] His subordinates mock him. The only reason he hasn't been sacked is apparently his ideas are good. HE WENT TO HARVARD, in case you didn't know.

The topic of this chapter reflects this concept—Diminishing Returns of Value, or DRV. But to understand DRV, we first need to understand the original concept—DR (Diminishing Returns).

Law of Diminishing Returns

It states that an additional amount of a single factor of production will result in a decreasing marginal output of production.

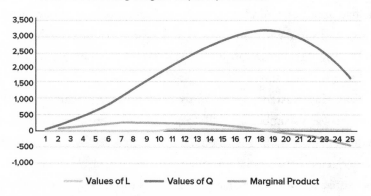

Let's clarify. First of all, those bottom two lines? Fuck them. They're dead to us. They cheated on you with the cleaning lady, those polygynous whores. Just focus on the top line and definition.

The definition lays out what the economic rule states and is explained in the top line.[226] As we've seen from the Value/Sacrifice Trade-Off, the more you value something, the more you will sacrifice to get it. The same scenario applies here. The more you put into something ("single factor of production"), the more you will get out of it ("marginal output of production").

At least for a time. After a while, you get to a point where all of that strain and work you put in gets you nowhere. You hit a wall. You plateau. You stop moving. That is the apex of the top line.

Then, after you hit said wall, you *decline*. The work you put in begins to work *against* you. And then, as shown by our friend the top line, you crash. And you crash hard. It's not pretty.

The greatest example of this in practice comes from Henry Ford,[227] the founder of Ford Motor Company and inventor of the Second Industrial Revolution.[228] Henry Ford created the assembly line.[229] Instead of individual workers building individual cars, all individual workers had to do was stay in the same place, wait for the car to come to them, put their part on, and do that for the entire workday.

It was the Life-Defining Principle in action. Henry Ford and Ford Motor Company went on to dominate the car market. The amount of volume Ford Motor Company could do brought the entire car market to its knees. No one could keep up.

Henry Ford also realized something else. Not only could he not delegate a large task to one person, he could also not delegate a *small* task to *more* than one person. Let's assume the optimal number for building a part was twenty people. But let's say Henry Ford wanted to ramp up production and double the amount of workers. He thought this would double the production. He, however, was wrong.

This is the "too many cooks in the kitchen" conundrum. The workers got so overwhelmed with who had what duty it derailed the whole thing. Ford got greedy, took his eye off the ball, and ended up wrecking the entire line. What was once an efficiency machine was now a clusterfuck.

Imagine this as the Value/Sacrifice Trade-Off. Value and sacrifice are directly correlated. You cannot have one without the other acting in tandem. Anytime you try to microwave it, bad shit happens.

The same thing happens when you get to the apex of the top line. You start to value things so much you end up crashing them by sacrificing everything. It's inevitable. It will always happen. That's the Wall

Street Guy, Sofia Franklyn, and Peter Nelson thing. You don't want to be like them.

"But wait," you might ask. "How could putting effort toward something lead to something bad happening? Doesn't that go against the Value/Sacrifice Trade-Off and Life-Defining Principle?"

No, it does not. Why? The reason is our friend Excessive Excess. Excessive Excess, if you remember, is what happens when you do something just to do something. You grow a company just because you can grow a company. You decide to sell everything you own and move to Tahiti just to sell everything you own and move to Tahiti. You decide to fuck that guy who is hovering somewhere around a four on your personal attraction scale on Tinder because you haven't been laid in two months. Doing things for the sake of doing things is a poor way to go about life. There's no value there. There is only the sugary-sweet satisfaction and teeth rotting of short-term indulgence.

When you plow every bit of your energy into something, it becomes easy to lose track of the why. That isn't valuable. It's an addiction. There is no balance there. There is only the thing you once valued but now obsess over. You become like Gollum salivating over the One Ring.[230] Everything else gets thrown away. Even though you once valued that one thing, everything else turns to complete and utter dog shit.

MAXIMIZE WHAT?

A lot of people don't know about Columbus, Ohio. To cite Fox Sports' Colin Cowherd, most people just "fly over it all the time."[231] Cowherd, subtle coastal elitism aside, has a point. The Midwest has always been the butt of the American joke. There are no vast oceans to look upon in wonderment. The cities that are magnificent are few and far between. There aren't many skyscrapers. Most corporations and young people move to areas where life is more dynamic. Some say it's better.

Columbus is a rare exception. It's home to the third-largest public university in America,[232] which provides a pipeline of young people to flow into the region. With those young people come young businesses—bars, clubs, restaurants—to capitalize on them. The overall wealth of that one area of the Midwest has skyrocketed, creating a quality of life that would be envied nearly everywhere else in the country.[233] You can get just as much fun in the city of Columbus for about a fifth of the price of living in San Francisco.

With energy and wealth comes investment. The second-largest commercial building in the world is located in Columbus and inhabited by JPMorgan Chase.[234] The first largest is the Pentagon.[235] Corporations like Abercrombie & Fitch, L Brands, and Progressive are headquartered there.[236] The startup scene has boomed, producing several mammoths that include Beam Dental, Loop, Olive, Path Robotics, and Root Inc.[237]

I know many people that have gone to work for these companies. HR departments devour them. Growth demands talent. Talent makes money. Ambitious YoPros are the key. They're a match made in heaven.

But there is one company in the above category that has gone off the deep end. In the last year, highly impressionable students have been driven in droves to this company, some as young as eighteen-year-old freshmen. This isn't atypical. College kids are cheap, hungry, and malleable. These are desirable qualities, especially for a tech startup. And that's exactly why this company hires them.

The company in question hires these kids to become SDRs, or sales development representatives. They all serve the same vital purpose. They do the grunt work. They cold call, email, and message people daily to get them to meet in person, where the account executives or managers can do the selling.

A company dies without sales. The most important question asked on Shark Tank is, "What are your sales?" When the aforementioned Shark, O'Leary, goes to invest in a company, the first person he meets with is whoever runs sales.[238] Good companies recognize this. Bad companies don't.

Entry-level sales is the hardest job across the wide scope of business. I know firsthand—I was an entry-level salesman. The job is 99.9 percent rejection, with a lot of those rejections not coming in the most kind ways. I've had people tell me to go fuck myself before. To never call again. One guy offered to have me cut his grass for him. If my manager wasn't on the line, I would have told him yes if he agreed to suck my dick first.

Due to the job's difficulty, it's necessary for sales teams to celebrate "small wins." This gets parodied a lot. There's fun in doing so because some can be ridiculous. But a good energy on a sales floor isn't a nicety—it's a necessity. Low morale is deadly to an organization that takes low blows so often.

But the opposite is true as well.

There are some teams out there that take this way too far in the other direction. The ones that are overly positive about absolutely everything. The ones who are "crushing it." There are plenty of examples of this out there. Self-help con artist Ed Mylett once posted a video titled *Who Is Ed Mylett?*, which featured a compilation of him driving cars, speaking at bizarre conferences, surfing, and wearing obscene clothing.[239] Exactly who Ed Mylett is remains to be seen. Grant Cardone once did something similar (although worse), publishing a video titled *5 Steps to Becoming a Millionaire*.[240] In it, he does nothing but rant, rave, and swear about his own success; tell people to push his bullshit books; and take the dry erase board away. The video lasts over thirty minutes, and he doesn't even have a fifth step. A shame—a couple of those people on his sales force might have become millionaires.

Back to the company in Cleveland hoovering up all the eager college kids. It capitalizes on this high and uses it to brainwash young wannabe moguls into selling products. It's hired an army. Recently, it was named by LinkedIn as one of the top fifty startups of 2020—a remarkable achievement. But what is the product? What is making this company so popular?

The product this company sells is an AI technology that helps generate sales. If the last sentence confused you, you're in the right place. The technology the company sells using their army of young salespeople to generate sales leads is a product that helps other salespeople at other companies get more sales leads.

It's an interesting value proposition, mostly because it's not a value proposition at all. It's a pyramid scheme. A pyramid scheme is when someone employs someone else to sign people up for something.[241] For example, John tells Jane if she gets Joe and Jim to buy a Product A, she will be rewarded for it. All she has to do is get people to sign up.

This company is nothing more than a bullshit sales-churning machine fueled by ambitious children, a coercive work environment, low-hanging quotas, and the possibility of LinkedIn clout from "crushing it." It's been taken to Excessive Excess with no sign of deflation. The culture of this company is not equally toxic. It's worse, specifically because it infects its own employees. Completely hooked on the drug of bullshit, their behavior embodies more of a cult than a company. For example, I posted a transcript of a LinkedIn post from a former high school lifeguarding coworker of mine who now interns for them. He grew up with me and graduated with my brother. He's hooked:

> I can proudly say after my first full month at <Company> I crushed quota!!! Huge shoutout to <Employee One>, <Employee Two>, <Employee Three> *rocket ship emoji*, and many more for leading the way and showing how to get it done!! Also a shoutout to <CEO> and others who made this internship possible for me!!! Very excited to see what this next month holds. Time to double last month's quota!!!!!!!! #LFG

This is bizarre to post on LinkedIn. Swap in Jim Jones–related terminology, and you'd be able to see where the whole "cult" thing comes into play.[242] LinkedIn is a social media site, a platform that people can use for whatever. But this type of post is highly inappropriate in the context of LinkedIn's mission: [243]

Connect the world's professionals to make them more productive and successful.

It's hard to say how a post by a brainwashed SDR masturbating to his own success while getting cheered on by his superiors fits that mission. That's because it doesn't. It's a site for professional networking and career development. Some fun is okay, but it's not the primary utility of what it's used for. Braggadocio should be left for cryptocurrency Reddit threads and Instagram models, not a wannabe salesman.

But this scenario warrants a question—who is doing the brainwashing, the influencing? The answer comes from the post—the CEO. Culture is set, as many will say, at the top. They are correct. So, naturally, when this company started becoming more prominent, I did a quick search to view the CEO's profile.

It was worse than I had imagined. Picture the Business Guy they talk about in the memes. He fit that description to a tee. He was in his late twenties and had founded another company before the one in question. His profile conveniently avoids that fact. The post that my former lifeguard colleague posted above? That was *all* of his posts, dozens per day. He wasn't a CEO. He was a self-promoter. It wasn't about the company; it was about his company. How he had built success. He published three books on sales within the same calendar year, each as non-differentiated as the last. He had a YouTube channel and a podcast, on which he hosted both Cardone and Mylett as well as a man who was indicted for fraud and market manipulation. The focus on that particular podcast? He made the sale. He "crushed it."

But the worst post of all, the one that sold me on how much of a con he was, was about goals. It read this:

Every night before I pass out after giving it my all...I force myself to write out my goals for the year...This helps me wake up energized ready to go make them a reality...What is one thing you do to help stay motivated? Good luck finishing the year out on top!!! PS -> if you enjoyed this post, please smash that like button and drop me your comments below!

Goals for 2020:

- Positively impact 1 billion people by helping the world connect to _____

- 100,000 users on <company>

- 100,000 President's Club Winners at <website>

- $1,000,000 in sales every day

- 1 million hours of content watch in <company> YT/LI/ Podcast

- 1 million subscribers on LinkedIn, YouTube, Podcasts

- World's best husband

- $1,000,000 donated to charity every year

- World's most fit plant-powered vegan, 155 pounds, and 7 percent body fat

In the same post, he attached a picture, which showed the world (on paper) he had accomplished some of his goals. Someone in the comments section asked about his goals being "unrealistic." He waxed condescension about how he wanted to "inspire people." Indeed, he has. He doesn't have employees; he has a cult. They *all* want to be like him. They all want what he has.

But they also want something else. One goal that comes from a deeply held value that Business Guy keeps closer than any other. He forgot to write it down after the whole "Most Fit Plant-Powered Vegan" one (probably because he was so busy "crushing it"), so I'll fill it in for him: "Look at me."

Look at me. Look at my goals. Look at all the things that I'm "doing." Look at what you're not doing. Look at how much better I am. I invite you to join me, but only if you obey me. I invite you to join me, but only if you buy my bullshit, worthless products and then come on my podcast. Look at me. I am the ideal, the goal, the everything. I am what you should seek. Look at me. Or else you will not crush it. Or else you won't reach your "full potential." Or else you are lesser. Or else you are nothing. Look at me.

* * *

THE DANGER OF PEOPLE LIKE that CEO is that they are maximizers. The Maximizer Mindset, which has hijacked my generation, is when you seek to squeeze every drop of water from the towel of life. When you rip it to shreds looking for one more drop, one more ounce, one more whatever. You drive yourself to obsession with one thing and stroke yourself off to the near-sexual ecstasy of accomplishment.

That CEO said he posted a list of goals. But he lied. Those are not goals. That is a wish list. And last time I checked, Santa stops coming when you're around thirteen years old. Seeking the past in the form of the present is not only immature but a lie.

This can be applied everywhere in your life. One common fixation of my generation provides the perfect example—dating apps. In yesteryear, you weren't exposed to that much. There was no internet, no social media. What you saw was, quite literally, what you got. And what's more important to see than your significant other? I can't think of many more important decisions to make than that, at least to me.

Evolutionary biology has made it very clear what men and women deem attractive.[244] Men are attracted to healthy women of breeding age. Women are attracted to men they perceive as powerful. In the olden times, there was a limited pool. There were women who were more attractive than others to men, and conversely for men to women. There was a defined border, terms of agreement. You couldn't maximize anything. You had to work with what you had.

With the adoption of technology, people are being turned into something else—commodities. Women are packaged up in a profile perused for about ten seconds, a meaningless clump of ass, body, face, and tits. Men bloviate their egos, afraid to show who they really are because they know another man will outdo them. As summed up perfectly by the Flatbush Zombies, love is now being trivialized into swipes.

This new mindset is winning over the one that had been proven to work. I've seen it both with myself and my friends. I always ask the same questions: "Why the fuck would you pick a girl that's hot over a girl that's down for you?" "Why would you go out and fuck that guy when a guy just shelled out $150 to buy you dinner out of an act of genuineness?" It makes no sense.

Maximizers lie and pretend they like things until something "better" comes around. Then, the old thing is dropped in favor of a new, better thing. You like the girl that does papier-mâché with her kindergarten class and runs marathons for breast cancer until you realize the marketing analyst who loves to lose count of the number of vodka crans she drinks every Saturday night has a fatter ass. You think your boyfriend is cute until you realize that a guy you saw at the bar wears mala beads and drives an eco-friendly car while not giving a fuck about his friends roasting him for driving an eco-friendly car.

These people are incapable of knowing when something is good enough. They cannot see past their own stupidity to know they're running their values into the ground. These people, my generation, are not happy. They're the exact opposite. They can't tell things to go fuck themselves. They're always looking for better. When they realize they're wrong, it's usually too late. They've, ironically, fucked themselves.

THE ART OF SETTLING

My junior year of college was the most hellish time of my life. I value my education. It's the reason I jumped through hoops like going to a satellite campus in Siberia (more on this in Chapter Eight) and working through my situation in Chapter Five. That's the Value/Sacrifice Trade-Off in action.

But something happened my junior year. I was concerned about the looming Big Boy internship I would have to land to be a "success." Put that in a fireplace along with a bottle of lighter fluid made of hard quantitative classes and other obligations, and you get a pretty roaring fire going under your ass.

I worked myself to near death. In addition, I had my physical health, volunteering, part-time job, and fundraising events to tend to. I got up at 5:00 a.m. and didn't go to bed until midnight every day for a year. I missed half of my school's football games (good seats too) to lock myself in study. I went out a grand total of two times that year, one time sober with a friend to an eighteen-and-up nightclub just to see what it was like. My twenty-first birthday was three whiskey Cokes and shitty food from BW3 on a Wednesday. Yes, it was that bad.

But it wasn't as bad as the next time I went to a BW3. At the time, I was part of RallyCap Sports, a charity that organizes sports for local children with disabilities.[245] I was invited by the leadership board and my university chapter president to serve as the ambassador for that chapter at a yearly outing to celebrate the year's achievements. It was set to take place on Friday, April 12, 2019, in the town where the charity was initially founded, a small suburb outside of Toledo called Bowling Green.

The town's university, Bowling Green State University, was the alma mater of a man named Paul Hooker, who had founded the charity decades ago after being inspired by a disabled little girl not being able to play baseball. Since then, he and his staff have helped spread the charity to dozens of local chapters. The operations director, Lily Alten, had known me growing up. We went to the same school, and I once had a massive crush on her sister. Luke Sims, their managing director, gave me the sign-off as well.

If it were at any other time of year, I wouldn't have gone. However, in that moment, I was feeling something I hadn't felt in a long time—calm. I had a very good internship. I had done well enough in all my classes, and all my exams except for my two easiest classes were done. The other two exams were more than two weeks away. I had more than enough time to study. Additionally, the charity party (with half the money raised going to RallyCap) I had coordinated had gone off without a hitch, relieving another gigantic source of stress. I was uncommonly carefree. I was going to have a nice weekend, go to this event, and then go to a fashion show for a girl who had helped me market my party. (By market, she must have meant just to show up, tell her mediocre amount of Instagram followers that she was there, and then bounce thirty minutes later—but whatever.) I was set to jet out to Italy for a global lab sponsored by a favorite professor, Doug Farren, immediately after exams. Life was good.

The event was a success. People from different chapters showed up, met one another, and told stories. Sure, the trays of food were cold, the wings were awful, and we ran out quickly, but it was a lot of fun. And this time, unlike the horrific sober eighteen-and-up nightclub experience, I was able to enjoy myself. Mr. Hooker came in, gave an emotional speech, told me I was doing a good job, and congratulated me on our chapter's success. That made me feel good, particularly coming from him.

After about an hour and a half, things began to wind down. I said goodbye, got in my 2014 Jeep Wrangler, and started down I-85 back to school. It was about 9:00 p.m., and I was scheduled to be back around 10:30. I wasn't worried. I plugged my phone into my aux cord, threw on Do Not Disturb, and settled in.

I woke up twenty minutes later to the sound of the hard rap of knuckles on glass. I stirred awake, confused at how I was asleep but still in my car. I didn't remember pulling off the road. When my door opened, I saw the gray cement median staring at me and two paramedics standing close by with a bodyboard.

My alertness immediately perked up. I didn't feel hurt, so why were there paramedics near me? Where was *I* near? Finding the ability to form words, I asked the lead paramedic what was going on.

"Uh, we're pretty sure you had a seizure."

I would have laughed if I wasn't so frightened. A seizure? It couldn't be. I was driving a car. Those happen when you're stationary, not when you're driving down the highway at 70 MPH. Seeing my bewilderment, the paramedic reaffirmed what he said and added that they needed to get me out of my car. I looked out my windshield and saw smoke. My hood was at an odd angle.

Panic began to set in. The first question I asked was if I had hurt anyone. Lead Paramedic said he didn't think so, at least seriously. The woman I had hit was being taken to the hospital, but it was thought she had only a neck sprain. I had hit someone? The other car that had hit me after my first collision with the woman was fine—shaken up, but fine. Two people? After I undid my seatbelt, I leaned on Lead Paramedic as he lowered me down onto the bodyboard on the side of the interstate. Working as a lifeguard for five years, I saw they did me up exactly how I was trained to[246]—stabilize the head, inside then out, no straps placed over the joints. I asked if it was necessary. They said yes.

They loaded me into the ambulance with Lead Paramedic riding in the back with me. He explained the situation. I was driving down the highway at 73 MPH on cruise control when I started seizing. The woman in front of me noticed my arms flailing and stopped along the median to call 911. My car, of course, didn't stop. It drifted toward the median, where it scraped along the wall before rear-ending the woman at full speed. My car then ricocheted into traffic, where I got hit by a station wagon and thrown *back* into the median, where the car finally stopped. After they took me away, they totaled my car. They had to saw the front axle in half with the Jaws of Life because they couldn't get it on the tow truck.

I was completely stunned. I didn't know what to say, so I said nothing. I still felt fine. But I knew what was coming. Lead Paramedic did too. And, being his cool, calm, and collected self, he whipped out his iPhone (mine was still in my heap of a car) and asked the question, "So do you want to do this, or do you want me to?"

I gestured for him to give it over, and I called the number of the person I knew would take it the second worst—my dad. It was around 9:45 at night, and my parents were in Florida with my sister. My dad had an apartment down there for when he had to go to his company's HQ on business. My family had lived down there for a year. But, given the subpar public school system and unprecedented homesickness, they had decided to re-relocate back to Ohio. That weekend was their last hurrah. Little did they know their party was about to end sooner and harsher than they could have expected.

My dad picked up on the third ring. I calmly said hello, asked how he was, and told him my situation ("Yeah, Dad, I kinda had a seizure while driving home. I'm fine, don't worry about me, they said I'll probably be out of the hospital by tomorrow morning, don't let me ruin your trip," is what I remember). My dad, the engineer and pragmatist, asked if I was okay, about the car, and if I was okay again then said he was giving the phone to the person who would take it the first worst—my mother.

My mom was calmer than expected, probably because she had heard me laugh and my dad stay calm. I could still tell she was frightened, so I did my best to reassure her. She asked to talk to Lead Paramedic, so I gave him back his phone so he could fill her in with the other details I had glossed over. He handed it back, and I told my mom not to come. I would be okay. She said she would talk it over with my dad and that she loved me. I told her that I did, too, and hung up just as we reached the hospital.

They kept me up until 2:30 in the morning. After two CAT scans, two MRIs, and two EKGs, I was allowed to sleep. When I woke up in the morning, I realized I was mostly blind—my glasses had been thrown off in the crash. However, a familiar voice said hi. I recognized it as my uncle Greg's, my dad's brother and my godfather. He had driven all the way from Cincinnati in one night just because my dad wanted him to. A second voice, that of my mother, was talking to my nurse in the hallway. She had been on the first flight out that morning.

My uncle handed me my glasses. They had, remarkably, not been damaged. I looked at myself clearly for the first time since the crash. I didn't look any the worse for wear except for a couple bruises, scratches, and a large bump on my head from my face saying an aggressive hello to the steering wheel. My uncle then set the salvage from the wreck on the bedside table (my phone, a Michael Jordan trading card, a two-dollar bill, a VFW coin, and my wallet) and told me my car was gone. They were in the process of scrapping it now. But it did its job. It protected me. Yes, this is an endorsement to buy a Jeep.[247]

My uncle left, and the doctors came in to check on me. The second-most remarkable thing was that, even after all their tests, nothing was wrong with me. Except for a larger-than-normal vestigial gland in my brain (probably exacerbated by the whole "face smashing the steering wheel" thing), I was in perfect health. It was a random event. Seizures happen more than people think. My brother had one when he was two, and my sister had one a little over two years after I did. My dad had one when he was a kid, and his boss had one while driving once. Given this non-diagnosis, I could leave that afternoon.

As my mom wheeled me out to her car, I realized the unspoken, remarkable thing: I was alive.

I was alive, and I was going to be okay. I'm not one to hype up anything about myself, but the fact that I survived the ordeal on Friday, April 12, 2019, on I-85 at 9:00 at night in northwest Ohio is pretty fucking amazing. When I tell people that story, they all express the same sentiment. Someone was looking out for me that night. I and everyone else involved walked out generally unscathed. I still have to take massive horse pills twice a day and stay away from strobe lights, but it's a small price to pay in my estimation.

I was alive, and people loved me. Both my grandmothers burst into tears when they figured out I was okay. So did my aunt Debbie, my godmother. My uncle had driven more than three and a half hours only to leave a half an hour later just to see that I was okay. My mom had interrupted upending her life again to dote on me unnecessarily. I didn't tell many of my friends because I didn't want them to worry. But whenever I did tell them, all they ever expressed was gratitude for my being alive. The RallyCap team sent me a card after they heard about what happened. I had never before been so touched.

I was alive, and I knew what almost caused me to not be. I can't prove it because there was nothing wrong with me (according to people much more intelligent than I), but to me it was simple: me.

I was alive because of sheer luck, happenstance, possible divine intervention, and a car built like a brick house. I was lucky that those four stars aligned. But the reason they had to was because I had run myself so far into the ground throughout the past year. My values had not diminished. They had been destroyed. I wasn't forging the identity of who I was; I was a slave of who I thought I wanted to become.

Diminishing Returns of Value occur when you don't value your values, when you subvert them for what they could potentially get you. However, when you do, you can create a whole mess of problems that aren't easily solved. But DRV can be avoided if you put emphasis not on what you can create from your values but on your values themselves. By focusing on the now, you give yourself the gift of loving what you have and not what you don't.

Because remember, when you ride that top line of death to the end of the graph, you crash against the side of the paper. You crash hard. Sometimes, while driving down the Ohio interstate.

* * *

I ORIGINALLY STARTED WITH SOMETHING of value (my education/schoolwork) and then drove the rest of my life into the ground by being greedy. That's DRV if I've ever seen it. When you value something too much, when you don't Essentially Diversify, when you let Excessive Excess run, bad things happen.

This reality of DRV leads me to what I alluded to when talking about the *Call Her Daddy* fallout—the Art of Settling. Settling, like I mentioned earlier, gets a really bad connotation in our culture. Why? Because we're Americans, baby! We build things. We put people on the moon.[248] We win World Wars.[249] We kick the shit out of the rest of the world in sports.[250] We don't get second place. It's almost blasphemous to think of not going all out, especially in a world driven by attention and social media.

If we settle, we're told, we will spurn striving. We will turn people off from reaching their potential. We will become unmotivated sacks of mediocre matter who don't do anything with ourselves. We will be average. We will stop innovating and making things better.

This is a fair point. But I don't think it's right. No absolute is. If we simply go all out on everything we encounter in life, I would actually argue we *inhibit* our striving and shoot our potential in the foot. Do some things work this way? They could. My parents went on a date to a Pizza Hut when they were sixteen years old and never looked back. I'd say it worked out pretty well for them.

But this isn't how life works holistically. It's ludicrous and wrong. If you allow yourself to become siloed in your values, it cuts off your vision from what could be better things to value in the future.

However, there is something worse that can and does happen. Our culture is obsessed with variety. It's wrong and detrimental to our well-being. In order to combat variety, we must consciously choose things to devote ourselves to. By confining ourselves, we are freeing ourselves from the slavery of variety.

The worst possible scenario for DRV is perpetual dissatisfaction and despair. When you go all-in on something, when you refuse to settle for the good that is happening to you at the moment, you get lost in the sauce. You are so consumed by your hubris and narcissism you fail to realize the consequences of what is happening to you as you dive further in.

When you're obsessing over the ideal, over the perfect, you're setting yourself up for disappointment and failure. Why? Because there is no ideal. There is no perfect. There is nothing that will totally sate you. Of all the life hacks and tricks you see on Buzzfeed,[251] none of them work in the long term. If there is one thing constant about human history, it is the imperfections of the humans that populate it.

When you pursue something that cannot be pursued, you open the door for a constant stream of dissatisfaction, ungratefulness, and unhappiness. Eventually, it will strip away the original value that enticed you in the first place. This is where the crashes happen. This is where Sofia Franklyn loses everything. Where Peter Nelson botches his credibility. Where Wall Street Guy gets arrested.

Let's go back to the example of my parents. A big insecurity of mine around romance and women is that story. "Well, shit," I think. "If they had this figured out so young, then I must really be some special breed of fuckup. My grandparents were like this too. So were my aunt and uncle who I'm close with. My brother has had a steady girlfriend for years, and he's three years younger than I am. What's wrong with me?"

The answer? Nothing. It was a story that was emotionally based and narcissistic. I thought I was special because I didn't get what other people had. Go cry about it. Get over yourself. You're not special. But our relationships are the single biggest offender when it comes to DRV.

I know a girl who would only date men who were four years older than her, were at minimum 6'4" could entertain her on Hinge for more than a week, and took her to a $40+ meal. So, being the good friend I am, I politely told her she was out of her fucking gourd. How could she expect this from one person? How could she do this to not just these poor Hinge men but herself? She was literally torturing herself with impossibility, creating Instagram posts about being "alone" and "unsatisfied" but then refusing to yield when the perfect guy didn't magically appear to jerk himself off on her carpet.

But that is exactly the point.

The sad reality is when we refuse to settle, we don't do it because we're upset with how we perceive others. That would be too easy. Our problems would be solved by now. When we refuse to settle, we do it because we're upset with how we perceive ourselves. We emotionally overcompensate for something we feel we lack and use all our energy to attempt to obtain it. When it doesn't happen, when perfection inevitably fails to be realized, we lose hope. We crash. We ride the top line into the abyss.

MOVEMENT VERSUS PROGRESS

I feel it's sometimes best to look at what not to do before realizing what to do. DRV is no different. It's an easy trap to fall into. It's easy to replace the material for the immaterial. Especially when the material is painted green, is cut from trees, and comes packaged in rubber bands and saran wrap.

But pretty paper is no substitute for what got you the pretty paper. That's the first reason that DRV happens. It's very easy to lose track of the value that got you to where you were. Don't be greedy.

The second reason the trap of DRV is easy to fall into is people don't know the proper pivot point. "Pivot" in business terms is used to describe when a company needs to alter their strategic vision. When companies don't do this correctly, they collapse in spectacular fashion. Ask JCPenney. Turns out, hiring the guy who created Apple Stores to run a fashion warehouse is a shitty idea.[252] Who knew?

The third reason the trap of DRV is so easy to fall into is your mind can trick you into the ends taking over the means. Justifying them, in all their glory, without a shred of common sense to hold you accountable. This is perhaps the most common excuse given. It's also the most dangerous.

Ever seen a mob movie? Like, literally, any one ever made ever? This is the ending of all of them. Sorry to shit in your cornflakes. The old Italian guy at the end of the movie said that all the killing, destruction, and pain he caused to rise to the top was all for nothing. His family hates him now. He has a lot of money but nothing meaningful to spend it on. He has a lot of power, but his power can be used only to hurt, not help. But, in his eyes, that's okay. He got to the destination. He crossed the finish line. He made it. That should mean something, right?

Wrong.

The ends should only justify the means if the means themselves are good. The value has to be good to derive anything worthwhile. If the value is corrupted, the ends will be corrupted. The mob boss could have chosen to become an accountant or dentist. That would have gotten him good money. And, aside from the possibility of him being an incredibly shitty dentist, the pain could have been avoided too.

How you get there matters. Just ask the Griswolds. When you make everything about the end goal, you'll sacrifice everything. You'll throw away your dignity, a dead relative, and sanity to get to Walley World only to find out it's all a sham. Only John Candy (may he rest in peace) is there to greet you.[253]

When you corrupt values, you automatically corrupt everything you get out of them. They must stay intact and be kept pristine. If they aren't, only disappointment and John Candy (if you're lucky) await you.

* * *

WE SHOULD ATTEMPT TO AVOID DRV. We don't want to crash. We don't want to spiral out of control because of a distorted view of the things that keep us grounded, which are our values. This can have a far worse effect than one might realize. If you suffer a DRV crash that is significant (see above examples), you might experience something worse than the crash itself: you could lose hope.

When you lose track of what grounds you to earth, you begin to lose your grip on earth itself. Your reality becomes falsified. You don't know what's real. You can't tell whether you're doing the right or wrong things. You lose control. You feel powerless. Because the fact is you're simply a perception of how you see yourself. Whenever that perception (your identity) is damaged, you are damaged.

That's why our values are so important. That's why this chapter is so important. We need to keep our focus on the values themselves, not what they could potentially provide us. Because (insert book-bound throat punch here) it's not about the destination, it's all about the journey that gets us there.

You need to know what you value, but you can never lose sight of the value itself. This is Excessive Excess. This is building for the sake of building and doing for the sake of doing. When partaking in indulgence, you deny yourself the opportunity to see how important the process is. Without the process, you cannot get to your goal. Without the process, that goal can become distorted and warped. You can't manipulate what doesn't want to be manipulated. You must let it play out in order to reap the benefits. If you get greedy, you risk tampering with something that could slam the door in your face on the way in.

If you don't know when to settle, you will most likely end up riding the top line of death into the abyss. That outcome can be avoided by knowing your inflection points. Knowing when the tides are turning is a skill that cannot be mastered without careful attention and patience. It takes a long time to master. I'm nowhere near there yet.

In my junior year of college, I succumbed to pressure and kept putting more and more value on my education and my schoolwork. I didn't socialize with people. I didn't go out. I'm surprised most of my few friends didn't drop me. A lot of them probably would have if I didn't help them with their homework.

But the thing is, I wasn't putting value on my education and my schoolwork. I thought I was when I wasn't. I was overcompensating by thinking I was doing more than I really was. I wasn't putting more value into that area of my life. I was bloating it. To quote my guy Denzel Washington, "Remember that just because you're doing a lot more doesn't mean you're getting a lot more done. Don't confuse movement with progress."[254]

I had never felt more indirectly attacked in my life than when I heard that quote. It hurt hearing I had wasted so much of my time being filled up with meaningless nothing that I had sacrificed my entire life (almost too literally) outside of school *for* school. Worst off, my GPA actually went down during this period. I didn't even accomplish what I wanted to accomplish. I had effectively tanked my entire life for nothing.

But after putting aside my victimhood, I began to reflect. I talked with my parents. I read some books that told me to get the fuck over myself and my narcissism. I came to realize the ultimate point that probably in some way led to the creation of my blog, podcast, and now, book: balance.

Balance is a tricky word. A lot of people say it can't be achieved. That we must sacrifice all of something for all of something else. Bullshit, I say. The reason for the bullshit is the other half of the "sacrifice" equation, which we covered in our introduction to Value Economics—value itself.

It all comes full circle, you see. Your values determine everything. What you eat, who you choose to call on a Thursday night, who you fuck, etc. Your values, if allocated correctly, act as a natural balancer to the rest of your life. They keep you balanced for the simple reason that they in themselves are balanced.

The next year, I fortunately was able to get my life back on track. At least a little bit. I got some new friends who replaced old and toxic friends. That's the Third out of Jordan Peterson's Twelve Rules for life, by the way.[255] I went out on a weekday or two (gasp). I started a blog to vent and talk about all of this shit with random people on the internet. My grades went up. It was awesome. By noting that inflection point, by knowing the tide of change I needed to ride, I was able to navigate it successfully to redefine what success looks like for me. Nothing else mattered.

You must always keep your Means of Value in mind. How you get there is just as important as where "there" is. Intent matters. How you get from Point A to Point B matters. If it didn't, the world would be a pretty shitty place. Awful values would run rampant, and shit would be on fire. Not good.

It would be different if I decided to be a heroin trafficker, made a ton of money, and pimped out a used 2005 Ford Taurus to get friends.

That wouldn't have solved my problems. It would have just made me a douche.

We must deal with real problems by seeing them as they are—real problems. The best way to get out of a hole is to stop digging. You need a way to get out of your current situation. That way is a process.

But processes are *hard*. It was hard to convince myself that I needed to stop. It was *hard* to say I needed to cut some people off to get where I wanted to go. It was *hard* to reorient my values in order to prevent myself from riding the top line of death off of a fucking cliff. But it was essential.

Only through self-awareness, the essential Factor of Value Production, can this be achieved. Only through deciding to embrace the hell you're going through can you dig yourself out and be better. Only by examining and orienting your values can you have a chance to maintain your position on top of them.

Intent matters. Don't think that it doesn't. Don't get greedy. Don't shove your problems under the rug. Deal with them.

CHAPTER SEVEN

GUNS AND BUTTER

"Money itself is not the reason to work hard. The reason is freedom. There is nothing more beautiful than getting up in the morning, even though you want to go to work, and knowing that you don't have to."

−KEVIN O'LEARY

EAT MY SHORTS

"Corner-boy, I prolly sold more rocks than a rock pit//Tryin to fill my shoes is like a armless man with chopsticks."[256]

ONLY A COUPLE PEOPLE IN MUSIC COULD PULL OFF A LINE this absurd. Gucci Mane is one of them.

When Gucci first came on the scene in Atlanta, the culture was engulfed in immense transition. Coming up with other rap pioneers such as T.I. and Young Jeezy, this new wave of music swiftly began to take over. Gucci was the most entrepreneurial, enlisting help from many collaborators to spread his music.

No one expected what happened to happen. Gucci Mane revolutionized the Atlanta rap scene into a powder keg of clout chasing, heavy drumbeats, and mumble rap. The explosion that resulted was nothing short of transformative. New artists popped up left and right to get a piece of the action. Gone were the days of aliens and zodiac signs spun up by OutKast.[257] An entire new subgenre of rap music was created that eventually became the dominant version of the art form: trap.[258]

Gucci Mane is rightfully recognized as the most important and influential pioneer of trap music,[259] which was a result of both his aforementioned ingenuity and patented hustle. Gucci put out (by his count) over one hundred tapes before he made it big.[260] That's an absolute fuck ton of music. For context, the Beatles only released twelve studio albums, and one motion picture soundtrack, over the span of seven *years*,[261] which is still a relatively frenetic pace. While his popularity took a while to take off, it finally did with the release of his song "Freaky Gurl" in 2007.[262]

After dropping "Freaky Gurl," Gucci decided to treat himself. In his autobiography (a fantastic read, by the way), Gucci stated he had one item in mind. A typical person would treat themselves to something relatively common but still enjoyable: a burrito, a piece of clothing, a milkshake maybe. But this is Gucci Mane—not your typical person by any stretch. Gucci decided to buy a chain. But not just any chain.

La Flare decided to blow $75,000 on a solid-gold chain adorned with a diamond-studded Bart Simpson riding a skateboard. Not your most orthodox flex by any stretch. It's a sick chain. No one denies that. But those same people probably won't deny the appeal of the alternatives either.

For the sake of argument, let's say Gucci didn't call his jeweler. Instead, he calls his broker. He tells him to drop that $75,000 into Microsoft, which was trading at around $30.25 on January 3, 2007, the time of Gucci's purchase. Gucci buys and holds the stock up until the day I finish this chapter.

Gucci then cashes out his stock on January 21, 2022, say to buy another absurd chain or something. Not including a broker fee and capital gains, Gucci would receive a total of $746,256.20.[263] That's almost ten iced-out Bart Simpsons.

If that's shocking, hold my lean. Let's say instead he threw that money into Apple, trading at $11.97 on January 3, 2007. Gucci would receive $1,028,320.80.[264] Almost fourteen iced-out Bart Simpsons.

Fuck it, let's get crazy. Let's say Gucci held his money because a huge fan of his, Elon Musk, really likes freaky girls (i.e., Grimes[265]) and lemonade.[266] So, as a favor, Gucci decides to save that money and dump it into his friend Elon's IPO of this company called Tesla that makes cars that can fly, or something.

Tesla went public on June 29, 2010 and began trading at a price of $17 a share. Gucci would receive $4,231,102.94 today.[267] Over fifty-six iced-out Bart Simpsons and in three years less than Microsoft or Apple.

These are startling numbers. If you factor in things like depreciation, wear and tear, and sociocultural trends (like that *The Simpsons* blows and giant chains made out of its characters probably aren't hot anymore), the chain would almost certainly not be worth $75,000 today. Maybe three quarters of the initial price. Maybe half. Maybe lower.

Gucci said in his book it was one of the dumbest things he's ever bought. He's wise. He's mentored current sensations such as Migos, Nicki Minaj, and Young Thug, among others. He constantly talks with other up-and-coming rappers about financial literacy, especially those from Atlanta.

Most people don't learn financial strategy until they're at least Gucci's age. Maybe older. Some never learn it. That lesson is essential to financial freedom. I'm not of the age, experience, or intellect to where I can pursue investing for myself (although your reading this book might help ☺), but I've been thankful to learn a lot of lessons from people I trust along the way.

I take this topic very seriously. I honestly don't know why more people don't. Maybe it's because a lot of people don't know how to define it. Not a valid excuse, but in our world that lacks definition and identity, it's one that gets thrown out a lot. Spending is spending, right?

Wrong. One hundred percent wrong. You can spend money on the good things or the bad things. Money is binary. You either save or spend, buy or don't buy, make it or don't make it. What makes it so awesome is that all of these decisions are entirely yours, which leads back to our definition problem and another money problem: what categories can we spend money on?

There are two. The answer is very simple in nature but complex in motivation. What's also simple is how it can relate to our values. Our value literacy, like our financial literacy, is essential. It's one thing to have money; it's another thing to use it properly. The whole point of this book is to not only have values but to understand Value Economics. This lesson is essential, which leads us to the two categories we can spend money on: guns and butter.

This analogy can seem strange at first. What I do want to say is this is one of the most important, if not the most important, single lesson I've learned to be true in life. And it doesn't just pertain to money.

GUNS AND BUTTER

Now for the Brain Hurt. I apologize in advance—I'll try to make this as painless as possible.

In "What Came Before," I explained how economics is the study of a shit ton of graphs. I'm going to introduce another, one that econ nerds splooge over daily: the Productions Possibilities Frontier.

Letters! Numbers! Partially *and* completely filled-in lines!

Let's start with the basics. Resources are finite. I like Brené Brown, but no matter what she tells you, this is an inescapable fact of life,[268] except for things like the sun and air (and depending on how cynical and/or woke you are, even those could be in jeopardy[269]). The way you use them is also finite. You cannot use more than what you have. That leaves a series of (wait for it) production possibilities.

Now for the Guns and Butter part. In the context it was originally used way back in the olden times, this was simply a choice between what the government could spend its budget on.[270] It could either spend on defense (guns) or civilian goods (butter). This is a trade-off, like the value/sacrifice graph.

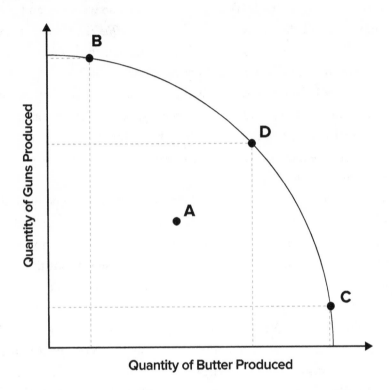

This is where the letters come in. Point A is simply resources being underutilized. You are not using all of your resources to buy either Guns nor Butter. Point B is leaning toward buying guns, while Point C is leaning toward buying butter. Point X is a point of impossibility. Resources are finite, remember?

You cannot use what you don't have. If you do not have the resources to make it to Point X, you cannot achieve Point X. Point D represents a perfect balance (Thanos voice)[271] between the two. You are completely equal in your priorities. You are spending equally on Guns and Butter. Everyone wins.

Or do they?

What would have happened if during World War II, we shifted to making anal beads and condoms instead of tools to help with the war? What if during the Cold War (you know, the one where us and the commies were a click away from sending us into *The Terminator*[272]), we spent all our resources testing missiles and manufacturing "Fuck you, communism!" signs rather than improving civilian life?

This would signal to the public that our priorities are *way* out of whack. Both options could improve society, depending on your love of country and/or sex. Both could be valued. But at certain points in time, some are more important to emphasize. So why don't we do the same with our own lives?

As a culture, we are fucking awful with enacting this type of discipline (Factors of Value Production Number Four, if you can remember that far back in the book). For the sake of this chapter, I'm going to talk mostly in terms of money to keep the consistency, but this is a universal concept. Money, in my opinion, just happens to be the one area where we set ourselves up to fail in the worst ways.

Think about it. When was the last time you bought something at Starbucks for approximately $278? Probably this morning. Online shopping for something you already have? Probably in the past few weeks. Blew money on an insane amount of alcohol that you yakked up? This past weekend.[273]

Now, most of us don't have the capital nor the desire to purchase massive weapons of war or large quantities of civilian goods. What we do have is the resources at our disposal and what we can use to buy them. Which leads me to what Guns and Butter mean for us everyday folks.

Guns are things that are scarce. There are only a finite number of them in the world. And (most importantly) when you spend money on them, they actively create value for you. It takes a lot to make a gun, and it sells for a lot more.

Butter is the opposite. Butter is easily duplicated. There is an almost unlimited supply of butter. And (most importantly) when you spend money on butter, it actively takes value from you. It takes relatively little to make butter, and it sells for a lot less.

You probably have a good amount of butter at your house. It usually comes in packs of four for about three dollars. I doubt as many people have a four pack of Glocks sitting in their fridge. Scarcity is key.

This brings me to the second part of the Guns and Butter rule. Other than the historical context, there is a little-known but famous scene from a film that explains it perfectly. In the film *Baby Boy*, directed by the great John Singleton, Melvin, the new boyfriend of Jody's mother, drops a rant of wisdom on his girl's son:[274]

> When you makin' paper you gotta learn some rules to go with it. You gotta learn the difference between guns and butter. There's two types of n***** in this world: there's n***** with guns and n***** with butter. Now, what are the guns? The guns, that's the real estate. The stocks and bonds. Artwork, you know shit that appreciates with value. What's the butter? Cars, clothes, jewelry, all that other bullshit that don't mean shit after you buy it. That's what it's all about, guns and butter, baby!

In essence, there is stuff that is worth spending money on, and there is stuff that isn't. It may not seem that way. But when you spray-paint that shit with gold paint, someone at a flea market will buy it.

CATFISHING, COCKBLOCKING, AND CORNERBACKS

But gold spray-painted shit is mostly harmless. There are many more things out there that are far worse.

Dating apps are up there with Kim Kardashian's ass[275] and the nuke we dropped on Hiroshima[276] as potentially the most devastating invention ever. For the most part, they do nothing but provide a daily dose of pain to all of their users. Well, most of them. My former best friend met his girlfriend there, and I think they're still together, but I'm not sure.

The first time I downloaded a dating app was my freshman year of college. I was eighteen and horny as fuck. I was a fat kid. I played the fat kid positions in sports. And if you recall, I wasn't even good. That makes for a devastating effect on your social life, particularly for a kid who didn't think that highly of himself. I didn't get a lot of girls. My prom date my senior year thought I was a creep, so she kicked me to the curb a month before. I practically begged her to reconsider, and she thankfully showed me mercy.

But being eighteen and horny as fuck really doesn't get you terribly far, depending on your environment. Much more on this in the next chapter, but my living situation wasn't good. My college was located in one of the most booming metropolitan areas in the Midwest. It was rife with thousands of college students.

The only problem was that my apartment wasn't there.

I had gotten deferred to what is called a satellite campus, which is a subsidiary of the main campus located in a city somewhere in my home state. The place my satellite campus was located was forty-five minutes away from Columbus, Ohio, in a dilapidated town called Newark.[277] In terms of women, I only interacted with one in particular, who was a single mom living next to my townhome apartment with two young boys. She was a nice woman, but I kept my distance after she admitted she was worried about "her boyfriend's wife finding out about her" when I offered to help her build a bedframe. I'm surprised Octavia Spencer didn't leap out of her closet and skin me with a kitchen knife right then.[278]

So my dick, already dry, began to shrivel even more. But thankfully, there was a way out. My aforementioned friend was generous enough to offer up a stay on his futon every weekend in his dorm. He paid for my meals and allowed me to crash in his already cramped dorm room with his two other roommates. It was one of the oldest buildings on campus in a room originally made for two. They later added a fourth roommate, a Chinese exchange student named Yidi who didn't speak a syllable of English. I played Four Loko pong with him one night while sloshed. He laughed.

It was in that dorm room where I learned the ins and outs of college life. My best friend had a high school girlfriend up until around Thanksgiving. After they broke up, he went on the biggest womanizing spree since Genghis Khan, whose descendants make up 8 percent of the Asian male population today.[279] His first roommate was the son of a Greek cardiologist. He blew money like crazy, partied harder than anyone I'd ever seen, and could pull women like it was nothing. I've never met anyone more fun. His second roommate was mostly asexual. He was a really fun guy too. He just chose to smoke weed, take psychedelics, and headbang to EDM rather than pick up girls. Yidi, of course, did none of these things. He was the best of us.

I certainly wasn't my best friend or Roommate One. But I wasn't Roommate Two or Yidi either. I was something worse. My confidence was nonexistent. I would go out in khakis; a short-sleeved, button-down shirt; and a dad hat every Friday and Saturday in negative-two-degree Ohio weather. I thought I looked like hot shit, but I always felt like shit. I felt like a poser. I would see a dude my age and even uglier than me walk up to a girl at a bar and have his tongue probing somewhere around her small intestine within about five minutes. I was astounded. But more than that, I was depressed.

Approach Anxiety is a real thing,[280] but I have it particularly badly. And I mean *badly*. I froze every time a girl looked at me. I didn't know how to interact with them. I had never kissed a girl in my life. I had barely hugged one that wasn't my grandmother. I had no idea what to do. My mom was very traditional, and my sister had autism. I didn't know how that whole "normal Gen Z female gender" thing functioned.

I occasionally got lucky. My first breakthrough came on the weekend of Halloween. The roommates and I, being idiots, decided to get absolutely shit-faced on three different types of alcohol. From what I remember, the combination was some mixture of Bacardi Dragonberry, Four Loko Gold, and Jägermeister, all bought from the local gas station with my best friend's shitty fake ID for about $22. I'm a lightweight. I've puked up my liquor more times than I can remember. But that night, amazingly, I managed to hold it in. I didn't have a costume, so I threw on a Michael Jordan Tune Squad jersey[281] and cutoff sweatpants and began falling and drooling over myself like the drunken buffoon I was.

There was a club at my university notorious for letting kids in underage. It was so bad that my best friend gave me his spare fake, and I got in. For context, my best friend is blond-haired, clean-shaven, and blue-eyed; I have brown hair, a full beard, and brown eyes. That's how many fucks they gave.

The two of us were meeting some high school friends (also drunken buffoons) and linked in the middle of the dance floor of the club. In a drunken stupor not unlike the hotel lobby scene from *Fear and Loathing in Las Vegas*,[282] I was in complete blackout mode.

In my haze, my best friend and I made it to the bar and, in a continued show of our dumbassery, ordered more alcohol. As soon as several bombs were downed, I locked eyes with a girl at the bar. She was similarly wasted. I'm not entirely sure what happened between time lapses, but five minutes later, we were making out and groping everything on each other's sweaty bodies in the middle of hundreds of other sweaty bodies. My best friend got it on video. It was an appalling sight. I ended up taking her back to the dorm room, miraculously being the first one of the group to accomplish that "milestone." I was quite proud of that. While I didn't slide into home, let's just say several firsts happened that night.

I had an epiphany as soon as I guided her out of the glass-plated lobby and sent the poor girl on a Walk of Shame in front of the RAs. That realization was this: I fucking suck at this. The only way I can score is apparently by downing an absurd amount and versions of alcohol, falling all over myself, and practically Me Too-ing a girl whose last name I couldn't remember? This is awful. I'm awful.

But there was an out, you see. That Out was Tinder. Roommate One had mastered this tactic and began to share his wisdom with me. He would match with a girl on Tinder, meet her out at a bar, and then do his best to make something happen. It was a brilliant strategy. He also suggested linking up with female friends of theirs and matching with *them* on Tinder in order to remove the awkward Approach Anxiety. My eyes lit up. My chances of rejection would be reduced to zero. This was amazing.

But the whole issue of "I don't live there" kept coming up. I was hopelessly stuck. I tried my best, but location is a big factor when it comes to dating, it turns out. However, I was persistent and eventually came to my second breakthrough. I found a girl who was a friend of one of my roommates' friends on Instagram who I thought was *insanely* hot. I followed her, and she followed me back. She also had her Snapchat in her bio. I added her, and she added me back. But Approach Anxiety, even virtually, still reigned supreme. I didn't message her for three months.

But one night, a golden opportunity opened up. She posted a story about a football player cutting the line at the same bar where I had tongue-fucked my prior Lucky Girl three months prior. He, like all football players, knew the bouncer and had cut the line of about two hundred people in negative-ten-degree weather. I thought that was bullshit, and I slid up and told her that. Unbelievably, she responded, and we started talking. Soon, we were Number One Best Friends on Snapchat for over three months.

It turned out this girl was unbelievable in other ways than just her hotness. She was the valedictorian of her class. She was a computer science major who wanted to take over the world. She hung out with really cool people. She was really fun. She was funny. I couldn't believe it. After three months, I finally got the nerve to ask her out to a local ice cream place that she loved from her hometown in Northeast Ohio. She accepted, and I left my satellite campus to go get her.

I parked my car and went into her dorm lobby to wait for her. It was a beautiful April day. I messaged her to tell her I was there, and she started down. I was both bursting with excitement and in a state of abject shock. The literal girl of my dreams was waiting to hop in my Jeep to go get ice cream with me. Me! A former fat kid who nearly shit himself every time he saw a girl breathe! It was incredible.

But all that excitement evaporated when she got out of the elevator. I've learned the hard way that I have the most horrible poker face of anyone I know. I have no control whatsoever. My face says it all. The girl who came out of the elevator wasn't the girl I had been Snapchatting. She was something else.

She was a whale.

Other than knowing that I was shitty at getting them, I knew one other thing about women—I *love* them thick. Love them. No offense to any skinny girls out there, but to me, you're overrated. Men, particularly eighteen-year-old, horny-as-fuck ones, tend to lose sight of the bigger picture when a woman they find attractive is involved. And when I say "lose track," I mean lose all common sensibility whatsoever.

My best friend tried to tell me. Every time I'd pull up a picture of her to explain how I had fallen in love with a thick yet inanimate object, he would bring me down to earth. He was really good at that. "Dude, she's fat." "Dude, she's not thick at all. She's just fucking obese." I spurned his warnings every time. He was wrong. Nothing was going to stand in my way.

But something was standing in my way, and it sure as shit wasn't the girl I had met over Snapchat. I didn't know it yet, but I had been officially catfished.[283] I mustered all of my self-control and forced a smile. My God, this was horrible. I didn't know what to do, so I stuck to my guns and led her to my car. I opened the door for her, she got in, and we sped off to the ice cream place, something that she obviously didn't need. This wasn't the Freshman Fifteen.[284] This was the Freshman Fifty-Pushing-Sixty.

I calmed down enough to make conversation. Somehow, that made it worse. The girl, as it turns out, was not intelligent at all, or at least didn't apply herself. She had gone from valedictorian of her high school class to a 1.9 GPA and a major switch to political science. I didn't ask her how she thought her GPA was going to support that level of supposed ambition. I was a good soldier, so I soldiered on.

The avalanche continued. Her "fun" was going out every Tuesday, Thursday, Friday, Saturday, and Sunday to drink and do drugs with her degenerate friends, who also were not fun. The only thing that comforted me was knowing that maybe with just a teensy bit less alcohol, she could look less whale-like. But, based on her current trajectory, I knew that was never going to happen.

The avalanche hit the bottom of the mountain just before we parked at the ice cream place. The girl of my dreams then began talking about her sex life. Our football team had a really good secondary that year. All four of them would eventually turn out to be first-round draft picks. She had fucked three of them, had a threesome with two of those three in her dorm room, and was actively trying to convince one of them to leave his current girlfriend for her. The girlfriend was later revealed to have been carrying that player's child.

I'm not one to sex-shame anyone (as hopefully evidenced by Ms. Cooper's story in Chapter Six), but I don't think it's unreasonable to be slightly miffed when the girl you spent the last three months pouring your soul into shits on your masculinity with several football players like some sort of cuck porn film. I nearly crashed my car through the front of the ice cream stand as we pulled into a spot. It would have given me something slightly more humiliating to get my mind off things.

I was a good boy. I sat down, paid for both of us, and made the same ridiculous small talk for another forty-five minutes before I damn-near threw her in my car (if I could even pick her up) to ship her back to her cesspool of disappointment. But even after all of that, I still held out hope. I still was hooked on that very same premise of some woman, any woman, paying any remote bit of attention to me. I whipped out my phone, sent a message saying thank you, and proposed another date before the end of school. The warm tide of hope slowly filled my body as I sped back to my apartment, hoping for a response by the time I got back.

I did get a response. She left me on "read." I tried again but got the same response—nothing. She had effectively cockblocked me.[285] She had only used me for attention and ice cream to pad both her ego and rolls. I was crushed. My ego, already small, was ground into a fine powder and snorted up someone's nose (probably hers, given her "fun activities"). I didn't hear from her for another four months. When I did hear from her, it was because she was revealed to be living on the same dorm room floor as I was the whole next year. She had an orgy with her roommate in that room.

She's still fat today, I think. She didn't study law. She's now a project manager for a software reseller. She's not running any type of world, much less the world. It's too bad. She seemed to really want to.

LIVING IN THE GRAY

The concept of Guns and Butter is one of the most difficult dichotomies people have to learn to balance within their lives. It's one that most people don't think about because we actively don't think about it. But we should. Because while we don't actively think about it, it can absolutely dick us in the long term, as evidenced by me dicking no one in the previous section.

Let's go back to our graph. We'll start where we don't want to be. We don't want to be at Point A, although it's better than some other alternatives. When we underutilize our money, we may not put it where it can create value for us in the long run, which will hurt us in the future. But hey, at least you're not blowing it on a fourth pair of white Air Force Ones or going out five nights of the week.

You definitely *don't* want to be at Point X. This is the point on the graph where you watch *Wall Street*, get high on bath salts, max out all twelve of your credit cards, call your broker, and tell him to dump all the money you don't have plus your daughter's college fund into a biotech company that's strangely headquartered out of a Winnebago on the outskirts of Albuquerque.[286] This is the point of overutilization/impossibility. When we do this, we overextend ourselves and can end up doing much more damage by leveraging our finances out further than they should be.

Now we get to the gray area of where on the curve we should be. Remember, it's called the Production Possibilities Curve. All points on the line are possible because they are in our means of production. In terms of Value Economics, they're on the spectrum of our Means of Value, which define the end points of where we can deploy our value capital, as discussed in Chapter Two. We are now officially on the Frontier and have an unlimited amount of spots where we could go. Only points B, C, and D are left.

Point B isn't ideal either. Yeah, you'd be throwing all of your finances into things that create value for you, but where's the fun? You wouldn't be disciplined. You'd be rigid. There would be no flexibility, no room for enjoyment out of life. Discipline leads to freedom, but rigidity leads to stagnation. Too much rigidity leads to a life of fulfillment in the sense that you accomplished the mission, but what did it cost to achieve mission success? (Gamora voice)[287]

Point C is another one of those "DO NOT FUCKING GO HERE" points. Not only are you creating no value for yourself, but you're actively destroying it. This is ice-cream-for-breakfast, strippers, and PCP-use territory. Stay away.

So Point D is where a lot of people assume you should go. It's perfectly in the middle, the equilibrium between the two extremes. It's natural to assume that.

But that's also wrong.

Think of it this way: if you took home $50,000 after taxes and split it right down the middle, you would still be blowing $25,000 on shit that does nothing for you. Half your money would go down the toilet, no one having gained anything except for the person who suckered you out of your money.

In any aspect of life, especially monetary, you should always lean toward the side where value is created and sought after. Always. A failure to do so will not only be betraying your current position but also betraying yourself and what you truly stand for. Only by first identifying your values and putting your proverbial money to work for them will you live a life of personal significance.

Gucci Mane obviously shouldn't have bought that giant chain of a cartoon character. The girl I met through Instagram obviously shouldn't have tanked her entire life by falling victim to her own shortcomings and vices. Yet so many other people fall into the same trap. Long before the beer virus was a thing, there was and still is another sickness that has infected and infested our culture. It has corrupted it for as far back as we know. One to which we are all guilty of falling victim, whether we like it or not: keeping up with the Joneses Syndrome (KUJS).

KUJS is a horrific affliction, one that is affecting more and more people in our society today than ever before. This is a direct derivative of what we went over in the beginning of this book. Excess is corrupting our culture, which is causing us to tribalize into groups based on identity while shunning any true individuality. Our Means of Value, driven by excess, are totally out of whack.

Our world has been completely transformed by this phenomenon. As alluded to in "What Came Before," our world is better off now by many statistical metrics than any previous point in history. This is not hyperbole. This is true. We live longer. We've found solutions to diseases that ravaged the world for thousands of years, including COVID-19 in under a year.[288] Those guys Bin Laden,[289] Hitler,[290] Saddam,[291] and Stalin[292] are dead. We aren't at war with anyone (at least as of this writing). These are good things.

But this has also led to some bad things. Solving those issues above left holes we need to fill. Humans are creatures that need conflict to survive. A world without problems is a world in which we don't want to live because problems inherently create meaning for our lives. Meaning itself is derived from values, which, as we have seen, are derived from what we deem personally important.

This leads us to the question of how we currently fill those holes. KUJS is a leading way humans currently do this. When there's no existential threat to the common good that people can get behind (with the exception of the first couple months of COVID-19), we make up threats in our mind to compete with.

These threats are our neighbors. The people we have around us. Our family and friends, maybe. In order to find meaning, we either consciously or subconsciously compete with our environment to prove our superiority. And the means by which we prove ourselves is incredibly fickle and destructive to our well-being: money.

How many people have you met in your life whose parents drive His and Hers Mercedes, but their kids still have to take out student loans? Girls that online shop in class to constantly purchase things to wear just to impress girls in their sorority? Guys who sift through StockX in search of a pair of Jordans they're not even planning to wear out that much for fear of getting them dirty?

There are many examples. I guarantee you there are many. When this misalignment of values happens, disaster occurs. Those kids might not get out from under that debt. That shirt might not fit. Those Js might get scuffed.

Do these things create value for you? In excess, they do not. However, it isn't fair to say they entirely don't, either. That would be coming from the philosophy of Point B, and that's too rigid. Value is in the eye of the beholder. Once you discover what you value, you can actively go forward to pursue it.

It would be different if the parents of the college kid actively contributed to their kids' higher education while also saving up to treat themselves to a (meaning one) nice car because they have worked hard and value what the car can bring to them. The reason is *internal*, not external, like we talked about in Chapter One with the hallmarks of good values. It would be different if the girl who likes to shop online only does so infrequently and for items she truly desires, not just ones that will allow her to keep treading water. Whether that's a luxury bag, a pair of shoes, whatever the fuck the popular legging brand is nowadays, it's all the same. As long as it comes from *her*, not from seeking the validation of others. It would be different if the kid who bought the Jordans didn't have a pair and was really saving up for ones so he could feel fresh. He would do so because it would enhance how he feels about himself. It would enhance his worth in *his* eyes, not others.

Excess dilutes value. And butter is modern society's excess when not mitigated properly. We must be cognizant of these things as a culture and actively work to move in the proper direction.

* * *

I TEND TO BE TOO literal. You've probably been able to sense that just a little bit throughout this entire book. I live in a very black-and-white world. For the most part, it's served me quite well. But I've learned the hard way, particularly in terms of my dating situation, that life isn't always a binary. Being too rigid leads to a very empty and sad life. People are not black-and-white creatures, and the quality of the lives we live depends highly on the quality of the relationships that fill them.

Being this type of person, most of my life has been very empty and sad. In a lot of people's opinions, I've lived quite the opposite. They see a lot of big things I've done and think it's automatically good. But cotton candy and popcorn come in big packages too, and they tend to not fill you up very much. I've pretty much ridden a constant sugar high. Nothing has ever truly sustained me.

My parents, being good parents, have tried to help with this. They can't fix my problems because they're my problems, but they did give me one piece of advice that has proven helpful: living in the gray.

This is, quite literally, the opposite of what provides a cotton-candy-filled life. Human beings, our relationships, and our values are not black and white things. They are constantly adapting, changing, and testing, as we went over in Chapter One. They're on a spectrum related to our Means of Value, as we went over in Chapter Two. And they are Essentially Diversified, as we went over in Chapter Three.

The topic of Guns and Butter in Value Economics is inherently gray. Not black or white, but very, *very* gray. And for the most part, people hate gray. We want things to be simple, for us to have the ability to take the path of least resistance. This topic of money and financial literacy is the complete opposite of that because every person and situation is different.

You should invest money into guns and scarcity—stocks, bonds, companies, good food, time with your family, etc. But you shouldn't invest all of your money into them. You should invest money into butter and duplicity—cars, jewelry, etc. But you shouldn't invest all of your money into them. My Instagram Girl did that, and we all know how that turned out.

Life is a duality, one that brings us in constant contact with the dreaded gray. It's incredibly hard to navigate and even more so with the noise of social media and other sources. But we must confront the gray and learn to live in it.

The people that learn to confront and live in the gray of financial literacy eventually win. The ones that don't eventually lose. That part of the equation *is* binary. Two plus two equals four.

We must decide for ourselves what the optimal point on our personal Productions Possibilities Frontier is. It is different for every person, but there are certain ways to go that help us successfully navigate it in the end. The means of getting there and what your Frontier looks like are up to you. And that personal Frontier will determine much of what the next chapter holds.

CHAPTER EIGHT

LACROSSE'S LAW

"You can't have a pain-free life. It can't be all roses and unicorns. And ultimately that's the hard question that matters. Pleasure is an easy question. And pretty much all of us have similar answers. The more interesting question is the pain. What is the pain that you want to sustain?"

—MARK MANSON IN AN EXCERPT FROM HIS BOOK
THE SUBTLE ART OF NOT GIVING A FUCK (2016)

ACID, ACID CHANGE YO LIFE

YES, I'M NAMING LAWS OF FAKE ECONOMIC SCIENCE AND theory after myself now. We're eight chapters in at this point—I fucking deserve it, okay?

On February 5, 2016, the Flatbush Zombies released their debut single "Bounce."[293] A song about braggadocio, corrupt police, and psychedelic culture, it was perfect to introduce the Zombies to the world. It was authentic, creative, unapologetic, and, like all their songs, sprinkled with cold, hard truth.

In the opening verse, the lead singer/rapper Meechy Darko (the greatest rapper who has ever lived, by the way[294]) spins an epic tale of bravado, flexing, and sexual prowess. It was a perfect imitation of his idol, whose face he has tattooed on his chest—the late, great Biggie Smalls. But even amid the flaunting of his gigantic dick and YSL jeans, he dropped the most powerful bar he's ever dropped: "Tag on your soul everybody got a price."

Then he raps more about drugs, specifically LSD. But let's stick with the point about our souls first.

What a powerful eight words. What truth they contain. What Darko was specifically referencing was other people in the rap game that sell their souls for money without caring about the artistry. With the rise of lo-fi and mumble rap (a lot of which was inspired by last chapter's hero), this has only gotten more prevalent. It can make money, certainly. But can it get you originality? Debatable at best.

However, let's be fair and flip this in reverse. How many of you reading this had ever heard of the Flatbush Zombies before this chapter? Probably not a lot of you.

The price lo-fi and mumble rappers pay is they don't have originality. They just blend in with the crowd, make an occasional good song, and maybe hit it big once or twice. They'll probably make a lot of money. Definitely more than they're worth. Afterward, they'll cycle out of music and fade away. There are far fewer Juice WRLDs and XXXtentacions than there are Lil Moseys and Sheck Weses.

Conversely, the price the Flatbush Zombies pay is not getting noticed at all. Their individuality is so insane it can be off-putting to most. Not many of their songs have charted. That's not a lot to put food on the table. They're not signed to a major label. They would rather be independent and control their destiny.[295] They have to pay for everything on their own. They don't get shout-outs from mainstream artists. There are few groups like A Tribe Called Quest. There are many like the Flatbush Zombies.

Mumble rappers would probably prefer that to be their model though. The Flatbush Zombies have expressed numerous times they have no desire to be a part of mainstream culture if that means sacrificing their artistry. They'd rather just chill, make great music, make enough money to get by, and call it a day. They are the starving artist incarnate. It's why their fans, while not as numerous as someone like Travis Scott has, love them so much. They change lives. They could care less about moving units.

But this trade-off (also a Zombies song[296]) does not just apply to music. It applies to *everything*. We talked about the bedrock of Value Economics, the Value/Sacrifice Trade-Off, in Chapter Four. It is the decision behind everything in our lives. It is a fundamental truth to the human condition. The more you value something, the more you will sacrifice to get it. This is a fact of life. It's human inertia.

The concept of price is just as powerful. *Everything* has a price. What matters is the price you pay and why. For rappers, it can be your soul for fans or money. For others, it can be many things.

As stated in Chapter Four, the most basic and foundational trade-off in economic theory is the one between quantity and price. However, basic and foundational does not necessarily equal the most consequential or important. And in my opinion, it is not.

Because, in "What Came Before," I said it is *not* the basic and foundational principles that always have the greatest effects on our lives. My mom was the inspiration for this. She told me that 95 percent of your life, at minimum, is boring. Nothing exciting is going to happen. It's going to be drab and dull and seem meaningless. You should see the LaCrosse family in person. We're a hoot, can't you tell?

However, she also said that a few events in life will be beyond consequential. Things like her first date with my dad at a Pizza Hut, finding out her daughter had autism, and getting her doctorate in physical therapy all count. Like Forrest Gump said, you can't find those things around the corner. They are rare.

Yet they drive so much. In some cases, they are incredibly hard to face. It's *hard* raising a child with a disability. It's *hard* getting a doctorate degree while raising three teenagers and working part-time. It's *hard* knowing at sixteen you want to throw your twenties away on the slim chance committing to this one person will work. You don't know any of them *will* work. But you do them anyway. You swing.

In 1975, economist Arthur Okun published *Equality and Efficiency: The Big Tradeoff.*[297] The thesis of this book is that the ultimate trade-off in a successful economy is managing both its efficiency and equality. It's an impossibly hard question. Do we want things to be better, or do we want things to be fair?

Efficiency and equality butt heads often. It's the key differentiator between liberals and conservatives in their views on economics. These are both hard decisions to make. Of course, people want things to be better. But also, people want others to be treated fairly. It is a simple matter of which *hard* you would like to choose.

I'd like to propose a spin on Okun's work. It's called LaCrosse's Law because I am, indeed, that much of a narcissistic asshole. But in all seriousness, this shit is useful. The hard things we choose in life have the most consequence. It is important we learn how this law rules so we can use it properly.

The seesaw of hard decisions, like efficiency and equality, can manifest itself in incalculable ways. But at the end of the day, we must choose. If we don't, we don't have values. If we don't have values, we are simply adrift, waiting on the hacks of our mob and ruling class to pummel us into submission.

The hard decisions define our lives. They are paradigm shifters we rely on to propel us toward the primarily boring and mundane lives we live more often than we admit. It is our values that drive these decisions. They allow us to choose our hard, see both paths, and force ourselves to choose.

LACROSSE'S LAW

In 2018, former *Wall Street Journal* columnist Morgan Housel released his article "The Psychology of Money,"[298] chock-full of around twenty principles on personal finance. The book that it eventually turned into in 2020 is the best book on personal finance (and one of the best books generally) I've ever read.[299]

Housel's thesis is that knowing about money doesn't do you any good. Instead, you should focus on your behavior around money. If your *behavior* around money is shit, your money will go to shit with it. What you know doesn't matter. It's about how you behave. For example, if you get a master's degree in finance from Wharton but still blow $20,000 a weekend of your ridiculously overpaid private equity salary paying hookers to smoke crystal meth out of your ass, you're going to have issues. You probably know about derivatives and Sharpe ratios. But you don't know how you ended up with a mound of credit card charges, two more STIs than you thought you had, and bizarre burn marks on your asshole.

But Housel's most important lesson in the book is not about crystal meth, derivatives, or third-degree asshole burns. Housel's most important lesson in the book is three simple words: "Tails drive everything."

Here's Housel's example.[300] Bill Gates went to middle school in the mid-1970s. At that middle school was a computer. He and Paul Allen, a friend of his, learned how to use it and were employed by the school to create an analytical model that would help schedule classes. The two began writing their own code. It became a passion for Allen and an obsession for Gates. They wanted to change the world. But there was also a third partner. A young man named Kent Evans, Gates' best friend, was even more into programming than Allen. He and Gates were the ones that wanted to change the world. Allen was, more or less, along for the ride. He was cool with smoking pot and listening to Jimi Hendrix while coding on the side. Evans and Gates were inseparable. They did everything together.

Except for one thing.

Evans wanted to learn to climb mountains. He signed up for a course where he could learn and practice during the summer. Gates abstained. The two friends would see each other after Evans got back.

But they wouldn't get the chance. Kent Evans died at that climbing camp. In a tragic accident, he fell off the mountain and was killed at seventeen. Gates' world was shattered. They were going to go to college together. Instead of Paul Allen, Kent Evans would have been the driving partner in his life before he met his future wife, Melinda. But that didn't happen. Tails drive everything.

A "tail" in statistics is an outlier of such extremes it hardly ever happens. In a normal distribution (or "bell curve"), this is the shit at the *way* far end of the graph. It's something so out of the ordinary no one even thinks of it happening. Events like this include 9/11, COVID-19, the Holocaust, and man discovering fire. No one thinks they can happen. But they do. Tails drive everything.

Think back to Bill Gates. How many "tails" were involved in just those few paragraphs? Being born in an intact and supportive family, in that location, in that school, in that time period, with those friends, and with that computer, which, at the time, was one of only a few in a school like that in the nation.

I don't have the exact figures, but my guess is his scenario is next to impossible. But man, did those collective tails drive everything. If you count the money Gates has given to charity (around $36 billion),[301] Bill Gates would be worth around $166 billion *before* compound interest on that $36 billion. If he didn't give that money away, he would be far ahead of the current richest men in the world, Jeff Bezos, Bernard Arnault, and Elon Musk.[302] All because Bill Gates rode a series of tail events that drove his whole life.

But let's also think of the inverse. How often do you hear of a child dying in a climbing accident? Kent Evans suffered a tragic fate that robbed him of a promising future. Who knows what would have happened. Would Paul Allen even be a thing? Would Gates have been forced out of Microsoft? Would the conspiracy theories and memes still be a thing?[303] Only a parallel universe could tell you.

This is an extreme example, but it shows a very powerful lesson. It shows how small decisions (Gates' middle school and Evans' climbing course) end up *dominating* our lives. For Gates, it propelled him to be one of the most important figures in human history, no matter your personal opinion of him. For Evans, it propelled him to an untimely death. They were the same kid, in the same situation, with the same ambitions. And yet, they experienced very different futures.

Let's look at one of Gates' Rich Asshole Guy contemporaries. A little-known guy from South Africa toils over an electric car that no one thought would work. He had a net worth of about $20 billion in 2019. But as soon as Tesla turned a profit and showed it could be a viable model, that tail drove everything. Tesla is now the most valuable automaker in the history of the world, and its founder has seen his net worth skyrocket by over 600 percent since.[304] This is how our entire life works. Tails drive everything.

Let's bring some examples down to Earth for us mere mortals. The gender parity of the earth is split roughly 50/50.[305] In theory, that's 3.8 billion people of the opposite sex to choose from. You have to meet only one you get along and share goals with to marry and have kids. Tails drive everything.

It takes only one cold LinkedIn message to a job recruiter to have them look it over, bring you in for an interview, and hire you. There are over 722 million people on LinkedIn.[306] Tails drive everything.

Your dad released roughly 280 million sperm when he came inside your mom.[307] It took only one of them to get her pregnant and give you the ability to be reading this chapter. Tails drive everything.

This begs the question—how do we position ourselves for these tail events to happen? The answer resides with Okun's Law. Okun's Law states that for every 1 percent increase in the unemployment rate of a country, its gross domestic product (GDP) will reduce by 2 percent.[308] The same is true inversely. Okun's Law says there are choices that must be made about the health of an economy. This is the efficiency versus equality argument in *The Big Tradeoff*.

Say a technology comes out that can automate jobs. It's more efficient for a company. You don't have to pay a technology benefits and a salary. But is it the *right* thing to do? According to Okun's Law, it may not be. When those replaced workers increase the unemployment rate, the GDP decreases along with it. A slowing economy will lead to less jobs, which will lead to an even further decline in GDP.

But where would we be without innovation and progress? Probably crushed on the world stage. China has been working feverishly to catch up to us, and they've begun to beat us.[309] India will likely be the next China due to their population.[310] And even though no one in Europe can ever seem to get their shit together, maybe they'll prove us wrong. After all, tails drive everything.

If I had to rename Okun's Law, it would be the Law of Creative Destruction. We must regress to make progress. It's up to the decision makers to make the impossible decisions. They have to choose their hard. Do we want to expedite a vaccine or do it normally?[311] Do we want to risk our reputation dropping an atomic bomb, or do we want to watch World War II rage on?[312] Do we want to have uncomfortable conversations, or do we want to let them fester and hope people don't reach a tipping point?

LaCrosse's Law is built on the back of the bedrock of Value Economics, the Value/Sacrifice Trade-Off. In order to value something, you must sacrifice. Otherwise, it would not be that valuable in the first place. In order to value progress, we must be willing to sacrifice something to obtain it. There is no free lunch.

LaCrosse's Law tells us we can't have everything. We can't have our cake and eat it too. Just ask Marie Antoinette; her severed head will tell you. Values require choices. Choices require sacrifice. Something given up means anger, pain, and sadness at the lost prospect of what could have been.

LaCrosse's Law tells us we must hurt people. Our relationships are the most important choices we make. To make the right ones, we must sacrifice the wrong ones. The act of pleasing everyone is an act of displeasing ourselves and our values. We must treat all with decency and respect. We are all equal. However, just because you treat everyone equally does not mean you treat everyone the same.

LaCrosse's Law tells us that to have a life we desire, we must sacrifice all the other alternative lives we could potentially live. It tells us to shun variety and instead consciously choose who we are and why. We need to choose our hard. Our values are the only way to navigate this due to the principles and truths that guide them, as long as we picked them correctly in the first place (see Chapters One–Three).

This is a simple concept. But it's impossibly hard to wrap your head around. Like Okun's Law, creative destruction is the way. But, like Okun's Law, there are many ways to do it. None of them are always pleasant. Each decision will lead to obstacles and problems. It's not a matter of avoiding things. That's impossible. It's a matter of choosing which load to bear. Tag on your soul, everybody got a price.

Bill Gates chose the hard of social isolation and shunning to create arguably the most consequential company in modern world history. The Flatbush Zombies chose the hard of niche music to create true art. Kent Evans chose the hard of climbing a mountain, which led to him falling to his death. Elon Musk chose the hard of trying to solve what had been an impossible problem for two decades before he achieved one of the great breakthroughs in recent memory. Tails drive everything. But choices lead to tails.

THE AMERICAN NIGHTMARE

Ohio is a huge football state. Texas gets a lot of the hype because of its palatial stadiums and *Friday Night Lights*,[313] but Ohio is right up there with it. We did invent the fucking sport, if you weren't aware.[314] But remember the part in Chapter Four about my not being good at sports? That never changed. I got a little better, but not much. It didn't help that I had incredibly skilled teammates, multiple of who went on to play Division I football and win national championships at the Division III level at the local University of Mount Union.[315]

Seeing this, I pivoted my attention to the one thing that potentially *could* set me apart—my academics. As noted earlier as well, I was really interested in writing. I was decent at everything else. But academics weren't the reason I wanted to be good at academics. It was the end goal that was the prize for me.

Due to the mostly horrific nature of non-LeBron-related Ohio sports, the Ohio State Buckeyes were almost a cult in Ohio. Saturdays in Ohio weren't just fun. They were religious. Ohio State was the pinnacle of excellence for everyone. I was mesmerized by the myth that surrounded not just the football team but the school. It was Willy Wonka's Chocolate Factory. All you needed was a ticket, and you were set.

This was my sole aiming point. Get to Columbus at all costs. On a college visit, I asked the requirements to get in. They told me the standard was a 3.8 unweighted GPA and a twenty-eight on your ACT. Roger that. I had everything I needed. A 3.8 unweighted GPA? Check. Twenty-eight on my ACT? Check. Time to roll out. I submitted my application in September and was told to expect a turnaround by the end of October.

I remember exactly where I was the night I got my response. It was Saturday, October 24, 2015, my Grandma's birthday and exactly one week after mine. My dad, brother, and I were going to see a film about the great Jesse Owens.[316] He medaled four times at the 1936 Olympic

Games[317] while basically giving Hitler the middle finger.[318] He was a badass. He was also an Ohio State Buckeye.[319] There are multiple gyms on campus that bear his name and a statue right outside the track and field facility.

As my dad's F-150 pulled into the theater, I whipped out my phone and saw an email. It was from the admissions office at Ohio State. My breath stopped. It had finally come. A smile broke out onto my face. This was it. I was going to open up my portal, see my results, and top off the greatest achievement of my life by basking in the greatness of arguably that same university's greatest alum getting his due in a feature film. It couldn't have been more perfect. I opened the email and saw its contents:

Application Status: Declined/*Deferred*.

I went numb. I sat there, holding my phone in front of me, the pale light reflecting the disbelief that was painting my face. My brother and dad had gotten out of the truck and were headed toward the theater when they saw I hadn't gotten out. "Sammo, let's go!" my dad said. I didn't move. My dad came over to the truck and told me twice, something he never liked to do. I said the only phrase that I could, one that had repeated in my mind over and over an impossible amount of times:

"I didn't get in."

My dad, completely oblivious to the context of my statement, asked for clarification. Not being able to say words, I simply showed him my phone. My dad, ever the pragmatist, looked it over, saw the elephant that had shit all over my proverbial room, and handed it back. He told me there was nothing I could do, and we would figure out a game plan after we saw the movie.

Even though he didn't express it, I could sense his shock. He was certain I had gotten in on merit. Engineers like processes, and I had followed this specific process to the letter. I could tell that didn't sit well with him. But I did what he said. I got out of the truck, walked in, and sat down, still completely numb.

I don't remember much about the rest of that night. I sure as hell don't remember a damn thing about the movie. That awful fucking movie. The only thing I remember is not a memory but a feeling: rage.

All-consuming, pure rage. Not only did I fail at the biggest aspiration of my entire life, which I had thrown my entire past four years into, I had to sit through a two-hour movie talking about how great Ohio State was. Like The Asshole and my wrestling teammates, it was mocking me. Making me feel like dog shit. Grinding what was left of my self-esteem into a fine powder and getting high off it by snorting it into their fat fucking nostrils. When I got home, my mom and her friend Dawn offered their sympathies. But I didn't want them. People pitying me didn't help. It only fueled the monster burning inside me.

The Monday after, I called the admissions office. I was more confused than anything else. I had done what they told me to do. I had the credentials. I volunteered with special needs kids. I was the vice president of the National Honors Society. I was in two sports. I had taken AP and honors courses and done well. I founded a club. I had never once taken a single drink of alcohol or an illegal drug. I never stayed out late and was always in bed before curfew. I respected authority. I had known other kids who had gotten in with twenty-fours on their ACTs and 3.5 GPAs. It didn't make any sense. I just wanted to know why.

I put the phone on speaker and asked if I could review my application with the woman on the line. She pulled my file. She said everything looked good on the application. She then went down to the Reviewer Notes section. She then said two sentences that would forever be burned in my brain:

"We don't think you're academically or psychologically ready to handle the rigor of Ohio State's campus. We're sorry."

I did a double take. White noise filled my brain. Everything was fuzzy. It was like someone had shaken up a can of Coke and blew it off in my frontal lobe. I couldn't feel anything. After about ten seconds of silence, I asked how they could possibly derive that from a common application, one that was supposed to be accessible and objective. She answered the question by not being able to answer the question. "I'm not sure," she said. "These things sometimes happen," she said. "Again, I'm sorry," she said.

I said thank you and hung up the phone. The Coke-explosion feeling was soon replaced by the familiar feeling of rage. My mom, who had been listening, didn't know what to say. She was just as stunned as I was. I exhaled, bit my bottom lip, walked up to my room, and burst into tears. My dream, the thing I had worked toward for four years, was gone because some admissions office person who didn't know a single fucking thing about me had made a subjective statement about an objective application.

They didn't even give me the courtesy of outright rejecting me either. My application status said "Declined/Deferred." Ohio State had several satellite campuses, small university subsidiaries that were alternative options for students. Their main purpose was to accommodate low-income students and students who didn't have the merit to get in on their credentials.

This bothered me for multiple reasons. First was pride. I knew kids from my school that had gotten in with worse scores and grades than me. I knew I was better. But that apparently didn't matter. The whole thing was a cheat, a con, a scam. Second was location. The satellite campuses were in the middle of buttfuck nowhere. The biggest attraction they had was the prison where *The Shawshank Redemption* was filmed.[320]

I don't like when people, particularly in collectivist institutions, look and punch down on others. The satellite campus situation felt like that. In fact, it was openly admitting to it. You're not rich enough to afford tuition? Off to Marion, Ohio, peasant. Not as smart as all the smart people at our main campus? Have fun in Lima, dumbass. We'll keep the kids that "earned it" in Columbus. While they're busy dropping $100 bar tabs and running frats, all of you lesser folks will simply have to watch from afar.

Beyond that, I was stuck. I had done the exact opposite of Essential Diversification. I had put all my eggs in one basket. I had only applied to two colleges—Ohio State and Michigan State. I had gotten into both but only really wanted one. Michigan State was a good university. It was a Big 10 school with a good football program and decent business school. Lots of successful people went there. It was a pretty campus. They had beaten Ohio State in several important football games recently.[321] No small feat.

My family went out to dinner at Red Robin later that week, probably to help alleviate my pain through bottomless fries. I went into the bathroom and looked at myself in the mirror. I made my face stone still and walked back out to the table. I told my parents I wanted to go to Michigan State. I didn't want to participate in the charade. I knew it was a blatant lie and a fraudulent meritocracy. I wanted no part of it. My parents supported my decision, and I formally sent all the paperwork in to register for classes.

Once I enrolled, I joined a GroupMe with dozens of incoming students. I met some dudes who I thought were cool, and we became roommates. We picked out a dorm we thought was in a good location. I slid into girls' GroupMe DMs (which, per last chapter, was a big deal for me). Most of the time, I was unsuccessful. But that was okay. I was doing what I always wanted. I was having "the college experience."

But something didn't feel right. I wasn't into it. It was cool to see I was doing "the right thing." But I didn't like how I felt. It was empty, hollow, and shallow. All of the fire was gone. I had no desire to be anywhere but Ohio State. It was showing. I wasn't excited about Michigan State. It was simply a school to me. Ohio State was an idea, something much more powerful. There were a lot of good colleges. But there was only one that meant anything to me. I tried to ignore it. "It'll get better in time," I told myself.

But it didn't. I knew for certain three weeks later. The two schools were playing each other in the biggest game of the year. It was a late-fall

Ohio Saturday. It was forty degrees and raining, making everything cold, miserable, and wet. I promised a friend of mine I'd go watch his local powerhouse high school football team play. I went with him and his parents to watch an absolute shellacking in freezing rain that didn't have the mercy to turn to snow. The Ohio State game was on. I didn't care. I would rather catch a cold.

We caught the very end of the Ohio State game as we left. They had not played well.[322] Ezekiel Elliott, the best player I've seen in a Buckeye uniform, had a pathetic thirty-three yards on twelve carries. The game was tied fourteen to fourteen late in the fourth quarter. Michigan State was in field-goal range. In a moment that went viral, MSU kicked a forty-one-yard field goal as time expired to end Ohio State's chances at the College Football Playoff and their twenty-three-game win streak. After he made the kick, the kicker sprinted around Ohio Stadium windmilling his arm. I should have been happy. My thirst for revenge should have been quenched.

But it wasn't.

I felt just like my family friends did in that car ride—awful. My team had lost. But my team had just won as well. "Congrats, Sam," the dad said. I said thank you but didn't mean it. I didn't know what to do. I was completely apathetic about Michigan State and unable to fulfill my dream at Ohio State.

At least at the main campus.

When I got home, I began to look into the satellite campuses more. The biggest and closest one was in Newark, Ohio, a small town about forty-five minutes east of Columbus. It couldn't be that bad, could it?

My dad and I took a tour and discovered some advantages. The tuition was less, making my financial burden easier. Smaller classes could provide more digestible information and access to professors. Local housing could provide an independence I couldn't get with dorm life. They wanted people to succeed, which meant professors wouldn't try to get students to fail. Plus, I could still buy discounted football tickets. I was not allowed to eat in main campus dining halls, use fitness facilities, join clubs, or get access to university buildings. I would still be a second-class citizen, but I still had some Civil Rights.

But there was the problem of the whole "Michigan State" thing. I had everything there that I wanted at Ohio State—roommates, connections, everything. We had already put a deposit down. But I couldn't shake the apathy. I called the admissions offices and informed my roommates. I was off to Siberia.

EVERYBODY SELLIN' DREAMS, I'M TOO CHEAP TO BUY ONE[323]

LaCrosse's Law states we must choose our hard. Lots of people ask whether others have dreams they are chasing. LaCrosse's Law informs them this is the wrong question. Instead of chasing dreams, we need to chase hardship. Dreams are the spoonful of sugar without the medicine. They sell ignorance, illusions, and life hacks. When following LaCrosse's Law, you can embrace the horror of your dreams through your values. Only then will you be more than likely to achieve them.

However, these decisions can be quite confusing in most of the situations they present themselves in. They are not always binary or black and white. A lot of times, they happen without us knowing these little decisions of whether to pick comfort or hardship matter. But if they happen multiple times over, they can compound and end up leading to a tail event unfavorable for us.

People from all walks of life tend to too easily demean those on the other side of the coin. They say they're either bad or wrong. They're "privileged" or need to "pick themselves up by their bootstraps." This is wrong. While these things could be true (though it's unlikely either are), we should avoid being ignorant and attempt to understand their perspective. We cannot judge someone without knowing their full story.

It's hard to be poor and barely making it. It's not fun. You need to focus on feeding yourself. There isn't time for Netflix binging or complaining about the environment while drinking your sixth vodka cran out of a plastic cup at your favorite dive bar. You have more important things to worry about.

But it's also hard to have lots of money and plow your entire life into making it. Elon Musk once said a person needs to work eighty to one hundred hours a week to "change the world."[324] That's either a sixteen-to-twenty-hour workday if you take weekends off or a twelve-to-fourteen-hour workday if you don't. Would you want that? Is "changing the world" that important to you?

It's hard to be out of shape. To be a fat slob whose health fails by the time you're forty. You're likely to develop cancer or cardiovascular disease,[325] the two biggest killers of Americans.[326] You're much more likely to die from the beer virus.[327] You get crushed by a sedentary lifestyle and waste away before your own eyes.

But it's also hard to craft an impeccable body. My uncle once had a guy who worked for him who did bodybuilding. He had to carry around a tub of raw broccoli with him. Broccoli *burns* calories when you eat it. Is that worth it to you? To be a constant slave to your routine? To worry so much about your calories and how you look that you have to weigh the pros and cons of eating a grape every two weeks?

It's hard to be married. To shackle your life to one person without knowing how it will end up. You must be completely vulnerable and love unconditionally. You must forgo all other potential paths with all other potential partners and isolate yourself. These are all very scary things. You can't afford to be careless. Everything you do in this area of life must be in the service of that commitment, or there *is* no commitment. It's not something you can break here and there whenever you want. It goes against the very definition of the word itself. This can lead to dissatisfaction for those who aren't ready to take the leap.

But it's also hard to be single. To be confined to the hellscape of modern dating. Bad things come from this. You start to treat the gender you're attracted to as simply a means to an end—something to have sex with, make you feel good, etc. With each person that goes in and out of your life, there is a feeling of failure attached. Why didn't that work? What's wrong with me? What could I have done differently? It's a very taxing process, one that leaves you exhausted more times than it leaves you fulfilled. That's why bachelors seem to have a new person on their arm every five seconds. They don't want to face the emotional hole of being empty, so they fill it as quickly as possible to avoid that feeling at all costs.

I'm not saying either of the two is right or wrong. It's up to the beholder. However, do not think that either of them is devoid of hardship or pain. They are not. As the universal constant of life, pain will rear its ugly and inopportune head whenever it gets the chance. But there is one alternative that is far worse: the pain of the middle.

It's hardest to be in the middle. To be perpetually dissatisfied, torn between two options and split in mind and soul by indecision. You aren't making any choices at all. You are simply wading in the water hoping to be pushed to one side or another by the tide of life. This is hardly a reliable model, even if Forrest Gump tells you that's half of what destiny is.[328] It could be. But it also could not.

This is the purpose of values and this book. Indecision is my generation's Fatal Flaw. We're a bunch of identity-less and stance-less zombies who get pushed to a side of the aisle by someone who had the balls to make a choice. There is no nobility in being a tweener. It only makes you're controllable and weak.

You cannot control everything. The only thing you can control are your choices. This begs the question—how do we make them? How do we ensure creative destruction to make it go as favorably as possible? How do we go about chasing the tail events through these choices? How do we choose our hard?

LIFE IN SIBERIA

I moved into my apartment in Newark, Ohio, in August of 2016. My parents had moved some of my stuff down, and I had toured the complex with my mom in the spring. But I had never been inside my specific unit nor met my roommates until the day I stepped foot in the place on which I had already put down a deposit. The roommates seemed like nice enough people, at least not heroin addicts or narcoleptics.

I remember deliberately wasting time, always finding one more thing to do. There was a small playground outside our apartment with a swing set. I cried on it when my family left me in the middle of nowhere, knowing nothing about anything within fifty miles or whether it was worth it to be there at all.

I used the week before class to do the one thing I knew could make my current state better—get busy. I enrolled at the local YMCA, where I could lift and work out. I got shit for my apartment. I found a Chipotle and a grocery store. I learned how to use my Foreman. I was determined not to drown in the adult ocean. I called my family twice a day, which eased the anxiety. At least someone cared where and how I was.

The great thing about moving someplace new is it gives you perspective. During that week patrolling the dilapidated Ohio-brand Siberia, I began to see why not a lot of people went there. My first glance was at the local Ford dealer. My engine light had come on, and that dealership was in network to get discounted mechanic services. I dropped my car off, talked a bit with the mechanics, and waited.

Outside, another car was getting serviced. The wife was in tears, completely emotionally broken. She didn't have enough money to fix the car. Inside of that car was her husband. Every inch of his bald head was tattooed. Every cell in his brain was fried from either crystal meth or fentanyl, if I had to guess. He was screaming at his wife in a belligerent rage, using every fiber of his being to tell her how horrible she was and that it was her fault they were in this situation. "Bitch," "cunt," and "whore" were some of his favorite words. The mechanic, obviously not knowing what to do, tried to work with the woman as best he could. I felt great anger when the woman got back in the car with that horrible man. It wasn't her fault it was broken.

I began to see things like that happen more often. I remember vividly coming home from a downtown CVS (the first and only time I went downtown) to see another couple on the street. I had stopped at a red light just in time for the argument's apex. This woman was also in tears, talking into a cell phone, desperately trying to explain something. Her husband, wearing a white wife beater and numerous needle marks across both of his arms, didn't like her conversation. He flew into a rage, ripped the phone from her, and slammed it screen-first onto the concrete. He left her to pick up the pieces.

Things weren't great around the apartment complex either. We were in the "bad" part of a bad town. It began to show. Around Halloween, there was a trend on social media about clown terrorists (2016 was a bizarre time[329]). One day, while studying, the fire department came to my door. Apparently, people dressed as clowns had threatened to detonate bombs inside the complex. No clowns were ever found.

One of my neighbors was a single mom. She had a boyfriend, but she was constantly worried about his wife finding out about her. Yes, you read that correctly. But despite her obvious issues, she was an incredibly nice person. She had two young boys that would hang out on the aforementioned playground all the time. I made sure to give them extra Halloween candy when they went trick-or-treating.

But those issues soon found her. Her ex-husband was a state trooper who liked alcohol too much. Over our Christmas break, he got drunk, broke down her door, and savagely raped her. After he left her broken on the floor, she banged on our front door begging for help in the snow and ice. We couldn't help her. No one was home. When my roommates and I returned, she casually told us about the incident. She acted like it was just another thing that had happened, like one of her kids getting sick. We didn't speak much after that. These things, apparently, are pretty common in places like Newark, Ohio.

Being off-campus and having no clubs, most of the students treated the satellite campus like community college. They would go to class and then leave. The smart ones got housing in Columbus and made the commute every day, so they didn't have to live here. The only "friends" I made were in the math tutor room, so I didn't fail calculus. They had been in college purgatory for about six or seven years, had changed their majors about five times, and were too deep in student debt to not get a degree. They were nice people. But they were also sad people. Their lives, like most in Siberia, left much to be desired.

My roommates didn't have these problems. Their hometowns were thirty minutes away. They went home to see their families every weekend. Their moms cooked all their food for them. Their girlfriends had sexy sleepovers often. My weekends were good, as mentioned in the last chapter, but most of my weeks were nothing but sitting in Siberia doing nothing but studying, watching everyone else seemingly have a better life than me. Social media was my worst enemy. Every hot girl I talked to was in Columbus. Every cool party was there. Every class worth taking was there. Every person worth knowing was there.

This was further backed up by the student body in Newark. I had come in with the impression that the majority of students there were like me. That wasn't the case. They came to Newark by choice. They wanted an "easy ride" into Ohio State. They mocked the professors. They didn't try. Nothing was their fault. They were, mostly, an incredibly unimpressive group of entitled and spoiled teenagers who didn't take life seriously. They weren't ambitious. They didn't strive. They only wanted a smoother path to alcohol, drugs, a good resume, and sex, one that was paved by cheating the system that had robbed so many other promising students of that exact same thing. I was disgusted by them.

I was miserable. I hated every second. You can't get your freshman year of college back, and mine was being pissed down the drain by multiple dicks. I hated everything. I hated the miserable and sad shithole town. I hated how people like me hated miserable and sad shithole towns. I hated Ohio State for not letting me in. I hated my family for letting me make such an awful decision. I hated my room-mates for not having the same struggles I did. I hated not feeling like I was pushing myself or getting better. But mostly, I hated myself because only I was to blame. I wanted to leave as soon as possible.

But I didn't. The thought never entered my head. My parents, par-ticularly my mother, grew understandably sick of my bitching. One Sunday night, on our weekly Facetime, my victimhood was too much for her. She cut me off and basically dared me to drop out, enroll at a local university, and just go into Ohio State the next year. The plan was reasonable. I knew about ten to twenty kids that were doing just that.

But I didn't. I chose to stay and grit it out. I chose to do what I believed was the right thing. I began to not see the utility of pinning all of my misery and problems on other things. Because in reality, it is useless. Not everything is your fault. But it is your life, and you should take responsibility for it.

I began to come around to the fact that my problems, and what had caused them, were on me. Didn't get into the main campus? You didn't do enough. Work harder. Don't like the people? Don't associate with shitty people. Don't like your surroundings? Well, why'd you move there in the first place?

My mindset shifted when I realized this simple law—you are always choosing. It's the hards of life that must be chosen with the most care. Complaining about how unfair your life is is consciously choosing to make it unfair. Directing your energy toward hards you do not want to undertake does nothing for you.

I put a large value on getting into Ohio State. That was my price. It was up to me to pay it. I'm happy to say that I did. It's a valuable experience to know you're in full control of how you live. Knowing that is a superpower. It makes you incredibly hard to stop and nearly impossible to quit. With proper values and knowing what you value, an incredibly powerful force forms. With LaCrosse's Law constantly powering that force, you always know what you have to do. When you constantly know what to do, you constantly know what you value. And that is a luxury not many people can say they have.

WE ALL WANT THIS

Our values, the bedrock of our decision-making processes, are the things that lead us out of the middle grounds and indecision of these hard choices into better and more profitable decisions. Our understanding of LaCrosse's Law should enable us to maximize our decision-making processes to most effectively navigate the specific hards that we choose in our lives.

Life is suffering. I know, more inspiration to lift you up—aren't I awesome? But in all seriousness, this is perhaps the most important piece of advice I can give to anyone. You should not exacerbate your suffering, because *everyone* suffers. Suffering doesn't care about your ethnicity, gender, wealth, whatever. It just cares that it makes your life miserable. It's really good at doing that.

This realization does one of two things to people. It either paralyzes or liberates them. For those it paralyzes, they feel life is not worth living because there is pain involved with everything. They hole up in their little shells and wait for things to happen. They take no action. They get dominated.

For those it liberates, it brings suffering down to earth. We, especially my generation, grew up and lived in a very coddled society, our minds being the most affected. We avoid suffering like the plague. But if you realize suffering is just as common as breathing, it becomes easier to come to terms with. You can maneuver and take it head on. You can bear the pain and tragedy of life.

You become objective. You see things with a clear and focused mind. You're not blinded by the Two Es. If you embody LaCrosse's Law, choosing your hard, you shouldn't worry about the hardships of life. You know they are common. That everyone will have to face them more often than they would like.

And that's okay. Because deep down, we know it's true. We don't make choices just to make choices. We make them because we think they can benefit us. The ones who commit to people are the ones who *want* to commit to people. The ones who commit to an unhealthy lifestyle are the ones who *want* to commit to an unhealthy lifestyle. The ones who live in their parents' basement and eat Oreos dunked in French onion dip are the ones who want to do that heinous activity.[330] They *know* what suffering they have chosen. It is up to them to accept it for what it is. It's your responsibility to do the same with your life.

Next, remember the Life-Defining Principle. Your life is defined by all the things others aren't willing to do. The person that works more than you has better odds of advancing higher and faster in the company. The parents who dedicate more time to their children versus going out for cocktails three nights a week will have a better chance at raising productive children. The more time you sacrifice working on your house, the better your house will look. Not a lot of people are willing to do things that are good for them because they are hard, but the ones that do will automatically fare better in life.

So knowing this, do yourself a favor and be the one to isolate yourself favorably. If you can choose the things that others go away from to get yourself ahead, you should have a similar advantage with your hard choices and suffering. You are ahead of the societal curve by knowing to put yourself in situations where you choose your hard to determine the quality of your life based on your values. So you can create a life and choices that define it that are optimized for success through your values.

This involves self-awareness, the most important Factor of Value Production. Only by knowing what you really value can you effectively apply the Life-Defining Principle and get further ahead. You must know yourself because there is no use in getting ahead in the wrong direction, as proven in Chapter Three by Essential Diversification. To get ahead effectively, you must know what you need to get ahead.

Bill Gates and Elon Musk put themselves on societal Mars (lol) to get ahead. The Flatbush Zombies did in music. There are countless others we can name. These tradeoffs take place in our daily lives as well. Fame does not always equal a life lived by the Life-Defining Principle. This is the exception, not the rule.

The best husbands I know actively spend time working on their marriages. The best coaches I know spend countless hours doing the little things to make sure they are coaching to the best of their ability. The best truth-seekers I know spend hours researching to get the proper information. It does not matter what the field is. What matters is the effort that goes into that field.

Ask yourself—what is my life defined by? Do I like what it is defined by? If not, what do I need to do to change it for the betterment of myself and others? What little things do I need to engage in more often to provide the choice that can lead to the tail events that can drive my life forward?

Lastly, on a more philosophical and/or cheesy note, one of the best pieces of advice I've ever received is to treat your life as an investment. The reason?

Because it is.

The purpose of investing is to make sure you get the most return on your capital while navigating the risks of the market. Your life is your capital. You can spend it however you wish. Only do with it what you know to be good. Then you will afford yourself the luxury of suffering constructively. Of choosing your hard. Of taking your life and creating optimization in ways that would benefit you and those you care about the most. This is the last step in Essential Diversification, the tipping point before we can effectively use our values to navigate life. It is important you get it right.

Just like a 401(k) or Robinhood account (if they don't stop the trading on you[331]), not a single penny nor second should be put to waste. Human beings were meant to solve and strive. If there is one overarching trend for our species, it's that. Humans have fucked up a lot. But humans have always gotten better.

If you treat your life as if it were following that same trajectory, you should find yourself on the path to improvement through greater decency and striving. Investment, when done right, is supposed to appreciate in value. The lesson about Guns and Butter taught us this. How you invest that allocated capital matters. Your life should be the same way. LaCrosse's Law is built so that as you go on in life through the choices of your hardships, you become stronger and more valuable to yourself and others.

You not only have a stake in your life but in the lives of others. Life is a team game, as Joe Namath once beautifully said. Your life has value not only to you but to the ones that love and support you. Your hardships mean a lot to them. As you define your life, their lives will be defined around you. An investment in your life is an investment in the lives of those you care for most.

So when someone says that money really doesn't mean anything, they're both right and wrong. Just like Morgan Housel so eloquently states in his book, money can teach us a lot about life. Knowing that your life is an investment can teach you a great deal about how you can most effectively use it to live one that yields high profits.

Everything in life has a price. LaCrosse's Law states we need to choose our specific hardships and sufferings through our decisions in life. By picking good options and deliberately shunning other good options, we embark on a process of creative destruction that forms the skeletons of our lives through our habits and routines. Through our habits and routines, we can then start to formulate a lifestyle that will lead to our tail events that will drive the most growth and expansion throughout the courses of our lives. Our lives are a series of choices, but it is the hard ones that matter most. They drive our lives, so it is important to have a framework for how to deal with them properly.

Through the examples we see and practices we embody in our own personal lives, we show ourselves the ways in which we should live. It is our duty as practitioners of the human race to light the way for ourselves, the ones we care about, and others around us. When we enlighten those around us, we can show that same light to the people that need it.

Or that light could be you frying on acid. Remember, it could change your life, according to Mr. Darko and Mr. Dirnt.

CHAPTER NINE

COMPARATIVE VALUE ADVANTAGE

"We have an idea of happiness. We believe that only certain conditions will make us happy...We have to look deeply into our perceptions in order to become free of them. Then, what has been a perception becomes an insight, a realization of the path...It is a clear vision, seeing things as they are."

—THICH NHAT HANH IN AN EXCERPT FROM
THE HEART OF THE BUDDHA'S TEACHINGS

FEELS LIKE THE FIRST NEIN

THERE ARE A COUPLE OF FIRSTS YOU NEVER FORGET IN LIFE:

- The first time you get laid. (I lasted over three hours due to the well-blended cocktail of embarrassment, fear, and shame I consumed both before and during. At least she did some local modeling and had the decency to talk to me for a few months after.)

- The first time you fall in love. (We both broke each other's hearts, tried to be friends for about a year and a half afterward, and failed miserably. She's with someone else now, who I think makes her happy. I recommend all of it.)

- The first time you crash the car that was mostly financed by your parents. ("I was just reaching in the backseat for my bookbag, Dad!")

But, for me, there is one first that stands above all the rest: the first time I was openly called a white supremacist.

In my junior year of college, I got a cold email from a recruiter who worked for a notable nonprofit organization called Teach for America. At that time, I had no idea what I wanted to do with my life. This is how a lot of third-year college students feel, I think. We're more than halfway to the finish line but not even sure what or where the fuck the line to cross is. We've seen what we like and don't. Both scare us. We feel like we're drowning in the middle of some vast ocean.

Teach for America, initially, was an appealing alternative. TFA is (on paper[332]) an organization that sends college students to teach in tanking public school systems. This seemed like a noble cause. In a world that has created an avenue for everyone to become a victim, children are one of the few groups that truly fit the category. Children are, by definition, innocent. They don't know what they're getting into coming into the world. All they can hope for is a chance. I think it's highly unfair and tragic that some don't get it.

I thought of my autistic sister. A year before this, my family had moved to Florida, so my dad could advance his career. The move was hard. My parents had never lived more than twenty minutes from their parents. This is not to say they weren't independent people. They were. But this is to say that, as with anyone, ripping your life up and planting it in a new and strange place can be a shock to the system. I've done it a few times. I know the feeling well.

One of the hardest things about the move was the strain it put on my sister's education. Our public school system in Ohio is well-funded due to our town's now-high tax dollars.[333] The school district in Florida wasn't. This caused problems. In Ohio, my sister was most often one-on-one with an aide in a classroom of about ten kids. In her classroom in Florida, there was one teacher and one aide for twenty students. Neither my sister nor her classmates got the proper attention. The teacher and aide were not at fault. There wasn't proper capacity. It was a zoo. It was a big factor in why my family went back to Ohio.

That experience sat with me. "How many other families and kids are there like this?" I asked. My answer? Probably a lot. My family was blessed to have parents who worked hard and made a decent living. We could afford to move, even though it set my parents back financially. A lot of other families can't. Therefore, one of the only things these folks could hope for was a better staff to help their kids learn. This intrigued me. I could make a difference. I could help.

Oh, and the other thing. It was a Golden Ticket to any avenue imaginable. The way the program works is you go into a school district for two years, teach, and then rotate out to your next endeavor. I looked at the opportunities on its website and was impressed. The candidates who entered the program were desired by some of the most reputable institutions in the world. Big Tech. Harvard Business School. Investment banking. Management consulting. Venture capital. All I would have to do was wave this organization's magic wand, and I would be into wherever my heart desired. It was a slam dunk.

Until I looked at the recruiter's LinkedIn profile. This guy had originally gone to the University of Wisconsin to study physical therapy. But when he got there, he discovered something about himself: his inherent privilege.

Upon discovery of his "privilege," he had a change of heart. He didn't want to be a physical therapist anymore. They were the problem. Instead, he leaned into a thing called "educational equity." Only by correcting "the system," you see, could it potentially be redeemed. On and on it went. Waxing philosophical about everything. Woke-shaming everyone who stumbled on his page about their inherent privilege because of trivial things such as gender and race. I was stunned at how much he hated himself.

When I got home, I showed his profile to my friend. He knew from the jump this could end up being a disaster. He asked if I was still going to take the meeting. I had thought about it a lot and decided I was.

On one condition. If the guy tried anything with me, I would light him up like a Christmas tree. I knew and respected myself too much to allow someone to repeat those lies. I agreed to meet two days later.

I made sure to get there fifteen minutes early to scope it out. I caught a glimpse of him on the second floor of the student union. It was worse than I had imagined. Capri-style pants that would only be acceptable on a nine-year-old girl. Leg tattoos going up his unmuscled calf. Some bizarre, large, and obnoxious ring necklace adorning his unbuttoned floral-print shirt. I braced for impact.

The first five minutes went surprisingly well. The guy seemed nice. He told me about his journey (inherent privilege and all) and how it had led to his own personal enlightenment. He told me about all the things he and his colleagues were doing and everything they hoped it would accomplish.

He finished by opening a folder he had brought with him. In it were resources about the program and several pieces of white stationery. He grabbed one and put it in the center of the table. He grabbed a pen and drew a line right down the middle of the long side. He looked up at me, flashed an almost-scary, toothy grin, and asked:

"So what do you know about the Walking Line of White Supremacy?"[334]

I didn't know what to say. I like to think I remained stoic. But my gut tells me the horrendous poker face I talked about in Chapter Seven revealed shock. I think I managed to utter an "Um, nothing."

Unfortunately, it probably came out as a Wookie-esque series of groans and yells.

With a Pleasure Island child smile painting his face, he continued. On one side of the Walking Line, he wrote David Duke, the Ku Klux Klan, and Richard Spencer. On the other side, he wrote Teach for America. The recruiter attempted to explain that if you didn't *directly* support the organization, you were indirectly supporting white supremacists in the suppression of minority communities. I'm surprised I even stayed conscious. I literally almost fainted from the stupidity. The fizzy-Coke feeling returned.

After I picked my jaw up off the floor, I asked him if he seriously thought what he was saying was true. He gave me an enthusiastic yes. He dropped a bunch of Mob buzzwords ("Reaganomics"[335] and "patriarchy" were two of his favorites) to persuade me. Only he was spared from the wrath. Only he could be saved.

I retorted with this: The friend I lived with had a black girlfriend. They had been dating for almost two years. She volunteered at two mental health hotlines to stop people from killing themselves. She raised money for minority mental health causes. She wanted to eventually open a psychology practice for the same issue. She, to my knowledge, had never heard of Teach for America. I asked the recruiter if he was bold enough to call her a white supremacist.

He, of course, had no answer. He babbled, dropped "Reaganomics" about sixteen more times, and tried to back out of the question. I didn't let him escape. I hammered him more. Quickly, his shaming turned to fury. The Pleasure Island smile disappeared and turned into the donkey frown.[336] He knew he had lost.

Mercifully, the interview finally ended. I shook his hand and left. I was shell-shocked for the next week.

CLOUT CHASIN' AND PATTY FLIPPIN'

Clout is a disgusting word. But sadly, we all chase it. "Clout" is defined by Merriam-Webster as simply, "pull, influence."[337] In Urban Dictionary (probably the better of the two in a case like this), the definition reads, "being famous and having influence."[338] Fame, influence, and pull sound like quite desirable things. They are.

But only to a degree. Like most things in our wonderful world, and as we've discussed many a time throughout this book, clout is just a tool. It's neither inherently good nor bad. It's in how a person uses said tool that determines its goodness or badness. But, as we've also talked about a ton, humans don't always use things well. Our imperfectness tends to screw stuff up on occasion, it turns out.

The main problem with clout chasing is that it skews our perception of what is really important to us. In Chapter Two, we talked at length about our Means of Value. In our culture defined by excess, we're getting hosed no matter what. We're getting brainwashed into thinking that in order to provide value to the world, we need to follow a specific formula.

But what is this value that people think they should pursue? I think a lot of people confuse clout with value. This is a sad mistake. Clout is the root for a lot of huge comparisons that don't mean shit. However, due to the factors mentioned in the previous paragraph, they're paid attention to a lot.

For example, I majored in finance in college. I can't find a place where clout is more relevant than business school. There were positives, for sure. It surrounded me with great minds. They pushed me. I hope I pushed them back.

But it wasn't without detriments. The business douche stereotype is rooted in fact. It's all about who has the "best" internship, who makes the most money, who eventually ends up working for which company. It's nothing more than excess-filled credentialing. It's the hierarchies of social dominance that have reared their heads throughout this book, only this time they're wearing Dockers and Vineyard Vines.

The main problem with this obsession our culture has with clout is it's not that simple of an issue. There are too many fields to account for. They all do different things and have different expectations. They're all determined by the person who wants to go into them. They may not have the same reasons you do. There's no way we can quantify what is immeasurable. There are too many variables. The sample size isn't big enough. Not only is this a tasteless thing to do (which it is), it's also dangerous.

The French Revolution evolved out of clout.[339] It was class warfare, clout warfare, between the haves and the have-nots, the bourgeois and the citizens. The peasants were sick of being constantly dumped on by the bourgeois, so they rose up. They were destitute, poor, and starving. Our friend Marie Antoinette, the then-Queen of France, allegedly responded to the cries of the outraged peasants with one of the most ignorant lines in world history: "Let them eat cake." Avoid saying that phrase in public at all costs. Odds are you'll get your head chopped off.

The effects were astronomical. Many died. Nearly three thousand were put to death by guillotine. In the end, the revolutionaries got what they wanted. The monarchy was toppled. But then a guy named Napoleon came along, and that wasn't pretty either.[340] Short-man syndrome is a motherfucker, lemme tell ya.

Now, I am in no way insinuating we are even close to a French Revolution-esque type of scenario. But what I am saying is this emphasis on comparison between clout is real. Very real, in fact.

There's a reason the film *Joker* was such a big deal.[341] In the movie, the haves and have-nots hate each other, and the have-nots eventually take to someone (the *Joker*) to ignite the revolution. It's about classism. The fact the film was so real to so many folks is disturbing. It was a slap in the face to how ignorant we've been as a culture to our clout-chasing nonsense. It was a warning against disparaging others who don't have as much as we do when they may not even want what we want.

A lot of people attribute Hillary Clinton's loss in the 2016 presidential election to the fact that she refused to go to places like Michigan to campaign.[342] Voters there didn't think she cared enough. They viewed it as a casual hair flip, a slight by the Ruling Class superiority. The people of West Virginia felt the same. Clinton wanted to take away coal, their primary industry.[343] It's not great for the environment. The data is in.[344] But they feel they don't have a choice—the haves are descending on the have-nots.

Fellow Ruling Class hack, businessman, mayor, and formerly atrocious presidential candidate Michael Bloomberg has taken these types of potshots as well. He thinks the have-nots are beneath him too. When giving a speech at Oxford University, he had this to say about farmers and manufacturing workers:[345]

> "I could teach anybody, even the people in this room, to farm. You dig a hole, you put the seed in, you put dirt on top, add water, up comes the corn…You put the piece of metal in the lathe, you turn the crank in the direction of the arrow, and you can have a job."

Non-failure-at-being-a-presidential-nominee Joe Biden said a strikingly similar thing in his 2020 campaign. He was asked a question about removing hundreds of thousands of Middle American oil and gas jobs in exchange for "green energy investment." "Well, the answer is yes,"[346] Biden replied. No concern for the lives this would destroy, the skills they shit all over, the money that would flood out of those areas. All in the name of something that wasn't even brought to the people this would most affect. The haves were descending on the have-nots. The Ruling Class hypocrisy was manifesting itself.

In a press conference after my Cleveland Cavaliers railroaded his Chicago Bulls, center Joakim Noah decided to condescend not to the team that just whooped his ass, but the city that it represented:[347]

> I don't know about this place, man. I just stay in my hotel room. Every time I look out my window, it's pretty depressing here,

man. It's bad. It's bad. No—no going out in Cleveland, man. It's all factories…

You think Cleveland's cool? I've never heard anybody say, "I'm going to Cleveland on vacation." What's so good about Cleveland?

The slander continued from sports commentator, frequent condescender, and vicious race-baiter Stephen A. Smith. "I'm not interested in doing SportsCenters in Cleveland in four-degree weather,"[348] said the highest-paid man in sports media.[349] Others followed. They felt Cleveland was "beneath" LeBron James. While that is certainly true of the organization (just ask me about my hatred for Dan Gilbert), it's not very nice to cast that shade onto the city and its citizens. The haves descending on the have-nots.

So what of those "have-nots"? The coal miners, excavators, manufacturing workers, and Middle American citizens? I know a lot of them. They don't like being shit on because of shit that shouldn't matter. The problem is some people make the shit matter in order to feel better about themselves. It's a shame.

But the problem is it's easy to buy into. Incredibly easy. I've done it more than a few times. But it's wrong. Very wrong. Because when you compare yourself to others and condescend someone else's career and/or occupation, you are directly comparing and condescending that person's values.

* * *

GROWING UP WITH A SPECIAL needs daughter and two sons, my parents were big McDonald's drive-through people. It was cheap, easy, and quick. The McDonald's drive-through, especially when we were younger, was our meal of the week when we went out. We almost always ate at home.

Being that my parents didn't work in fast food, I was curious as to why someone would work in that industry or others like it. Construction. Grocery stores. Trades. Welding. It was foreign to me. I didn't understand why some people did and some didn't. When I asked my dad, his response was this:

"Sammo, someone's gotta flip the burgers."

I used to think this was condescending. But it wasn't. My dad wasn't demeaning the work these people do. He wasn't comparing himself to anyone. He was simply stating that these employees were doing a job. They were contributing. They were necessary to the functioning of our country.

I had an epiphany after that moment. I learned you should *never* condescend to anyone unless they aren't following the law or aren't contributing to society. A McDonald's cashier follows the law and contributions to society. Good. An underground bath-salts dealer fails at both of those criteria. Bad.

Every job that meets those two criteria is important. *Every* one. That's what the people in those examples earlier didn't understand. They didn't know nor care for those people. They looked down on them. They casted shame from their ivory towers of virtue. It's embarrassing, and it's wrong.

As I got further in school, the "someone's gotta flip the burgers" story became more prominent. This was reflected most in an economic theory: comparative advantage. It's maybe the most important economic theory ever. It's basically defined the world since we created advanced international commerce and trade. It's a pretty big deal. At least maybe for first-time authors who are looking for a way to sell books.

THE THEORY OF COMPARATIVE ADVANTAGE

Who's ready for the *last* theory of this book?! I know I am. It's tiring writing one of these things.

However, this one is easy, even for those of you who don't speak econ. The theory of comparative advantage applies when an economic agent has a lower opportunity cost for something over another.[350]

If you remember from earlier, opportunity cost is the "cost" incurred by an economic agent by not doing something. For example, your girlfriend corners you after five minutes of "no, you pick" banter and forces you to make a decision on where to go for dinner. You've gotten it down to two options: Applebee's or Chili's. Considering she's going to dump you if you can't nut up and make a decision, your brain shits itself and defaults to the start of the alphabet. You go to Applebee's. The opportunity cost of this scenario is not going to Chili's. And, if you were a Vine junkie, that might be a bad idea.[351]

Agent A has an "advantage" over Agent B. Therefore, it only makes sense to have Agent A produce that good while Agent B looks to find somewhere *they* have a comparative advantage.

Let's use two countries as an example: Country A and Country B. Country A is located on an island. Its soil is cock. However, it has mountains that are rich in minerals such as iron ore. It also has decent fields—it just can't farm them. Country B is located on the mainland. Its soil is awesome. It doesn't have a lot of mineral-rich mountains, but it has wide-open spaces with some wheat bushels growing sparsely.

The two work out a deal. Country A will use the resources it has to build factories and trade steel with Country B, which will take the wheat, make bread, and trade with Country A. Country A's advantage is steel, and Country B's advantage is baking bread. They fill holes they wouldn't have been able to fill themselves. Country A gets to eat, and Country B gets stuff built for them. Everyone wins.

At least in theory.

While this theory may not seem like a big deal, it actually was a *gigantic* deal when it came to the Industrial Revolution and globalization. When we didn't all have to be hunters and gatherers anymore, we saw there was other cool shit out there we wanted our hands on. Therefore, we started picking things by the country where we could have a competitive advantage. This led to problems.

An example is the offshoring of manufacturing. Manufacturers saw it was cheaper to manufacture things in China, so they moved production there.[352] China had a comparative advantage related to wages. Their labor was cheap, so they got the business. It turns out the 401(k) market isn't quite as rich for slaves.[353]

But America didn't go totally off the rails after that happened either. Entrepreneurship blossomed. Tech companies started appearing in the 1970s, exploded in the 2000s (quite literally, early on), and now reside in proverbial cities on the hill like Austin and Silicon Valley.[354] Did we make the economy inefficient? The argument could certainly be made, particularly with what we learned in Chapter Two. But we have developed a new comparative advantage—our entrepreneurs. It almost seems to be baked into the American cake, especially since COVID-19 crippled the world economy and boomed the start-up market.[355]

Comparative advantage works (again, in theory) because it allows different agents of the economy to specialize in what is best for them. Whether that be bread, entrepreneurship, steel, tech, or wheat, everyone can find their niche and create their thing that can provide the most value to the market.

It's sad this is disappearing within our society. The main reason I think this is happening, especially for young people, is our dreaded Fatal Flaw. We've become brainwashed into thinking certain things are bad and good without experiencing for ourselves what those things mean to us.

"But what do we conform to?" you ask. Various things. Pleasing our parents. Making "good" money. Getting a "good" job. But what defines "good"? Hint: *you* do. You define what good is in those cases. It's mostly arbitrary. It's completely made up. That is, unless you're running off stabbing people with dull spoons or impeding on their rights or that sort of thing. That's not cool under any circumstances.

We look to our culture for a lot of things, especially to celebrities and social media. But what we see in celebrities and social media does not equal what is good. I would argue it's the opposite of good, but I'm a cynical fuck, so maybe I need to check myself.

But there's no denying the influence of celebrity and social media. We see people in nice cars and apartments and with other luxuries and immediately associate it with clout. But then the question arises—how do we get these things? The answer? Money. *Lots* of money. How do we get that money? Well, that's an issue. There really aren't a lot of ways where we can buy a Ferrari and live in a penthouse on Madison Avenue.

Which leads me into a second trend I find disturbing—the Absolute of going to college. Absolutes are bad—only Sith deal in them. But it's a narrative that continues to get pushed, and get pushed hard.

It's not the narrative itself that's the problem. It's the other side of the narrative that's worse. Besides encouraging us all to get college-educated, we're discouraging, and in most cases condescending upon, those jobs I mentioned earlier. Farmers. Manual laborers. Manufacturing workers. Tradespeople.

This is skewing America's young people to bend *heavily* toward college. And, more importantly, *heavily* in certain areas. Computer science and finance are exploding.[356] They're filled to the brim with ambitious young people foaming at the mouth to get that Ferrari and Madison Avenue penthouse.

This wouldn't be a problem if it were our comparative advantage. But we must remember our friend Excessive Excess. It's an incredibly dangerous vice to fall into because when that Excessive Excess fails, the clapback is incredibly destructive. Societies, ranging from the freest of markets to the horrors of communism, collapse when there's too much excess. Read history. There are examples aplenty.

Our individual comparative advantages are being skewed and wrecked by comparisons. We're all going toward the same things. We all want to be the highest of profiles, the most valuable of influencers, the biggest drivers of change.

But what of those that don't? What if there are some people that don't want this? Shouldn't they have the freedom to choose anywhere along that spectrum too? To feel valued for what they value?

Not everyone can be a banker at Goldman Sachs or a consultant at McKinsey. Not everyone should be. It's a problem if we try to force a square peg into a round hole with a hammer composed of comparisons and condescension.

We need to get back to what we value as individuals. To take back our *rights* to those values. To our individual comparative advantages. The theory works. Well, at least in theory.

So I fucked around and made up a new theory of comparative advantage that, if worked properly, will right the ship and put us back on course for a more balanced society. One that values everyone and everyone's values. That doesn't succumb to potshots and put-downs. Let the fuckery begin.

THE THEORY OF COMPARATIVE VALUE ADVANTAGE

Okay, so I'm not going to come up with a *totally* new theory. That's a lot of fucking work. But what I am going to do is take the old theory, add a word, and turn it into something similar. That counts, right? Well, I think it counts. The book's almost over; deal with it.

The theory of Comparative Value Advantage is simple yet effective. Comparative Value Advantage occurs when a noneconomic agent puts a greater personal emphasis on a value than another agent.

Comparative Value Advantage works for the same reason comparative advantage works. It allows every agent within a Value Economy to specialize in what they do best. It doesn't corner everyone and force them to decide between Applebee's or Chili's. The simp of a boyfriend would simply pick between restaurants, not feel some misplaced sense of pressure to pick "the right one."

This term deals with an awful topic—our friend variety. People have become afraid of specializing in something because of the perception it will not make them "well-rounded." They don't want to go all in and invest out of some fear of missing out on something that could be gained.

That is something to consider. However, if you're an avid practitioner of Value Economics (as you should be—if not, wyd?), you would know this fear is unwarranted. The Value/Sacrifice Trade-Off debunks this fear. So does Guns and Butter. So does the Life-Defining Principle. So does Essential Diversification.

It's not that you should be ignorant to the possibilities. Instead of *ignoring* other things, practitioners of Value Economics simply see alternatives, acknowledge them, and decide something else is more important to *them*. They appreciate other values and people's rights to them. But they don't conform if they don't believe them to be of merit, even though other folks do (and should, if they truly value them).

An adoption of Comparative Value Advantage would be awesome. Humans think so differently before they conform to others that we would cover all our bases. Our individual Essential Diversifications of values would create a broad spectrum of values, like the painting Cameron stared at in *Ferris Bueller's Day Off*.[357] Our own individual dots contributing to the larger whole of our society. It would be awesome.

Unfortunately, through comparison by way of conformity, we're going away from this. Humans are flawed. We suck sometimes. We make poor decisions. It's easy to stray from what we truly value if we feel society scorns us for it. We've felt these pressures in the past, but I think it has been amplified tremendously by other factors—polarization, mainstream/social media, idiotic elites, etc.

Through these vehicles (and the enormous amounts of money they reap), we're losing our minds over this tribal value warfare we engage in. We know it's hurting us, yet we do it anyway. It's a mind-blowing study in The Two Es and the power they have over the human mind.

I have a family member whom I won't name (not like I haven't outed enough people in this book, what's one more?). Let's call this person Family Member One. This person is older, with a strong opinion of who they view as worthy of society's value. I have another family member whom I *also* won't name. Let's call this person Family Member Two. This person is much younger and just starting out. Family Member Two does not fit the description of Family Member One.

Family Member One strongly values intellectual prowess and stature, such as great grades and high status in the social hierarchy. Family Member One really doesn't give a shit about people who don't value those things and choose to do other things, particularly the things stated in the first part of this chapter.

Family Member Two does not fit that description. Family Member Two has always tried hard in school, but it just isn't their thing. Family Member Two puts in more time than I've seen most do. It just doesn't click. So, they said fuck it, realized it didn't benefit them, and decided to go into a trade.

Now, this scenario would normally be fine. Except for one thing. Family Member One *disparages* people like Family Member Two, much like our disembodied elites. If you don't fit the values of Family Member One, you aren't worthy of their appreciation. You don't belong. You don't have value. From our definition, if you do things the right way and don't infringe on anyone's rights to do the same, *everyone* has value. That's what Comparative Value Advantage is. That's why it's important.

I had a friend once who was very into environmentalism. She got into an excellent master's program for it. But strangely, she turned to something called "envirofeminism," which basically says that capitalism and men are to blame for everything. We didn't speak much after that because I don't care about envirofeminism, and that's okay. My old friend didn't care about special needs kids as much as I do. That's okay as well. The reason that's all okay is because of Comparative Value Advantage. Everyone cannot care equally about envirofeminism or special needs philanthropy or kids with cleft palates or whatever the fuck. A man who values everything values nothing. Someone's gotta flip the burgers.

The same goes for nearly every cause out there in the world. Black Lives Matter. Breast cancer. Down syndrome. Education inequity. Saving the _____. You simply can't care about everything. You can't. It's impossible. The people who lie by saying they do are the most dangerous people in our society.

We should encourage Comparative Value Advantage individually in order to get people to express authenticity about who they really are. We should shed the comparison of conformity with other individuals because other individuals are not our individual selves. In doing so, we will create a wide variety of value-oriented folks who can go about bringing meaning to the world through their own individual differences and not simply succumbing to the dogma of groupthink and tribalism.

When we don't practice Comparative Value Advantage, there are consequences. The current tension of the conservative/liberal political dynamic, for example. Sorority girls forcing other women to sit in their underwear on washing machines. Frat bros making pledges cum on a cracker and drink their own piss in order to become "a man of ___ frat." People feeling ashamed of having an opinion or a difference in their sexual orientation. The Nazis and the Final Solution. Mao's Great Leap Forward. The Columbine kids. The list could go on for pages.

Comparative Value Advantage is the answer. It's how we defeat the comparison of values and discourage conformity and groupthink. We need to encourage and nurture it, especially in our young people, who grew up in this reality. But how will they do it if we can't?

DEFEATING THE TYRANNICAL COLLECTIVE AND SELF

A year after the interview with Pleasure Island Guy, TFA's recruitment chair cold emailed me and asked to speak. She said I was one of their top recruits in the country and wanted to know if I was still interested. I was confused. I had given feedback for the organization in an email survey. I didn't hold back in the "Would you like to tell us anything else?" section.

But I took the call. Why? Because she seemed nice. It seemed like she was coming from a good place. I gave her a chance. We had a very nice conversation and talked for about half an hour. We focused on the message, not the messenger. There was no narcissism at all. There was just a quality proposition from a quality person. Much different this time around. The woman admitted the organization's fault. I showed them sympathy. It was just a mistake. They happen. It probably doesn't happen that often.

But that doesn't mean I forgot about it.

A lot of people, when their values are insulted and/or when they come into contact with ones that so drastically conflict with theirs, get defensive. They succumb to outrage. They let the Mob bully them and win.

But their biggest fear is you not bowing. You not shutting up and obeying. You sticking to your values while respecting theirs. If you want to truly take their power, hold your tongue, allow them to feel, and then do nothing. They'll destroy themselves. There is immense power in refusing to stoop to their level.

The answer to how we defeat our Fatal Flaw, the answer to the question this book has (hopefully) provided the road map to answering, is to forgive but not forget. We must be better to others. We must forgive. We must come together in an attempt to see the good in all people because we are all people.

But we cannot forget. We should not hold grudges, but there must be a system of accountability held in place in order for us all to move forward after such an incident occurs. Fool me once, and all that.

The woman's pitch the second time was much better and much more honest. But I couldn't shake the feeling from the first. Impressions really do matter as much as everyone says. My "interview" with Pleasure Island Guy stands as the most dog shit first impression I've ever gotten. I emailed the woman thanks, but no thanks. I didn't see an alignment in our values. She, being a reasonable person, understood.

You should forgive people. You should forgive yourself. They (and you) deserve and need it. We should honor that need. We should allow them and you to pursue meaning in our own ways.

But we should not so easily forget their (and your) sins. We should always be aware of them. Because when we forget them, real ones emerge. There are actual racists, anti-Semites, pedophiles, murderers, sex criminals, and a whole lot of bad shit out there. Only by noticing trends can we hope to fix them. Only with self-awareness, the most important Factor of Value Production, can we snuff them out.

* * *

WE NEED TO *ENCOURAGE* COMPARATIVE VALUE ADVANTAGE, not discourage it. We need to lift others up, even if they're different. We need to challenge ourselves with opinions rather than be frightened by them.

We need to leave our comfort zones to encourage the defeat of the comparison of values and realize the importance of ours. It's hard to leave conformity and groupthink. It's much easier to go along and create avenues where we can be included, even though those inclusions can result in the defeat of our values.

Speaking out in public to a group of family or friends when something conflicts with your values is difficult. You'll probably get looked at like you're stupid or weird or have a dick growing out of your forehead.

But, according to Value Economics, our values are our most important resource. We cannot afford to waste our limited time living on someone else's value agenda. To not express ourselves authentically and be unable to reap the benefit of having other people (hopefully) meet us where we are and accept us.

When someone shares their values with you, try hard to compliment them. It takes a lot of courage and effort to put yourself out there. To make a big claim or take a stance on something that can come off as controversial or off the cuff. It happens, fortunately, in a lot of the various circles of people I associate myself with—from my family to the few friends I have to my coworkers and colleagues.

But when someone does make that leap to put themselves in the center of the conversation and say what they believe, too often they are merely shoved to the side. "Oh, that's cool man," "Oh wow, interesting," "Ooh, love that for you"—that type of thing.

That's nice, but it really doesn't *encourage* that person in that opinion. You're just acknowledging that they, indeed, are breathing, have a pulse, and can converse. But you're really not creating any rapport with that person. You aren't inviting them to explore and really go in depth with what they want to say.

This is one of the reasons I believe long-form content (including this book, if I may be so bold :D) is becoming the preferred method of getting information. It's really fucking hard to sound stupid for more than about ten minutes before people decide you're spewing absolute nonsense and turn you off. It's why mainstream news cycles and the stories that fill them are condensed.[358] A lot of people in the media are not talking about things of merit but instead what makes money.

This is where the "try hard" part comes in. Your job as a practitioner of Value Economics is to vet a person by inquiring about their values. Ask them the root questions—the "why" questions. The other person will open up about their values and stances. Conversation will ensue. We need to use more of our empathic listening skills, paired with psychological safety, to foster this. This is a good place to start. Drop the judgment, open the holes in your head, and listen.

Unless the person is talking about lighting small children on fire with a blowtorch or something of the like, empathize with them. Make them feel secure. Make them feel their values matter to not just them, but to you. You're an advocate for Comparative Value Advantage, after all. You want other people to be able to express their values. You *don't* want comparisons to matter. Because when we're all able to express ourselves without fear, meaning can assert itself.

Trying hard while complimenting someone shows your care and investment in that person and their values. You want them to open up. You want them to know they matter. By investing in their values, you also indirectly give them permission to do the same. And according to the Life-Defining Principle, it's that repeated investment in all the things around what you value that will orient your life around your values. So when in doubt, don't just acknowledge someone. Try hard to listen to and compliment them.

Tune out the noise and tune into yourself. One of the good things about the beer virus pandemic and the lockdowns that followed was it enabled us to look in the mirror with no distractions. While this is uncomfortable, it can also be an opportunity for a reset. It all depends on how you look at it.

Don't let the end of the pandemic (update: it's over) stop you from tuning back into nonsense. Clean up the nonsense in your own life before you worry about cleaning up the world's. That's Rule Number Six of the first Twelve Rules, by the way.[359] Don't let the comparisons of the world influence your values and direct your attention.

It's easy to get distracted by the noise and succumb to conformity and groupthink. What if I miss out on this? What if I need to hear someone say this specific thing? What if this can inspire me today?

But will the sun rise? Will you drink some type of beverage today? Will DJ Khaled absurdly shout his own name at an outrageous volume?[360]

The answer to all three of these questions is yes. These things *happen*. You will miss things. You will not be in the loop on everything. You will completely draw blanks on cultural references. You won't get every single meme on the internet. Sorry to shit in your cornflakes.

Become okay with missing out on things. Become *comfortable* with missing out on things. Because when you miss out on things for the right reasons, it's not missing out on anything at all. You're simply gaining another opportunity to build something new in an area only *you* are privy to. Other people should be envious of *you*, not the reverse. Tune out the noise. Tune into yourself. You'll find it more rewarding.

Children can be cruel. Most times they don't know any better. They are children, after all. Most of that cruelty comes from bullying. Being a sibling of a special needs child, I saw this firsthand. Thankfully, my sister is very jovial and social. People like being around her. I am very happy about that.

But a lot of her friends weren't so lucky. No one wanted to sit with them at lunch. No one wanted to say hi to them in the hallways. No one talked to them. They didn't have touch points with other kids where they could have these relationships. Most of these children were segregated into their own rooms without anyone to branch out to. They had no one outside of that to interact with. They felt alone.

In high school, I was fortunate enough to be selected to help found a group called Friendship Group. In this group, we would hang out with special needs kids in a setting that wasn't forced. We wanted to be there, and so did they. We wanted to help. We wanted to sit with the lonely kids at lunch.

This turned out to be one of the most rewarding experiences of my life. I bonded with kids whom I would have never had a single touch point with. I learned about their families, their lives, who their favorite superhero was (Superman and Batman were most common, another discussion for another day[361]). You'd be surprised what happens when you interact with someone who just needs a friend. When you break that bubble and extend your bright and beautiful values, you'll be surprised what you get back.

You don't have to reach out to anyone who is an actual victim. Those are few and far between, thankfully. It can be a coworker, a family member, a neighbor, or a person in your community. Unfortunately, anyone can feel like their values are alone and unappreciated. When you encourage other people to share themselves and their values with the world, you remind them that they and their values matter. That they're important. That they can contribute to this sometimes-beautiful and sometimes-ugly society in which we live. Because as Comparative Value Advantage and the study of Value Economics prove, *everyone* is important. They *all* matter. *Everyone* has value. Everyone has a right to express *their* values.

The comparative sins of condescension, conformity, group identity, and groupthink remove this individual importance. Fight it. Grow a spine. Stand up for yourself. Stand up for others, particularly the weak. Don't let the vices of the world break you and your stride. Don't let them deter you from helping someone that might need it. You'd be surprised what can happen if you just decide to sit with the lonely kid at lunch.

Comparative Advantage and Comparative Value Advantage draw together the most important aspects of the human condition. As long as you're contributing to society in an honest and respectful manner, and you aren't telling anyone else to do differently, your values have value. Somebody's gotta flip the burgers.

It doesn't matter whether you're a patent attorney or a crane operator or a dominatrix. Your Comparative Value Advantage serves a purpose. I challenge you to find and express it.

THE END?

I was told of Pleasure Island Guy's fate during my second interview with the woman from TFA. It turns out he was a radical Marxist. Oof. He was fired from the organization when they found out he had been blamewashing and brainwashing other students with the same horrible nonsense he attempted with me. At least I'm told that's why they fired him. I'll never know. I frankly didn't care enough to dig further.

I sometimes think about Pleasure Island Guy. Shortly after I declined my second opportunity with TFA, I looked him up on Facebook. His profile picture was him looking at a graffitied wall in awe, probably thinking of some way he could topple it. He seemed to revel in the incomprehensible artwork that adorned it. There's something poetic about that, I think. On his feed were several enraged and incoherent rants. He was planning to "eat the rich" and "topple the patriarchy."

I pity Pleasure Island Guy. He'll probably never be happy.

* * *

I WAS GOING TO END the book here. I didn't think there was much more to say. But things change when you're writing a book. About yourself. The way you think. What you want to leave people with.

I realized there's one thing we still have left to cover. The most important tenet of Value Economics still has to be discussed. If you can recall all the way back to Chapter Three, I listed six values I personally hold. Well, technically five. I left a blank spot for the sixth one.

The sixth value is what the last chapter of *Value Economics* is dedicated to. Throughout the process of writing this book, I realized it was the one concept that strung everything together. It is, at the end of the day, what this book is trying to accomplish. It is the centerpiece. The linchpin. The nucleus.

The Ultimate Value.

CHAPTER 10

THE VALUE-SCARCITY PRINCIPLE

"And on that pedestal, these words appear:
'My name is Ozymandias, king of kings:
Look upon my works, ye Mighty, and despair!'
Nothing beside remains. Round the decay
Of that colossal wreck, boundless and bare
The lone and level sands stretch far away."
–PERCY SHELLEY IN AN EXCERPT FROM HER POEM "OZYMANDIAS" (1818)

THE END

CHRIS FARLEY WAS BURIED IN A PRIVATE CEREMONY ON December 23, 1997, at Our Lady Queen of Peace Catholic Church in his hometown of Madison, Wisconsin.[362] Over seven hundred people attended. The one notable absence was David Spade, Farley's best friend. While some thought there may have been a falling out between the two, Spade quickly squashed that rumor. It simply was too much to bear.[363]

As much as those seven hundred people didn't want to admit to Farley's Fatal Flaw, it couldn't help but hang over the final resting place of the man who carried its burden. During the funeral, Reverend Tom

Gannon, a friend of Farley's who preached in Chicago, was the first to bring up the elephant in the room:[364]

> "I remember a man who loved to work and loved to make people laugh. But I also remember a man never fully at ease with his talent and celebrity. He often felt trapped by people always expecting him to be funny or always the most outrageous person in the room."

Before Farley died, he was lined up to continue his meteoritic ascendance. He had recorded between 85 and 95 percent of the dialogue for a then-little-known film called *Shrek*.[365] After his death, the role went to his friend Mike Myers. *The Cable Guy* was initially meant for Farley. Other projects included a TV show about *Captain Underpants* and the films *Dinosaur*, *The Gelfin*, *A Confederacy of Dunces*, *The Incomparable Atuk*, and a biopic about Fatty Arbuckle.[366] The last three of those films had been offered to two other men, John Belushi and John Candy. They both died before the age of forty-five, the causes of death being derivatives of obesity and substance abuse.[367]

Much has been made of Farley's beyond-tragic demise. Most remember him quite fondly. This was a man that brought an incredible amount of joy and innocence to a world that can, at times, seem dark and foreboding. He was a reminder that there are still people out there that are innately good. That there are still people out there that could relieve others of their pain.

But for those who did know him well, Farley brings another emotion—sadness. Chevy Chase and Dan Aykroyd, two of the original *Saturday Night Live* cast members, knew where this train was going—to the same place their friend John Belushi ended up. Chris Rock, as alluded to earlier, knew as well. I can't help but feel sorry for David Spade, whose relationship with Farley ran so deep he's asked about it in nearly every interview. You can still see the pain in his eyes. He admits it will never leave him.[368]

But one observation stands above the rest. Bob Odenkirk, before finding incredible success in a starring role in *Breaking Bad* and *Better Call Saul*, first found traction as a writer at The Second City. The most famous sketch he ever wrote was called "Matt Foley the Motivational Speaker." The club did the sketch every night during Farley and Odenkirk's tenure. It killed every time. It's regarded as perhaps the greatest sketch in the organization's history.

However, Odenkirk saw behind the curtain too. And, in the most harrowing example of DRV I've ever heard, he didn't like what he saw:[369]

> "With Chris, there's a limit to how wonderful it is to me. And that limit is when you kill yourself with drugs and alcohol. That's when it stops being so fucking magical."

KICK SIX

Greatness is rarely planned. It's usually something forced on you in a moment of sheer magnitude. Most can hardly comprehend it, particularly the person whom it's forced on. For a young man named Chris Davis, greatness claimed him on the evening of Saturday, November 30, 2013.

That night, the University of Alabama and Auburn University played the seventy-eighth annual Iron Bowl at Jordan-Hare Stadium in Auburn, Alabama.[370] Frequently cited as the greatest rivalry in college football, Alabama was coming off back-to-back national championships.[371] With a victory over its rival, it was guaranteed a spot in the SEC Championship Game. Auburn, which at that time was ranked fourth, was looking to play the spoiler as a ten-point underdog. It was a highly competitive game, with the score tied twenty-eight to twenty-eight going into the end of the fourth quarter.

Auburn, who had rallied from behind to tie, kicked off to Alabama with thirty-two seconds remaining in the game. Alabama raced down the field. As time expired, running back T. J. Yeldon was forced out at Auburn's thirty-eight-yard line. Nick Saban, Alabama's head coach, sprinted out to the official to ask them to review the amount of time on the clock. The referees determined there was exactly one second left. Saban, trying to seal the game, sent out his field goal unit for an astronomically long fifty-seven-yard attempt.

What made this choice even more strange was that Alabama was on its backup kicker, a redshirt freshman named Adam Griffith. Stranger still, this substitution was not due to illness, injury, or any other set of circumstances. The reason Adam Griffith was put in was because Alabama's starting kicker, Cade Foster, had missed three kicks during the game. Saban, a notorious perfectionist, benched Foster for Griffith to hopefully right their special teams ship.

Auburn noticed this. Ellis Johnson, Auburn's defensive coordinator, suggested to his head coach, Gus Malzahn, he put a defensive back in the end zone. In football, a kick is considered a "live" play.[372] This means that, if the ball stays in bounds, any player can get their hands on it and do what they want with it in their possession, including score. Johnson's idea was that if Griffith missed the long kick, Auburn could have a moonshot attempt to return it for points, similar to a kickoff or punt. Malzahn agreed and sent the aforementioned Chris Davis, who had been the player that pushed Yeldon out of bounds, back into the end zone to receive the kick should the opportunity arise. He was the obvious choice. He was an incredible athlete who also doubled as Auburn's punt returner.

The two teams took the field. The referees blew the whistle. Adam Griffith lined up to kick. Ozzy Osbourne's "Crazy Train" boomed across the night sky. The dueling fan bases roared. The snap was clean. The hold was good. Griffith's steps and technique were perfect. He hit the ball clean, booting it over the line of scrimmage toward destiny. As the 87,451 fans in attendance watched, it looked good.

But it fell just short. Right into the hands of Chris Davis.

Davis fielded the ball nine yards deep in his own end zone, the farthest legal distance you can go within the boundaries of a football field. His adrenaline, athleticism, and instincts all simultaneously clicked into place. Davis began to loop around to his left sideline, quickly accelerating into a straight-line sprint. His teammates, playing their roles perfectly, formed a tightly knit wall to block for him. Alabama's field-goal unit, made up of mostly offensive linemen, never had a chance.

Davis saw the opening his teammates gave him and graciously took it. He cut left, veering past the mass of bodies, and nearly going out of bounds around midfield on the sideline. He tightroped and tiptoed just inside the green to see a miracle occur right in front of him: no one was there.

Davis cut back inside to the right, the only people in front of him being his own teammates. He had left everyone in the dust. Rushing into a sea of blue and orange, Davis waltzed comfortably into the end zone with no time left on the clock, upsetting Alabama and winning the game for Auburn thirty-four to twenty-eight. The sound of Jordan-Hare Stadium during the play was so deafening it registered on a seismograph.[373]

The Kick Six completely melted the sports world. Two ESPYs were awarded, one for the game and one for Chris Davis' return.[374] The final half hour of the game rated an astonishing 11.8, the highest rating ever for a college football broadcast at the time.[375] Writers from *The Huffington Post*,[376] *The New York Daily News*,[377] and *New York Post*[378] called it the greatest moment in the history of sports. Gary Danielson, the color commentator for CBS Sports who called the game, compared it to the Miracle on Ice.[379]

My parents were out that Saturday night. My brother, always awe-struck by everything, went ballistic. He jumped up and down and screamed his head off like everyone else, unable to comprehend what he had just seen. My sister, completely indifferent, asked if we could change the channel to her show. She did not care for the single greatest college football play of my lifetime. When my parents came home, they were astonished. As big fans of football themselves, they had never experienced anything like it before. When they asked me what I thought, I said the same.

But I lied. I didn't see the Kick Six. I was too busy jerking off.

THE FALL

I like to think that everything has a starting point. Insecurity is no exception.

I don't remember much about my early life. I don't think many people do. One memory, however, has never left me. We moved to my soon-to-be-excess-filled town that I described in Chapter Two when I was around five years old. Before that, we lived in another town about twenty minutes away, one much more affordable for a young family attempting to get their bearings.

In that town was an old-fashioned barbershop. Cracked, old leather seats, crude humor, hole-in-the-wall aesthetic, red and white pinwheel, the whole nine yards. My dad got his hair cut there. We were both due for one at the time of this memory, and he took me with him, so we both could get properly trimmed up.

There is a quote by Carl W. Buehner, often misattributed to Maya Angelou, that says, "They may forget what you said—but they will never forget how you made them feel."[380] All I remember from that day was the barber that trimmed me up. I don't remember what he looked like, how old he was, or even if my haircut was any good. But I'll never forget how that barber made me feel.

I didn't know what getting my balls busted felt like at that point. For one, I was only five, and two, they hadn't even dropped yet. I had just enrolled in kindergarten, the prime cooties era of any young child's life. The barber knew this and began ribbing me about it. He asked me how many girlfriends I had, if I had held hands, that sort of thing. I had never been exposed to this type of talk before. I vehemently denied all of it. I didn't know what to do. I felt trapped. (He was cutting my hair, in my defense.)

Then the laughter started. Everyone in the barbershop began laughing at how flustered I was. I looked over to my dad, completely overwhelmed, only to discover he was laughing too. I begged them to stop. They didn't. None of this, of course, was done maliciously. But I didn't know that. I learned what shame was that day. I felt humiliated. Like I was walking on eggshells. Like I had just been disrobed.

When I got home, I told my parents I never wanted to go back to that barbershop again. I didn't know how to describe what I felt, but I knew I hated it. I never wanted to place myself in that situation again. I thought if I simply removed myself from it, I wouldn't have to feel that feeling again.

But I did. Immediately after that fateful day, my behavior began to change. I didn't talk with the girls in my class much after that. I didn't want anyone to throw the anvil of shame down on me again. Soon, it spun into a raging fear. This was completely irrational. Women, particularly young girls, are not anything to be afraid of at all. But not many things are rational when you're a child.

Fear, when left unattended, inevitably turns to anxiety. While I didn't notice until later, I soon started to feel that "walking on eggshells" feeling every time I was put into a social situation. I cried at nearly every single one of my childhood birthday parties and holidays. I developed a paralyzing fear of doing anything in public, such as singing in a school show or playing a solo in a band concert. I distanced myself further from girls. I didn't want to stand out. Every time I stepped out of the crowd, all I could feel was the fear blinding me, like a car with its brights on coming at me from both sides of my vision.

My anxiety reached its peak in the fifth grade. I, without a doubt, went through the greatest awkward phase of anyone I knew (for proof, the dude who played Coconut Head in *Ned's Declassified School Survival Guide* liked my Instagram picture when I tagged him in it[381]). I started to come up with justifications in my head about why my social anxiety was a thing. It was because I was ugly. It was because I was scared to put myself out there. It was because I was scared to live.

The real world terrified the hell out of me. Everything in my life made me afraid. Everything made me anxious. Everything made me nervous. I needed an escape. Unfortunately, I eventually found it.

I had a friend in the fifth grade whose parents were, for lack of a better word, "loose" with how they supervised him. He played violent video games at will, drank Mountain Dew by the twelve pack, ate pizza four nights a week, and was basically allowed to roam the house unsupervised. This, naturally, made sleepovers at his house the shit. I loved going over there. I could escape. My parents were very strict and, in my opinion, very overprotective. I constantly felt suffocated by them. The sleepovers were a welcome reprieve.

One night at around 12:30 at night after playing *Halo 2* (I never played due to my anxiety of my parents finding out), my friend took me and the others at the sleepover up to his family's computer. He pulled up a website I had never seen before. When the video came to the screen, I was disgusted. A random man was putting his penis in a woman's mouth on camera. I nearly threw up on the spot. My friends, all being typical fifth-grade boys, were transfixed.

I went home the next day and figured that would be the end of it. I still had no idea what I had seen. This was before "the movie" and "the talk." I couldn't understand the motivation behind those strange things the people did on the screen. But I had a family computer. So, naturally, I looked it up.

At the time, I had no idea the internet was awash in an ocean of pornography.[382] I didn't get the same video. This one was different—it was just two people having sex. This video hit me for different reasons. Didn't people spank others when being bad? Why are adults doing it to one another? Why is a man being mean to a woman? Why are they taking each other's clothes off? Without knowing that my innocence was slowly being ripped from me, I began to sense something come over me: desensitization.

I was ten years old when I first started watching pornography. I had no idea what it was. No child does. But at the time, it was exactly what I needed. I hated everything about the real world. I hated how it made me feel. I hated how the pattern at the barbershop repeated itself. With The Asshole, the wrestlers, my school admissions, my failures with women, everything. So I simply decided to stop participating in it. Porn made me feel accepted. It made me feel a connection. It made me feel, if even just for a moment, that I could plug into my own individual Matrix and escape the pain of my everyday life.

Because my everyday life was, indeed, getting more painful. My sister's disability was starting to take more time and toll on my family. My sister, even though she's cognitively set back, is easily the most emotionally intelligent person I've ever met. She knew and knows how to get under people's skin. She would push my buttons day in and day out. I couldn't respond in the same way. It simply would roll off her shoulders. So I would respond differently. I would hit her. Push her. Pin her to the ground. Scream in her face. She would set my anxiety off so badly I would lash out when I felt cornered. I terrified my brother and babysitters when they saw this. They didn't know how to handle me.

My dad began to travel more. He was gone for a lot of my preteen and teenage years. I had to step up and help my mom. I became a third parent. I had to grow up quicker, furthering the already wide gap between myself and my peers. My brother wasn't as naturally gifted or talented as I was in school. He got more margin for error and patience from my parents, as well he should. My sister, obviously, did too.

But I didn't see it that way growing up. I felt my parents were favoring my siblings over me. I didn't feel they loved me as much. Their behavior showed it, in my opinion. Nothing I did was ever good enough for them. The pressure was enormous. I didn't have anywhere to hide anymore. I used to feel safe within my own home, but my anxiety shook me to my core every time I brought home a B on a test or got my ass handed to me at football practice. Both happened incredibly frequently.

I think I began to realize a trend throughout all these events, albeit unconsciously. I don't like to hurt people. I didn't like what I was doing to my sister or not living up to my parents' expectations or being an anxious kid who couldn't be a normal teenager. So I simply began to take that harm out on myself. The way I inflicted it, even though I was ignorant to it at the time, was through sex addiction.

I discovered masturbation in the seventh grade (after watching *Chronicles of Narnia: Prince Caspian*, oddly enough) and the missing link as to why pornography was so attractive to so many people. After that, my consumption kicked into high gear. By my senior year of high school, I was able to list every porn star in the mainstream rolodex. I was jerking off daily and viewing, at minimum, nearly an hour of porn every single night. I was able to cite hundreds of scenes. I knew when certain ones dropped. I was excited for them to come out. I set timers on my phone. I never missed a single one.

Simultaneous to the rise in my digital world, my real life began to crumble. I began to whore myself out for attention by going with the flow of everyone else. I agreed with everyone. I didn't want to ruffle any feathers because I knew what would happen between my ears if I dared to cross any line. I wasn't in the slightest bit authentic. I was never true to myself because I was petrified of facing the reality that my entire persona was completely and utterly fake. I valued myself so little I didn't make a single decision about my life for myself until writing this book. Every single one, literally every other decision, had some sort of peer pressure attached to it. All of it was a lie, a false idol.

I favored the digital over the real world. Why waste your time trying to get real girls to like you? You can watch fifteen of them get fucked in the ass with two dicks on demand. Why make yourself vulnerable trying to connect to people? These people are kind of real. They make you feel things. They can't hurt you.

But they can. Pornography is not "sexual liberation." It's not "expressing your intimacy." Those are lies. Pornography is a drug and an extortion racket.[383] It abuses and uses vulnerable and weak people.[384] It hooks into the neurological pleasure center in your brain and wrings dopamine out like a wet towel. When it gets wrung out often, you need to douse it in higher quantities to get it soaked again. Just like there are harder forms of chemical substances, there are harder forms of pornography.

I reached peak self-loathing my sophomore year of college. At this point, I was masturbating twice a day and watching porn for a minimum of two hours daily. My addictive behavior worsened. I memorized my roommate's schedule to know when he would be in class. My sleep schedule was beyond fucked. I missed things. I didn't socialize. Instead, I traded it all away by stowing away in my college dorm to eagerly look over new uploads like a child looking over a pillowcase full of Halloween candy. My sexual proclivities expanded from blow jobs and stepmoms to puke jobs and toilet sex.

The funny thing was, I didn't enjoy any of the heinous shit I was watching. I was often disgusted after I did the deed. I nearly threw up several times. I wouldn't dare think of doing these things with an actual girl. I was still too afraid to even talk to one. But I couldn't stop. The self-imposed torture continued.

It was at this point that I discovered anxiety's sister—depression. I knew I had a problem, like all addicts do. I knew what I was doing was incredibly disturbing, immoral, and unhealthy. I knew I had to stop. But I couldn't. I was imprisoned by my own doing. I couldn't break the cycle. My virtual world had devolved from the Garden of Eden into the roaring Lake of Fire.

My self-hatred increased rapidly. There was nothing I liked about myself. What was there to like? I was a glorified incel. I was addicted to pornography. I was giving my dick blisters from jerking off so much. My social life was evaporating, 100 percent of that being of my own doing. I was lonelier than ever.

But the thing that made me the angriest was that other people told me I wasn't pathetic. I was the Golden Child. I could do no wrong. I got good grades. I went to a good college. Everything about me was great.

I would fume when people would say these things. I always felt they were lying to me because they indirectly were. I was a piece of shit, a pitiful and vulgar excuse for a human being whose greatest joy came from watching women get exploited on camera. This was not anywhere near good. So much so, in fact, that I didn't know why I was even still trying to keep going.

I think every young person thinks of a reality where they don't exist. They've at least thought of the possibility before. I always wondered if I would get cold or warm if I slit my wrists. Would the blood loss make me cold? Or would my body so rapidly warm up that I would die in a slightly better euphoria?

Thankfully, I didn't take any of these thoughts with any degree of seriousness. I always viewed suicide as selfish. I thought it would do more harm to my family than it would myself. But that didn't stop the feeling of me continuing to live within the confines of my misery. I drowned in pornography. I felt completely worthless and unloved. I was petrified of socialization. I couldn't even make eye contact with a girl, attractive or not, without paralyzing fear overtaking me. Nothing could make me happy.

This seems, on the outset, like a pointless and worthless existence. I can validate that claim as true. I lived it. It was. I felt like I didn't deserve to be taking up space on the earth. There were other people who weren't as irredeemably forsaken as I was. They would do a better job. I was on a downward spiral. I had nothing to show for all that everyone told me I had "accomplished." I could very well have decided to end my life, to bring an end to my suffering.

But I didn't. For the longest time, I couldn't figure out why.

A PROBLEM DOG

Aaron Paul's Jesse Pinkman remains to this day my favorite live-action television character of all time. The evolution of his character, which was created by Vince Gilligan and the crew of *Breaking Bad*, is something so rare I don't think it will ever have a chance of being recreated.

But Jesse Pinkman is not my favorite character for the reasons one might think. Jesse Pinkman is my favorite character because of his impossibility. His inability to heal himself, to cure his trauma, to fix up his life was one of the most heartbreaking things I've ever seen. Jesse Pinkman is so broken, so hopeless, so lost, that only a person like him can reveal the flaws about our own human nature. And none did so more than his greatest scene of the series.

In the season-four episode "Problem Dog," Jesse is coping with a murder he was forced to commit on behalf of his partner and father figure, Walter White.[385] He does so by relapsing into drugs, partying nonstop, and letting his life descend into untethered chaos. He also leans further into the meth-dealing underworld, being tasked by White with expanding their list of customers. He does this by going back to his old Narcotics Anonymous meetings to prey on the attendees by selling these poor folks the very thing they were looking to escape. It's a truly diabolical act.

Jesse's spirit is close to breaking. He pays a visit to the twelve-step group one night. But this time, he does not go to the program to sell meth. For the first time since it happened, he speaks honestly about his sin, admitting he committed murder in front of the group by saying he killed a "dog" that was a problem for him. Just a problem. It didn't hurt anyone, do anything dangerous, nothing. It was just an inconvenience for him. Jesse did not want to. But, for reasons he obviously could not explain, he had to.

A woman in the group, understandably, begins to harshly reprimand him for this. Jesse takes it in stride, feeling incredibly glad that someone is finally telling him what he did was wrong. But the group leader thinks otherwise. He immediately tells the woman to back off. He tells her not to judge Jesse for committing this horrible act. Jesse, finally seizing the opportunity to vent, asks him this:

"Why not?"

Taken aback, the group leader says that judgment and self-hatred are not conducive to healing from trauma. Jesse's will finally breaks. He can't take the lies and broken logic anymore. He begins to rant about judgment. What's the point of doing anything? Why even do things at all? If you just do things and nothing happens, what does it all mean? Why not have consequences for our actions?

The group leader pushes back further, telling him that beating himself up over it will not allow him to heal. Jesse, his guilt and shame turning to rage, claps the group leader back personally. He asks the group leader if he forgave himself for once backing over his own daughter with his truck while high.[386] The group leader, finally, starts to display some disapproval. Jesse then goes in for the kill. He tells the group the real reason he comes—to sell them crystal meth. He menacingly turns to the group leader and asks this:

"I made you my bitch. You okay with that, huh? Do you accept?"

"No," the group leader replies, completely defeated and in shock. Jesse, finally satisfied, unloads the weight from his shoulders. "About time," he says. He then leaves, never to return.

* * *

WHAT MAKES THE PROBLEM DOG speech so powerful is that it absolutely obliterated the stupidity of self-acceptance. It totally unraveled the false notion that it is okay to not have standards for what people do. That it is okay for actions to not have consequences attached to them. Jesse Pinkman successfully, and refreshingly, flipped tolerance on its head. He did not do this in a way that was constructive to his well-being, certainly, but it completely unveiled the bullshit for all of us to see.

The sad thing is, I think we all know it's all bullshit, just like Jesse did. The reason I've been so pessimistic throughout this book about the positivity nonsense is because it doesn't focus on real problems. Happiness may be a convenient solution, but that does not mean it is the right solution.

Sometimes things need to suck before they can get better. We can't all sit around a campfire and sing "Kumbaya." We need to disagree, or complacency can set in within the culture. Once complacency sets in, anyone can come in and hijack it from us. Selective intolerance, as shown by Comparative Value Advantage, must be used to successfully coexist with our other nonobjective citizens.

Increasingly, this doesn't happen. But we don't have a reason as to why. If we all know it's bullshit, why do we still put up with it?

SELF-VALUE

In June 2011, self-help author Mel Robbins gave a TED Talk at TEDxSanFrancisco titled "How to Stop Screwing Yourself Over." It currently stands at twenty-eight million views on YouTube.[387]

During the talk, Robbins pulled research from trusted scientists. The most astounding fact of all was the fact of basic human existence. Based on the estimates from the data, Robbins told the audience the probability of any one person being born is approximately one in four hundred trillion. That's a very large number.

But it's also incredibly inaccurate and incredibly wrong.

The data Robbins cited included only the base probability of your successfully getting shot out of your mother's vagina, nothing else. Recall our conversation in Chapter Eight around tail events, the concept of abstract outcomes developed by our friend Morgan Housel. Think of your personal life and all the tail events it has contained. There may not be a lot of them because there never are. But they certainly are significant. Now, take that same methodology and multiply that across every single generation of your family. Your parents, your grandparents, your great-grandparents, and everyone beyond.

And those are just the extreme cases. There are multiple other ones that need to be considered. What if you were born in an undeveloped nation? What if you were born with a birth defect or disability? What if you didn't learn how to read? What if you were so impoverished the last fucking thing you would ever think about doing is buying a book from some wannabe, self-published author?

The odds of your birth may be one in four hundred trillion. I'm not good at math (nearly flunked college, remember?), but I would estimate the odds of you getting this far in life are exponentially lower.

Human life is the most valuable thing that exists in our universe. You're more likely to strike oil in your backyard, be struck by lightning, get abducted by aliens, or become a billionaire than you are to be alive. That's a truly astounding thing. The luck that had to take place for the bizarre reality of our consciousness and existence is the most extraordinary thing that can be perceived by human beings.

* * *

PSYCHOLOGIST SCOTT BARRY KAUFMAN KNOWS this. Kaufman does not embody the toxic self-esteem that poisons most of our popular culture. He doesn't run from the problem. He confronts it head-on and addresses the difficulties it creates and the delusions that permeate its modern meaning.

In his 2020 book *Transcend: The New Science of Self-Actualization*, Kaufman theorizes that this comes to a head when we start putting our self-esteem in front of our other needs of security, such as feeling connection to people and making sure we don't starve.

Understandably, this is a problem. When we put our own self-esteem at the center of our Needs Universe, it can easily destabilize. It's hard to argue that eating and feeling connected to something do the same thing. In his own words:[388]

> "Indeed, when self-esteem is too much of a concern relative to other needs, this is an indication that one's self-esteem has become unhealthy—highly insecure, unstable, and highly dependent on the validation of others."

Sound familiar? It does to me because that *was* me. I didn't identify with the positivity movement because there was nothing my brain could comprehend that *was* positive. I didn't love myself. In fact, I hated myself. But I still couldn't get the guts to do anything about it. Without knowing it, the reason I didn't harm or kill myself was the realization Robbins and Kaufman had. Even though I didn't like or love myself, I realized I *valued* myself.

So no, you shouldn't *always* love yourself. But you should always value yourself. It is the only way to avoid the clutches of those nefarious enough to use people as tools to shape their own lives. Loving yourself is not enough. Telling yourself you're fine no matter what you do and what the consequences are is not the answer. Telling yourself you love yourself in a mirror, regardless of if you're worthy of that praise, isn't either. Only by acknowledging your inherent value can you transcend that low-level gratification for something far greater.

Because when you look at the data, how could you not? Think again of all the obstacles you had to overcome. Your parents had to be mostly non-pieces of shit. You had to have at least one somewhat-stable income.

You had to be born relatively healthy. You were born in the most free country with the most inherent rights the world has ever known. It is not perfect, but it's more than most have ever even sniffed. You can afford access to this book. You have to be able to read in general. Put those odds in the oven at 350 for half an hour, and that's pretty much a motherfucking miracle.

And not only that, you've read this *far* into this book. That could say a lot of things. But the thing I believe outweighs all the others is that you value what you could potentially get from reading this far into a book written by a nobody with a media company that gets zero traffic and has made no money.[389] You must be seeking something to better yourself. You must agree that self-esteem, or our modern perception of it, is a little bullshit. You're making an effort. You're trying. And, in a world where not a lot of people try, where many people do things just to boost their "self-esteem," that's saying a lot.

If you do indeed value yourself, and not just shallowly "love yourself," you will inherently develop confidence and every good trait that comes with it. This cannot be done in reverse order. Like the chapters in this book, it must follow a chronology. This is the starting point. Those without a sense of self-value cannot accomplish anything. They're simply adrift, purposeless balls of bleh that are completely at the mercy of something way stronger and way beyond their level of comprehension.

However, when you value yourself, when you acknowledge that because of the sheer luck of the universe you turned out to be as un-fucked up as you are, you can discover the abilities of competence. You can pursue mastery, which is half the equation of real self-esteem, according to Kaufman. You can become something. You can build on your own inherent value to create more of it.

This is not something you should do. This is something you need to do. It's an obligation. It's a duty. It's a must. The world needs people who don't succumb to the crowd. It doesn't need any more purposeless balls of bleh. It needs people with actions, ideas, and opinions to shape discourse and drive the world forward. It needs people with values. Simply following mindlessly does nothing but add to the potential of the Mob. The great Jordan Peterson sums it up in his typical beautiful fashion:[390]

> We deserve some respect. You deserve some respect. You are important to other people, as much as to yourself. You have some vital role to play in the unfolding destiny of the world. You are, therefore, morally obliged to take care of yourself. You should take care of, help and be good to yourself the same way you would take care of, help and be good to someone you loved and valued. You may therefore have to conduct yourself habitually in a manner that allows you some respect for your own Being—and fair enough. But every person is deeply flawed. Everyone falls short of the glory of God. If that stark fact meant, however, that we had no responsibility for care, for ourselves as much as others, everyone would be brutally punished all the time. That would not be good. That would make the shortcomings of the world, which can make everyone who thinks honestly question the very propriety of the world, worse in every way. That simply cannot be the proper path forward.

Self-value is the only way out of the maw of self-esteem. It is the shunning of liking and hoping that you're a good person in favor of actually *being* a good person. It is rejecting the false notion of the rose-colored glasses in favor of seeing clearly and objectively who you are and what you need to get better at. It is letting go of the false notion our culture promotes that nothing you do matters. It is knowing the consequences of all actions and facing them with fortitude because they *all* matter.

When self-esteem takes precedence over self-value, the notion of feeling good becomes more important than *doing* good. The Two Es hijack your brain and insinuate chaos and disorder in every factor of your life. When self-value is imposed, you allow yourself to be checked. Do not know what you don't know. See if there's anything else that can be done to make you and everyone else better. If scarcity is what defines value, I'd say that's headed in the right direction.

THE ULTIMATE VALUE

I hit rock bottom in March of 2020. The beer virus had just rocked the world,[391] and I was sitting in my house on my extended spring break doing work in my dad's office. The state of the world was a horror. People were dying and getting sick in droves. Businesses were scrambling to avoid foreclosures. People in adverse financial situations were having to make life-altering decisions by the second.

But what impacted me the most (and, if I can hazard a guess, a lot of other people) was the feeling of abject and pure powerlessness. I had spent every second of my life since the moment I discovered insecurity living a lie. A lie that I completely controlled. From my motivations about my grades to the people I hung out with to the types of Four Loko I bombed on weekends in college, all of it was held up on strings by my fingers. My self-concept and perception of who I was totally resided within my control.

Until that control was robbed from me by something that was completely outside of it. When COVID-19 escaped from China and took a giant shit on the world, it completely shattered my perception of who I was. For the first time in my life, I was forced to look honestly at myself. I was forced to be truly vulnerable. I didn't like what I saw. But I couldn't look away.

My mom entered the room. She and I began talking, and my anger began to rise. My frustrations that had been building up my entire life that I hadn't been able to express were nearing a boiling point. I picked a fight with her, one that I had no business being in and much less winning. My mom defeated me decisively and swiftly, throwing my ego right back into its own vulnerability. Unable to bear it any longer, I sobbed harder than I had in my entire life. I cried like only a young man can cry in front of his mother. I cried because I was more afraid than ever. I had no idea what to do. I had no idea who I was.

I hadn't watched porn in over a year and had drastically (and thankfully, for my dick's sake) cut my masturbation down a good amount also. I felt a lot better in that regard. But the problem was, I hadn't done anything to replace it. I was just empty, which was infinitely worse. I was hollow, collapsing from the inside. There was nothing there. I was a purposeless ball of bleh. I had no identity. I had nothing.

But shortly after I apologized to my mom for being a narcissistic asshole, I remembered something. There's a concept that has been cycled throughout the realm of psychology called ego death.[392] Ego death is a complete loss of subjective self-identity, a finite separation of consciousness from where you were to who you could be. It's been cited by titans across cultures and philosophies as a crucial part of human development, ranging from Native American tribesmen to Eckhart Tolle[393] to Joseph Campbell[394] to Carl Jung.[395] My beloved Flatbush Zombies apparently experienced it and incorporated it into their name.[396]

That appealed to me. The concept of disassociating yourself from who you were, of experiencing true rebirth, of crafting a new identity opened up a new frontier of possibilities for me to see firsthand. I realized we have so many chances to be who we want to be. It's almost entirely within our control, particularly if we're lucky enough to be in this position in life. You can't make yourself invincible, but you can make yourself better.

There is only one you. If you don't value yourself above everything else, there is no possible way anything can get better. I don't care if you liked this book or want to throw it Nazi-style into a burning pyre. None of it means a fucking thing if you don't apply it with yourself at the forefront.

That's the thread that ties all of this shit together. That's why the sixth value in Chapter Three was left blank until now. If you don't get it through your head that this starts and ends with you, you won't be able to fill out the shit in the middle. And being at the opposite ends of an extreme is never a good thing.

What you do with your identity is up to you. It's your decision. Your values, the bedrock of your identity, are at the center of that decision. *That's* why you get to decide. Because you get to decide what you value. Almost no one is a victim because almost everyone has sovereignty over themselves and their decisions. We all have our circumstances, predicaments, and struggles. But so does everyone else.

And that's beautiful.

* * *

I HAVEN'T WATCHED PORNOGRAPHY SINCE October 24, 2021. I pray to God every day for that date to stay the same. My life is so much better without it.

But I know the temptations will never leave me. My life has been forever altered due to my addiction and past existence. I can hardly use social media. The two platforms I do use I only download on the weekends. I got rid of my dating apps because they reminded me too much of the thing that helped destroy my brain and my life. I can't even trust myself with a simple internet browser on my phone. Google Maps doesn't even have a place—I'll find a way around it. I have to pay for accountability blockers and on-demand counseling help on all my devices.[397]

But some positive things occurred also. I started an internet blog shortly before my breakdown to help me reinvent who I was and help me cope with the tragedy of my life. It worked. So I leaned into it harder. I expanded it into a podcast.[398] I began to form the idea for a book from the shit I wrote on my blog to hopefully help other people do the same. That finished idea is what you're reading right now.

The monsters will always reside in my closet, just like yours will. That's the thing I've realized about addiction. It never leaves you. I'll always be addicted to masturbation, pornography, and sexual deviancy. So will other people with their various vices. I'll never beat it, and neither will they.

But I do know that all of us can choose to live in spite of them. You can't be anything you want to be. But you can certainly be better than you are. Your values, your internal compass, can point you in the right direction toward your desired identity. Value Economics, the study of identity, can show you how to create your map.

Use both well. They're all we have, and all we are.

WHAT COMES AFTER

ON OCTOBER 11 OF 2021, JON GRUDEN RESIGNED AS THE HEAD football coach of the Las Vegas Raiders.[399] In a leak from an anonymous source, emails spanning from 2011 to 2018 sent by him were revealed to contain "homophobic, misogynistic, and racist" material.[400] The contents were certainly unbecoming of a head football coach, particularly one of Gruden's stature. It didn't help that he coached a team of which a good portion was black and on which the only openly gay player currently in the NFL, Carl Nassib, was on the active roster.[401]

The "homophobic, misogynistic, and racist" material contained in the emails is as follows. He called NFL Commissioner Roger Goodell a "faggot" and "a clueless anti-football pussy." He said that Goodell shouldn't have "pressured" the then–Saint Louis Rams to draft "queers," in reference to Michael Sam, a sixth-round draft pick of theirs who at the time was the first openly gay player in the NFL. Jeff Fisher, who was the coach of the Rams at the time, denied being pressured by Goodell.[402] Gruden stated that NFL players who protest the National Anthem should be fired. He specifically laid into Eric Reid, a former NFL safety who was the closest and most vocal ally of quarterback Colin Kaepernick during that saga.[403] He called former Executive Director of the NFL Players Association DeMaurice Smith, one of the most influential people in the NFL at the time, "Dumboriss Smith " and said he had "lips the size of Michelin tires." He called then–Vice President Joe Biden a "nervous clueless pussy." He also received naked photographs from disgraced former NFL Executive Bruce Allen, one photo containing two topless cheerleaders for the then–Washington Redskins, of which Allen was the general manager at the time.

This, naturally, caused problems. There are not many things worse in sports than a locker room in turmoil. When the man in charge of leading the team is caught in a position of such suspect behavior, particularly in the era we're in now, things tend to go off the rails quite quickly. Under immense fire and pressure, Gruden resigned in disgrace. He received no sympathy from anyone. He was immediately blacklisted from professional football. The Tampa Bay Buccaneers, which he led to a Super Bowl (over, ironically, the then–Oakland Raiders) in 2002, scrubbed his name from its Ring of Honor.[404] He was simultaneously erased and remembered with near ubiquity.

This type of thing is enough to drop a nuke on a team's season. But remarkably, the Raiders kept pace. They didn't fall off the rails. They won the following two games after Gruden's resignation. All seemed to be well.

Until it wasn't.

A little more than a month later, on November 2, Las Vegas Raiders star wide receiver Henry Ruggs III slammed his Chevrolet Corvette into a parked Toyota RAV4 at 3:40 in the morning. He was driving 156 MPH and collided with the Toyota at around 120. His blood-alcohol content was more than twice the legal limit.[405] He had been at a TopGolf with his girlfriend that night. He texted both his quarterback and a fellow wide receiver, Derek Carr and Hunter Renfrow, earlier that evening. He wanted them to critique his swing.[406]

In that Toyota RAV4 was a young woman named Tina Tintor. She was twenty-three years old and lived only a few blocks away. Her three-year-old golden retriever was with her. Remarkably, the collision didn't kill either of them. However, the collision left her pinned inside the car, unable to escape. In eyewitness testimony from a pedestrian, she was claimed to have been begging and screaming for help when the witness arrived at the scene. He was unable to do anything.

Tina Tintor and her golden retriever both burned to death that morning.[407] Henry Ruggs was apparently belligerent at the scene when he was taken away. His girlfriend and the mother of his child was seriously injured and taken to the hospital for emergency surgery on her arm. Ruggs was taken to court in a neck brace and wheelchair later that week and charged with two felonies. He currently faces up to fifty years in prison.[408] His life, as he knew it, is effectively over.

The professional sports world rightly grieved for Henry Ruggs following the tragedy. Henry Ruggs is, by all accounts, a good person. He didn't get into trouble. He treated people with respect. He had a charitable foundation. He took care of his family. He seemed to be a good boyfriend and a good father. He didn't deserve the grave fate he now faces.

But he still faces it. Like I said in "What Came Before," you don't get what you deserve. You get whatever you get. It doesn't matter that Henry Ruggs was any of those things or that he was a first-round draft pick or that he made millions of dollars or anything else. All that matters is that Henry Ruggs caused the death of two living things. It's not fair, but the reality is that some mistakes have bigger consequences than others. Henry Ruggs made one mistake, but that one mistake cost him everything.

Something strange happened after both of these two events. Following the leak, the world exploded. Jon Gruden was called mean names, just like those aforementioned people he called mean names in his emails. Randy Moss, a grown man and bona fide NFL legend, cried about it on national television.[409] Jon Gruden, who never before had been accused of being any of the things mentioned in the first paragraph, was automatically labeled all of them.

Following the tragedy involving Henry Ruggs, nothing of the sort happened. No one cried for Tina Tintor and her golden retriever. They were too busy crying for people far more powerful and far less helpless. The Henry Ruggs situation, remarkably, was forgotten almost as quickly as it happened. No one talks about it anymore. The same team, the same city, the same locker room, within the same month, and nothing. It seemingly isn't as important a lesson to hold up as an example as calling people mean names in an email thread with an entitled dumbass like Bruce Allen.

Maybe that person did the right thing in leaking those documents. Maybe they wanted to be virtuous. But maybe they wanted the Raiders to shed that $60 million salary over the next six years they were slated to pay Gruden too.[410] Maybe they realized the Raiders got in way over their skis by hiring a man who hadn't coached professional football in a decade and signing him to one of the most lucrative and tenured contracts the sport had ever seen only for him to underperform. Maybe they just didn't like him. Just maybe.

We should hold people accountable when they do things wrong. Just as our values tell us what is important, they also have corresponding consequences when we fail to meet those standards. Maybe Jon Gruden should have been forced out of the NFL in a blaze of shame. Maybe he deserved it.

But something strikes me as troubling when we as a society view leaked emails with mean words and naked pictures with greater severity than the murder of two living things. Henry Ruggs didn't mean to kill Tina Tintor and her golden retriever. But he did. No matter what those emails contained, it is completely and objectively better than someone killing a woman and her dog. This is the truth. Anything that says otherwise is a lie. Words can hurt. They often do. But they can't kill.

Put yourself in the shoes of both men, particularly if you're my age. How many of you have said derogatory things about somebody? Made a stereotypical comment? Sent a naked picture or video to someone? Showed others those same pictures? Probably close to all of you, myself included. But how many of you have horrifically killed someone? Probably close to none of you, myself included.

Think of how you would want to be treated in either scenario. If you can't, think of a family member or close friend. How would you want to be judged and viewed? What would you feel would be of greater benefit to your overall character and makeup as a person?

What we value is the most important question we can answer, both in the context of ourselves and the context of our society. What we prioritize is the only thing that matters. When these priorities shift, they do so at our peril.

What Came Before matters. But What Comes After is far more important. We should never change, erase, or forget the past. That's always a mistake. But it's a bigger mistake to not exchange something that is worse for something that is better. That's inexcusable. That's ignorant. That's lazy.

When we upend what we deem important, we upend society itself. And based on what has transpired during this book's writing, I don't think we can afford any more of it. We're not good at it. There is no more important question than this one. There is no more important thing to put into action than this. The non-tyrannical collective must begin with the non-tyrannical self.

Both Jon Gruden and Henry Ruggs deserve our forgiveness. So do the countless other people in the countless other scenarios that pop up seemingly every day, including the ones in this book. But more importantly, we need to take it upon ourselves to lead by example. Because if we don't, what else is there? What kind of society will we be forced to live in if there's nothing more than destroying people for whatever we deem their sins to be at the moment?

* * *

I CAME UPON THE INSPIRATION for this book when having a conversation with my mother about belief. "You guys don't really believe in anything," was her response when I asked about my generation. What a sad truth that is. But as with Jon Gruden and Henry Ruggs, the truth doesn't care about how you feel.

My ask of anyone who has read this far is simple—think about these things. Inquire about them. Ask yourself questions. Make them hard. Take an inventory, and then act upon it. Encourage as many people as you can to do the same. Be respectful of them. Ask them to be respectful of you. Don't bow to the Mob. You're not a purposeless ball of bleh. You're better than that. You're better than them.

If enough people do this, then maybe, just maybe, we can get somewhere. Maybe we're not as hopeless as I and others fear we are. Maybe things can get better. Maybe all this shit that I wrote will miraculously be worth something. And maybe your own life will be too.

ACKNOWLEDGMENTS

THIS BOOK IS A CULMINATION OF ALMOST THREE YEARS OF intense emotional and intellectual strain. There were countless times when I wanted to pull a massive "fuck it," send it all into the Nether Region, and spend my time watching cartoons or UFC. I'm glad I didn't, and all of the people following this paragraph deserve high praise for their encouragement, inspiration, and support throughout that process.

First, a massive thank you to the team at Scribe Media. I can't imagine the kind of balls it takes to both invest in and publish a book like this from someone no one has ever heard of, but I am forever grateful that you did. A special thanks goes out to Miles Rote and Eliece Pool—thank you for believing in me and telling me I could do it. Your support means the world to me.

I owe a deep gratitude to the inspiration for the introduction of this book, Chris Farley. I didn't know that when my parents brought home your "Best of *Saturday Night Live*" DVD my life would change forever. Like your friend Adam said, you ended up just like Belushi and Candy. And I can tell you that, like you said, it is indeed just dandy. Thanks for showing a fellow chubby kid from the Midwest it can get better. Love you, man. My dad's mayor.

If there was one act applied across all of our society's Fatal Flaws (and one that hopefully will be applied to ours) to ameliorate them, it would be the act of telling the truth. Telling the truth, particularly in the face of relentless opposition, is the hardest thing we can do. This, therefore, makes the people that tell it, and tell it consistently, the bravest among us. While I know none of these people personally, I want to acknowledge all of them for inspiring me and hopefully many others to tell the truth in order to take on the world and make it a better place. To Joey Bada$$, Krystal Ball, Hafeez Baoku, Glenn Beck, Russell Brand, Bill Burr, Tucker Carlson, Dave Chappelle, Alex Cooper, Colin Cowherd, Dan Crenshaw, Meechy Darko, Joey Diaz, Tim Dillon, Erick Arc Elliot, Saagar Enjeti, Enes Kanter Freedom, Lex Fridman, Tulsi Gabbard, David Goggins, Glenn Greenwald, Greg Gutfeld, Jonathan Haidt, Cameron Hanes, Tristan Harris, Heather Heying, Andrew Huberman, Zombie Juice, Andrew Klavan, Megyn Kelly, Tim Kennedy, Michael Knowles, Michael Malice, Mark Manson, Pat McAfee, Douglas Murray, Andy Ngo, Candace Owens, Jake Paul, Logan Paul, Mikhaila Peterson, Jordan Peterson, Dave Portnoy, Joe Rogan, Dave Rubin, Abigail Schrier, Andrew Schulz, Ben Shapiro, Akaash Singh, Debra Soh, Matt Taibbi, Matt Walsh, Bret Weinstein, Eric Weinstein, Bari Weiss, Kanye West, Jocko Willink, Andrew Yang, and Zuby—thank you. You've saved me from a lot of bad shit and taught me how to own the day and open my mind. You guys are my fucking heroes.

To all of the people in the stories I told throughout this book who have injured me in one way or another—thank you. Through the suffering I endured, I've become invincible. Nothing can hurt me now. I hope you have found or are on your way to finding the peace that is slowly finding me.

A massive thank you goes out to my professional network, all of whom have supported me immensely throughout my time navigating both that world and this one. To Carly Beitman, John Chaves, Trey DeJohn, Abby Raftery, Maudee Samarrippas, Luis Sanchez, Miranda Silva, and Tim Stansky—thank you for your excellent leadership, management, and mentorship. Additionally, a special shoutout goes to these colleagues—Audrey Bagarus, Jennifer Booher, Olivia Chamness, Julianna Cox, Cayman Hardy, Bristyn Leasure, Kelly Look, Pat Masi, Sara Miller, Kevin Ramos, Kristin Ratermann, Nick Ricci, Alexandria Quinn, Taylor Robichaud, Monika Schulz, Sam Vancia, and Kayla

Ventura. I'm grateful to consider all of you not just coworkers but friends. Finally, Lily Alten, Paul Hooker, and Luke Sims deserve praise for both their influence on me and the special needs community with the work they are doing with RallyCap Sports—it is nothing short of valiant.

I would be remiss if I didn't thank the various coaches, professors, and teachers I've had over the years. I was fortunate to have many who were instrumental in the foundation of my life and, therefore, my values. Many thanks goes out to Alexandra Bee, Holly Botos, Jared Cecchetti, Seth Cramer, Mike Elder, Paul Eldridge, Doug Farren, Kim Fitch, Melissa Gadomski, Jessica Hall, Todd Kacher, Lauren Kume, Jim Mulgrew, Jim O'Leary, Jason Ochs, Brianne Reinhard, Paul Reeder, Greg Rowe, Mike Ryan, Steve Salopek, Marc Smith, Jim Strang, and James Violand for the profound influence you all had on my life. A special thanks goes out to the wonderful folks who instructed me in English throughout my time; you formed my foundation and love for the written word, which was (hopefully) reflected in this book. These people—Kelly Getz, Nancy King, Lisa Mauser, Heather Pelphrey, and Preston Postle—all deserve phenomenal praise.

If there is one person who deserves outsized credit for this book's existence and (again, hopefully) quality, it would be Leisa McClellan. This wonderful woman instructed me in my AP Language Arts courses my final two years of high school and, quite frankly, whooped both my ass and writing into shape. It is in large part due to her patience, support, and tutelage that this book came into being. She represents the best of us, and I am forever indebted to her. Thank you.

I'm a horrifically damaged, flawed, and fucked-up person. I'm very difficult to get along with and understand. That said, my closest friends deserve all the credit in the world for putting up with me. To Lanay Brentley, Mara Enderbury, Dillon Franciscus, Sam Gerak, Taylor Johnson, Adrian Price, Hope Robinson, Hannah Stewart, and Nader Zidan—thanks guys, I love you.

To my extended family, thank you for being both my first friends and my first insight into what I wanted out of life: the Tomassis—Aunt Pam, Uncle John, Bryan, and Michele; the (other) LaCrosses—Uncle Greg, Aunt Julie, Ryan, and Crysta; the Goetzs—Aunt Debbie, Uncle Mike, Austin, and Abbey; the Snyders—Aunt Shelly, Uncle Jerry, Brenden, and Chase; the Franciscuses—Lee, Angie, and Devon; the Evanses—Dawn, Neil, Brooke, and Kristen; and finally, my grandmother, Marge Renney. I love you all, and thank you for everything.

Lastly, and most importantly, to all that taught me about values:

- My dad, Tim, for showing me the way to live through them

- My mom, Kris, for showing me the strength they embody

- My grandpa, Samuel Larry, for showing me the life that can be lived because of them

- My grandma, Lil, for showing me the love they exude

- My sister, Jackie, for showing me the bliss they provide

- And my brother, Jacob, for showing me the pounding they can take

I could go on for pages about how much you mean to me. But I know you know, and that's good enough for me. I love you all from the bottom of my heart. Thank you.

ENDNOTES

1   Chris Farley, "Matt Foley the Motivational Speaker," *Saturday Night Live*, YouTube video, May 8, 1993, https://www.youtube.com/watch?v=Xv2VIEY9-A8.

2   Selwyn Raab, Five Families (New York: Thomas Dune Books, 2005).

3   Civil Rights Act of 1964, 42 U.S.C. § 2000D et seq. (1964).

4   Akos Lada, "How Does News Feed Predict What You Want To See?" Meta, January 26, 2021, https://about.fb.com/news/2021/01/how-does-news-feed-predict-what-you-want-to-see/.

5   Adam Gollner, "XXX-Files: Who Torched the PornHub Palace?" *Vanity Fair*, January 18, 2022, https://www.vanityfair.com/style/2022/01/xxx-files-who-torched-the-pornhub-palace.

6   Encyclopedia.com, s.v. "The Evolution of the U.S. Healthcare System," accessed March 23, 2022, https://www.encyclopedia.com/science/encyclopedias-almanacs-transcripts-and-maps/evolution-us-healthcare-system.

7   Max Roser and Hannah Ritchie, "Maternal Mortality," Our World in Data, 2013, https://ourworldindata.org/maternal-mortality.

8   Max Roser, Esteban Ortiz-Ospina, and Hannah Ritchie, "Life Expectancy," Our World in Data, 2013, https://ourworldindata.org/life-expectancy.

9   Max Roser and Esteban Ortiz-Ospina, "Global Education," Our World in Data, 2016, https://ourworldindata.org/global-education.

10 Max Roser and Esteban Ortiz-Ospina, "Literacy," Our World in Data, 2016, https://ourworldindata.org/literacy.

11 Tessa E. S. Charlesworth and Mahzarin R. Banaji, "Patterns of Implicit and Explicit Attitudes: I. Long-Term Change and Stability From 2007 to 2016," *Psychological Science* 30, no. 2 (February 2019): 174–192, https://doi.org/10.1177/0956797618813087.

12 Jean M. Twenge, "Increases in Depression, Self-Harm, and Suicide Among U.S. Adolescents After 2012 and Links to Technology Use: Possible Mechanisms," *Psychiatric Research & Clinical Practice* 2, no. 1 (March 2020): 19–25, https://doi.org/10.1176/appi.prcp.20190015

13   Des Spence, "Bad Medicine: The rise and rise of antidepressants," *The British journal of general practice: the journal of the Royal College of General Practitioners* vol. 66,652 (2016): 573. doi:10.3399/bjgp16X687793.

14   Aisha Chottani, Greg Hastings, John Murnane, and Florian Neuhaus, "Distraction or Disruption? Autonomous Trucks Gain Ground in US Logistics," McKinsey and Company, December 10, 2018, https://www. mckinsey.com/industries/travel-logistics-and-infrastructure/our-insights/ distraction-or-disruption-autonomous-trucks-gain-ground-in-us-logistics.

15   Bruce Einhorn, Siegfried Alegado, and Ditas B. Lopez, "Empathetic Robots Are Killing Off the World's Call-Center Industry," *Bloomberg*, March 17, 2021, https://www.bloomberg.com/news/articles/2021-03-16/ artificial-intelligence-chatbots-threaten-call-center-industry-human-operators.

16   Mark Gold, "The Role of Alcohol, Drugs, and Deaths of Despair in the U.S.'s Falling Life Expectancy," *Missouri Medicine* 11, no. 2 (March–April 2020): 99–101, https://www. ncbi.nlm.nih.gov/pmc/articles/PMC7144704/.

17   Elizabeth Arias, Betzaida Tejada-Vera, Farida Ahmad, and Kenneth Kochanek, "Provisional Life Expectancy Estimates for 2020," Vital Statistics Rapid Release 015 (July 2021), https://www.cdc.gov/nchs/data/vsrr/vsrr015-508.pdf.

18   Michael Bang Peterson, Mathias Osmundsen, and Kevin Arceneaux, "The 'Need for Chaos' and Motivations to Share Hostile Political Rumors," *PsyArXiv*, forthcoming, doi:10.31234/osf.io/6m4ts.

19   *I Am Chris Farley*, directed by Brent Hodge and Derik Murray (Canada: Network Entertainment, 2015).

20   Tom Farley Jr. and Tanner Colby, *The Chris Farley Show: A Biography in Three Acts* (New York: Viking, 2008), 109.

21   James Barron, "Chris Farley, 33, a Versatile Comedian-Actor," *The New York Times*, December 19, 1997, https://www.nytimes.com/1997/12/19/us/chris-farley-33-a-versatile-comedian-actor.html.

22   Chris Nashawaty, "Chris Farley's Sad, Drug-Fueled Final Days", EW, January 9, 1998, https://ew.com/article/1998/01/09/chris-farleys-sad-drug-fueled-final-days/.

23   DMX, "Ruff Rider's Anthem," written by Earl Simmons and Kasseem Dean, track 2 on *It's Dark and Hell Is Hot*, Ruff Ryders/Def Jam, released May 5, 1998.

24   *Merriam-Webster*, s.v. "value," accessed March 23, 2022, https://www.merriam-webster. com/dictionary/value.

25   *Merriam-Webster*, s.v. "economics," accessed March 23, 2022, https://www.merriam-webster.com/dictionary/economics.

26   U.S. Const. amends. I–X.

27   *Forrest Gump*, directed by Robert Zemeckis (Los Angeles, CA: The Tisch Company, 1994).

28   Chris Farley, "The Chris Farley Show with Jeff Daniels," *Saturday Night Live*, YouTube video, October 5, 1991, https://www.youtube.com/watch?v=iK-04wOy2BM.

29   "Green Day Discography," AllMusic, accessed March 23, 2022, https://www.allmusic.com/artist/green-day-mn0000154544/discography.

30   Martin Cizmar, "Oral History: Green Day's 'Longview,'" *Willamette Week*, February 4, 2014, https://www.wweek.com/portland/article-21941-oral-history-green-days-longview.html.

31   Chris Mundy, "Green Day: Best New Band," *Rolling Stone*, January 26, 1995, https://www.rollingstone.com/music/music-news/green-day-best-new-band-246152/.

32   "1994 Grammy Winners: 37th Annual Grammy Awards (1994)," Recording Academy Grammy Awards, https://www.grammy.com/awards/37th-annual-grammy-awards.

33   "Best Singles of 1994," *Rolling Stone*, https://web.archive.org/web/20100723004927/http://www.rocklistmusic.co.uk/rolling.htm#94.

34   Green Day, "Longview Lyrics," Genius.com, January 28, 1994, https://genius.com/Green-day-longview-lyrics.

35   VH1, "Green Day—*Dookie*," Ultimate Albums, YouTube video, March 17, 2002, https://www.youtube.com/watch?v=N2jvcr1qUkA.

36   *Shane*, directed by George Stevens (Hollywood, CA: Paramount Pictures, April 23, 1953).

37   Lee Ann Potter and Wynell Schamel, "The Homestead Act of 1862," *Social Education* 61, no. 6 (October 1997): 359–364.

38   *Shane*, directed by George Stevens (Hollywood, CA: Paramount Pictures, April 23, 1953).

39   *Shane*, directed by George Stevens (Hollywood, CA: Paramount Pictures, April 23, 1953).

40   "Factors of Production—The Economic Lowdown Podcast & Transcript," Federal Reserve Bank of St. Louis, August 22, 2012, https://www.stlouisfed.org/education/economic-lowdown-podcast-series/episode-2-factors-of-production.

41   Erica York and Clifton Painter, "Sources of Personal Income, Tax Year 2018", Tax Foundation, August 19, 2021, https://taxfoundation.org/publications/sources-of-personal-income-in-the-united-states/.

42   *Encyclopaedia Britannica Online*, s.v. "Microsoft Corporation," by Gregg Pascal Zachary and Mark Hall, last modified November 12, 2020, https://www.britannica.com/topic/Microsoft-Corporation.

43   Matt Weinberger, "WHERE ARE THEY NOW? What Happened to the People in Microsoft's Iconic 1978 Company Photo," *Business Insider*, January 26, 2019, https://www.businessinsider.com/microsoft-1978-photo-2016-10.

44   "Prospering in the Pandemic: The Top 100 Companies," *Financial Times*, June 18, 2020, https://www.ft.com/content/844ed28c-8074-4856-bde0-20f3bf4cd8f0.

45   Nitin Lahoti, "Uber Business Model Explained: From Start to Finish," MobiSoft blog, January 2, 2019, https://mobisoftinfotech.com/resources/blog/uber-business-model-explained/.

46   Dan Blystone, "The Story of Uber," Investopedia, September 19, 2021, https://www.investopedia.com/articles/personal-finance/111015/story-uber.asp.

47   Fidelity Learning Center, "Investing in IPOs and Other Equity New Issue Offerings: What Is an IPO?" Fidelity, accessed March 23, 2022, https://www.fidelity.com/learning-center/trading-investing/trading/investing-in-ipos.

48   Annie Palmer, "Uber and Lyft Close at Record Lows as Investor Skepticism Grows around Recent IPOs," CNBC, October 1, 2019, https://www.cnbc.com/2019/10/01/uber-closes-at-record-low-worth-less-than-50-billion.html.

49   Becky Peterson, "Uber Wanted to IPO with a $120 Billion Valuation But Ran into Trouble When Some of Its Biggest Shareholders Held Out For a Lower Price," *Business Insider*, May 16, 2019, https://www.businessinsider.com/ubers-desired-120-billion-ipo-valuation-scared-off-big-shareholders-2019-5.

50   Erick Burgueno Salas, "Leading Ride-Hailing Companies in U.S. by Market Share 2017–2021," Statista, October 20, 2021, https://www.statista.com/statistics/910704/market-share-of-rideshare-companies-united-states/.

51   Corrie Driebusch and Maureen Farrell, "Uber Prices IPO at $45 a Share," *The Wall Street Journal*, May 9, 2019, https://www.wsj.com/articles/uber-prepares-for-ipo-at-midpoint-of-target-range-or-lower-11557422774.

52   *Reuters*, "Factbox: The Biggest U.S. IPOs of All Time," *Reuters*, November 10, 2021, https://www.reuters.com/business/biggest-us-ipos-all-time-2021-11-10/.

53   Mike Isaac, Michael J. de la Merced, and Andrew Ross Sorkin, "How the Promise of a $120 Billion Uber IPO Evaporated," *The New York Times*, May 15, 2019, https://www.nytimes.com/2019/05/15/technology/uber-ipo-price.html.

54   Kate Conger, "Uber Founder Travis Kalanick Leaves Board, Severing Last Tie," *The New York Times*, December 24, 2019, https://www.nytimes.com/2019/12/24/technology/uber-travis-kalanick.html.

55   "Our History," U.S. Steel, https://www.ussteel.com/about-us/history.

56   Jacob Davidson, "The 10 Richest People of All Time," *Money*, July 30, 2015, https://money.com/the-10-richest-people-of-all-time-2/#:~:text=That%20sum%20equates%20to%20about,to%20%24372%20billion%20in%202014.

57   "The World's Real-Time Billionaires List," *Forbes*, accessed March 23, 2022, https://www.forbes.com/real-time-billionaires/#4338b7aa3d78.

58 Katy George, "This Is a Now or Never Moment to Make US Manufacturing More Competitive," McKinsey Global Institute, May 19, 2021, https://www.mckinsey.com/mgi/overview/in-the-news/this-is-a-now-or-never-moment-to-make-us-manufacturing-more-competitive.

59 "United States Steel Corporation Stock," *Yahoo! Finance*, accessed March 23, 2022, https://finance.yahoo.com/quote/X/.

60 Kimberly Amadeo, "2008 Financial Crisis: Causes, Costs, and Whether It Could Happen Again," *The Balance*, last modified February 10, 2022, https://www.thebalance.com/2008-financial-crisis-3305679.

61 Frank Olito, "The Rise and Fall of Blockbuster," *Business Insider*, August 20, 2020, https://www.businessinsider.com/rise-and-fall-of-blockbuster.

62 *Encyclopaedia Britannica Online*, s.v. "Netflix," by William L. Hosch, last modified March 16, 2022, https://www.britannica.com/topic/Netflix-Inc.

63 Minda Zetlin, "Blockbuster Could Have Bought Netflix for $50 Million, But the CEO Thought It Was a Joke," *Inc.*, September 20, 2019, https://www.inc.com/minda-zetlin/netflix-blockbuster-meeting-marc-randolph-reed-hastings-john-antioco.html.

64 "Netflix," Market Cap, accessed March 23, 2022, https://companiesmarketcap.com/netflix/marketcap/.

65 Danielle Garrand, "The Last Blockbuster in the World Will Soon Be Available to Rent on Airbnb—for Just $4 a Night," CBS News, August 12, 2020, https://www.cbsnews.com/news/last-blockbuster-airbnb-4-dollars-night/.

66 Rebecca Aydin, "The History of WeWork—From Its First Office in a SoHo Building to Pushing Out CEO and Cofounder Adam Neumann," *Business Insider*, October 22, 2019, https://www.businessinsider.com/wework-ipo-we-company-history-founder-story-timeline-adam-neumann-2019-8.

67 Rosemary Carlson, "The Fixed and Variable Costs of a Small Business," *The Balance: Small Business*, November 9, 2021, https://www.thebalancesmb.com/a-guide-to-fixed-and-variable-costs-of-doing-business-393479.

68 Alex Sherman, "WeWork's $47 Billion Valuation Was Always a Fiction Created by SoftBank," CNBC, October 22, 2019, https://www.cnbc.com/2019/10/22/wework-47-billion-valuation-softbank-fiction.html.

69 Annie Palmer, "WeWork's Adam Neumann Wants to Live Forever, Be King of the World and The First Trillionaire, Says Report," CNBC, September 18, 2019, https://www.cnbc.com/2019/09/18/weworks-neumann-wants-to-live-forever-and-be-the-first-trillionaire.html.

70 Michael Kaplan, "The Shocking and Rude Ways WeWork's Ex-CEO Adam Neumann Treated Staff," *New York Post*, July 17, 2021, https://nypost.com/2021/07/17/the-shocking-ways-weworks-ex-ceo-adam-neumann-treated-staff/.

71 Edward Helmore, "WeWork Founder Adam Neumann Received $445M Payout in Exit Package," *The Guardian*, May 27, 2021, https://www.theguardian.com/business/2021/may/27/wework-founder-adam-neumann-enormous-exit-package.

72 Theron Mohamed, "WeWork's Value Plunges More Than 80% to Below $5 billion Last Quarter, SoftBank Says. Here's Why That's a Staggering Drop," *Market Insider*, November 8, 2019, https://markets.businessinsider.com/news/stocks/softbank-wework-valuation-5-billion-staggering-drop-2019-11-1028673855.

73 *The Wolf of Wall Street*, directed by Martin Scorsese (Los Angeles, CA: Paramount Picture, 2013).

74 Sabrina Nawaz, "To Achieve Big Goals, Start with Small Habits," Harvard Business Review, January 20, 2020, https://hbr.org/2020/01/to-achieve-big-goals-start-with-small-habits.

75 University College London, "Humans are Hard-*Wired* to Follow the Path of Least Resistance," *Science Daily*, February 21, 2017, https://www.sciencedaily.com/releases/2017/02/170221101016.htm.

76 Jocko Willink, *Discipline Equals Freedom: Field Manual* (New York: St. Martin's Press, 2017), 68.

77 *The Goonies*, directed by Richard Donner (Los Angeles, CA: Warner Bros., 1985).

78 *Merriam-Webster*, s.v. "constructive," accessed March 23, 2022, https://www.merriam-webster.com/dictionary/constructive.

79 *Merriam-Webster*, s.v. "destructive," accessed March 23, 2022, https://www.merriam-webster.com/dictionary/destructive.

80 *Merriam-Webster*, s.v. "habitual," accessed March 23, 2022, https://www.merriam-webster.com/dictionary/habitual.

81 *Merriam-Webster*, s.v. "sporadic," accessed March 23, 2022, https://www.merriam-webster.com/dictionary/sporadic.

82 Robert Robert, "Nothing Gold Can Stay," in *The Poetry of Robert Frost*, (New York: Henry Holt and Company, 1923), line 8.

83 Center for Women's Health, "The Benefits of a Healthy Sex Life," Oregon Health and Science University, accessed March 23, 2022, https://www.ohsu.edu/womens-health/benefits-healthy-sex-life.

84 *Merriam-Webster*, s.v. "controllable," accessed March 23, 2022, https://www.merriam-webster.com/dictionary/controllable.

85 *Merriam-Webster*, s.v. "uncontrollable," accessed March 23, 2022, https://www.merriam-webster.com/dictionary/uncontrollable.

86 Greg Lukianoff and Jonathan Haidt, *The Coddling of the American Mind* (New York: Penguin Press, 2018).

87 Brad Stone, *The Everything Store* (New York: Little, Brown and Company, 2013).

88 Mark Manson, *The Subtle Art of Not Giving a Fuck* (New York: Harper, 2016).

89 *Shane*, directed by George Stevens (Hollywood, CA: Paramount Pictures, April 23, 1953).

90 Plain Dealer Staff, "Chardon High School Shooting: A Guide to What Happened and How Word Spread," *Cleveland Plain Dealer*, last modified January 12, 2019, https://www.cleveland.com/metro/2012/02/chardon_high_school_shooting_a_1.html.

91 CNN Wire Staff, "Prosecutor: Suspect Admitted to Shootings at School," CNN, February 28, 2012, https://www.cnn.com/2012/02/28/justice/ohio-school-shooting/index.html.

92 Dan Lieberman and Christina Ng, "Ohio School Shooter Allegedly Killed Ex-Girlfriend's New Boyfriend, Students Tell ABC News," ABC News, March 2, 2012, https://abcnews.go.com/US/ohio-school-shooting-victim-dating-tj-lanes-girlfriend/story?id=15834378#.T1fV8Hmy_cg.

93 Anna Maria Gibson and Justin Weaver, "Notorious High School Shooter T.J. Lane in Custody after Prison Escape," ABC News, September 11, 2014, https://abcnews.go.com/US/notorious-high-school-shooter-tj-lane-escapes-prison/story?id=25446686.

94 Christina Ng, "Ohio School Shooter TJ Lane Laughs, Gives Finger at His Sentencing," ABC News, March 19, 2013, https://abcnews.go.com/US/ohio-school-shooter-tj-lane-victims-families-finger/story?id=18763554.

95 "Town Hall with Alexandria Ocasio-Cortez. TRANSCRIPT: 3/29/19, All In w/ Chris Hayes," MSNBC, March 29, 2019, https://www.msnbc.com/transcripts/all-in/2019-03-29-msna1214456.

96 Lisa Friedman, "What Is the Green New Deal? A Climate Proposal, Explained," *The New York Times*, February 21, 2019, https://www.nytimes.com/2019/02/21/climate/green-new-deal-questions-answers.html.

97 Deborah D'Souza, "The Green New Deal Explained," Investopedia, last modified February 26, 2022, https://www.investopedia.com/the-green-new-deal-explained-4588463.

98 Tucker Carlson, "Tucker Carlson: Here's Why Awful Ocasio-Cortez Has a Following—and It's Not Because She's Impressive," Fox News, April 2, 2019, https://www.foxnews.com/opinion/tucker-carlson-heres-why-awful-ocasio-cortez-has-a-following-and-its-not-because-shes-impressive.

99 Tucker Carlson, "Tucker Carlson: Here's Why Awful Ocasio-Cortez Has a Following—and It's Not Because She's Impressive," Fox News, April 2, 2019, https://www.foxnews.com/opinion/tucker-carlson-heres-why-awful-ocasio-cortez-has-a-following-and-its-not-because-shes-impressive.

100 Tucker Carlson, "Tucker Carlson: Here's Why Awful Ocasio-Cortez Has a Following—and It's Not Because She's Impressive," Fox News, April 2, 2019, https://www.foxnews.com/opinion/tucker-carlson-heres-why-awful-ocasio-cortez-has-a-following-and-its-not-because-shes-impressive.

101 Andrew Yang's 2020 presidential campaign website: https://2020.yang2020.com/.

102 Kevin Sullivan, "Andrew Yang Was Groomed for a High-Paying Job at an Elite New York Law Firm. He Lasted Five Months," *The Washington Post*, October 28, 2019, https://www.washingtonpost.com/politics/2019/10/28/andrew-yang-was-groomed-high-paying-job-an-elite-law-firm-he-lasted-five-months/.

103 Joe Anuta, "Yang Describes Himself as a Serial Entrepreneur, But He Often Worked for Someone Else," *Politico*, May 1, 2021, https://www.politico.com/states/new-york/city-hall/story/2021/05/01/yang-describes-himself-as-serial-entrepreneur-but-he-often-worked-for-someone-else-1379608.

104 Venture for America's website: https://ventureforamerica.org/.

105 Andrew Yang, *Smart People Should Build Things* (New York: Harper Business, 2014).

106 Andrew Yang, *Smart People Should Build Things* (New York: Harper Business, 2014), xiv–xv.

107 Joe Rogan and Andrew Yang, "#1245: Andrew Yang," February 12, 2019, in *The Joe Rogan Experience*, podcast, 1:52:02, https://www.youtube.com/watch?v=cTsEzmFamZ8.

108 Todd Spangler, "Joe Rogan Had the No. 1 Podcast on Spotify in 2021 (Podcast News Roundup)," *Variety*, December 1, 2021, https://variety.com/2021/digital/news/joe-rogan-experience-most-popular-podcast-news-roundup-1235123361/.

109 "opportunity cost." *Dictionary.com*, accessed April 7, 2022, https://www.dictionary.com/browse/opportunity-cost.

110 Jocko Willink and Leif Babin, *The Dichotomy of Leadership: Balancing the Challenges of Extreme Ownership to Lead and Win* (New York, St. Martins Press, 2018).

111 "narcissism." *Dictionary.com*, accessed April 7, 2022, https://www.dictionary.com/browse/narcissism.

112 The Holocaust Explained, "The Aftermath of the First World War," The Wiener Holocaust Library, accessed March 23, 2022, https://www.theholocaustexplained.org/the-nazi-rise-to-power/the-effects-of-the-first-world-war-on-germany/.

113 "Research Starters: Worldwide Deaths in World War II," The National WWII Museum New Orleans, accessed March 23, 2022, https://www.nationalww2museum.org/students-teachers/student-resources/research-starters/research-starters-worldwide-deaths-world-war.

114 *Encyclopaedia Britannica Online*, s.v. "Great Leap Forward," last modified February 18, 2020, https://www.britannica.com/event/Great-Leap-Forward.

115 Norman M. Naimark, Stalin's Genocides (New Jersey: Princeton University Press, 2012).

116 Nolan McCarty, Keith T. Poole, and Howard Rosenthal, "Political Polarization and Income Inequality," SSRN, January 27, 2003, https://ssrn.com/abstract=1154098 or http://dx.doi.org/10.2139/ssrn.1154098098.

117 Center for Disease Control and Prevention, "Covid-19," accessed March 23, 2022, https://www.cdc.gov/coronavirus/2019-ncov/index.html.

118 *Ultimate Fighting Championship*, "UFC 239: Jones vs. Santos," aired July 6, 2019, https://www.espn.com/espnplus/player?id=babb948c-d5f1-457b-ac03-09f206d55772

119 James Chen, "Real Assets," Investopedia, updated May 22, 2021, https://www.investopedia.com/terms/r/realasset.asp

120 Tim Grant, "Definition of Derivative Assets," PocketSense, last modified July 27, 2017, https://pocketsense.com/definition-derivative-assets-8791705.html.

121 "The Classical Gold Standard, World Gold Council, accessed March 23, 2022, https://www.gold.org/history-gold/the-classical-gold-standard.

122 Sandra Kollen Ghizoni, "Nixon Ends Convertibility of U.S. Dollars to Gold and Announces Wage/Price Controls," Federal Reserve History, November 22, 2013, https://www.federalreservehistory.org/essays/gold-convertibility-ends.

123 Taylor Tepper, "Why Does *Money* Have Value?" *Money*, March 3, 2016, https://money.com/why-does-money-have-value/.

124 DataLab, "Federal Debt Trends over Time," USASpending.gov, accessed March 23, 2022, https://datalab.usaspending.gov/americas-finance-guide/debt/trends/.

125 Brad DeLong, "The Trillion Dollar Coin—or, More Sensibly, 10000 Hundred Million-Dollar Coins—Is the Only Way for Obama to Fulfill His Oath of Office," Grasping Reality by Brad DeLong blog, September 30, 2013, https://delong.typepad.com/sdj/2013/09/the-trillion-dollar-coin-or-more-sensibly-1000-billion-dollar-coins-is-the-only-way-for-obama-to-fulfill-his-oath-of-offi.html.

126 Marcela Escobari, "Made by Maduro: The Humanitarian Crisis in Venezuela and US Policy Responses," Brookings, February 28, 2019, https://www.brookings.edu/testimonies/made-by-maduro-the-humanitarian-crisis-in-venezuela-and-us-policy-responses/.

127 "In Venezuela, a cup of coffee now costs a million bucks," Conde Nast Traveller, July 6, 2018, https://www.cntraveller.in/story/venezuela-cup-coffee-now-costs-million-bucks/.

128 Peter Thiel and Blake Masters, *Zero to One: Notes on Startups, or How to Build the Future* (New York: Crown Business, 2014), 71.

129 John Weinberg, "The Great Recession and Its Aftermath," Federal Reserve History, November 22, 2013, https://www.federalreservehistory.org/essays/great-recession-and-its-aftermath.

130 Michael Lewis, *The Big Short: Inside the Doomsday Machine* (New York: W. W. Norton & Company, 2010).

131 *The Big Short*, directed by Adam McKay (Los Angeles, CA: Paramount Pictures, 2015).

132 Hans Wagner, "Analyzing a Bank's Financial Statements," Investopedia, updated September 13, 2021, https://www.investopedia.com/articles/stocks/07/bankfinancials.asp.

133 *Merriam-Webster*, s.v. "ethics," accessed March 23, 2022, https://www.merriam-webster.com/dictionary/ethics.

134 Johnny Cash, "I Walk The Line," track 9 on *Johnny Cash with His Hot and Blue Guitar!*, Sun Records, released May 1, 1956.

135 Quote from a poem widely attributed to Oscar Wilde.

136 *The Wolf of Wall Street*, directed by Martin Scorsese (Los Angeles, CA: Paramount Picture, 2013).

137 *Good Will Hunting*, directed by Gus Van Sant (Los Angeles, CA: Miramax Films, 1997).

138 Dave Ramsey, *The Ramsey Show*, https://www.ramseysolutions.com/shows.

139 Dave Ramsey, Financial Peace University, https://www.ramseysolutions.com/ramseyplus/financial-peace.

140 Greg McKeown, *Essentialism: The Disciplined Pursuit of Less* (New York: Currency, 2014).

141 Harry Markowitz, "Portfolio Selection," *The Journal of Finance* 7, no. 1 (March 1952), 77–91.

142 "Press Release: This Year's Laureates Are Pioneers in the Theory of Financial Economics and Corporate Finance," The Nobel Prize, October 16, 1990, https://www.nobelprize.org/prizes/economic-sciences/1990/press-release/.

143 "Systematic Risk," Corporate Finance Institute, accessed March 23, 2022, https://corporatefinanceinstitute.com/resources/knowledge/finance/systematic-risk/.

144 "Idiosyncratic Risk," Corporate Finance Institute, accessed March 23, 2022, https://corporatefinanceinstitute.com/resources/knowledge/other/idiosyncratic-risk/.

145 Sam Swenson, "Day Trading Definition: Why It Differs from Investing," *The Motley Fool*, March 8, 2022, https://www.fool.com/investing/how-to-invest/stocks/day-trading/.

146 *Encyclopaedia Britannica Online*, s.v. "Enron Scandel," by Peter Bondarenko, last modified November 30, 2021, https://www.britannica.com/event/Enron-scandal.

147 James S. Kunen, "Enron's Vision (and Values) Thing," *The New York Times*, January 19, 2002, https://www.nytimes.com/2002/01/19/opinion/enron-s-vision-and-values-thing.html.

148 "Explore Holacracy," Holacracy, accessed March 23, 2022, https://www.holacracy.org/explore.

149 Eminem, "My Name Is," written by Marshall Mathers, track 2 on *The Slim Shady LP*, Interscope, January 25, 1999.

150 "What We Live By," Zappos.com, accessed March 23, 2022, https://www.zappos.com/about/what-we-live-by.

151 Championxiii, "Becky," Spotify, track 1 on *Champion Status*, Party Label, released June 3, 2019.

152 Christopher Rosa, "The College Cheating Scandal: Everything You Need to Know," Glamour, December 28, 2020, https://www.glamour.com/story/the-lori-loughlin-and-felicity-huffman-college-cheating-scandal-is-too-fascinating.

153 *Home Alone 2: Lost in New York*, directed by Chris Columbus (Los Angeles, CA: 20th Century Fox, 1992).

154 "Hinge Fail," Instagram profile, accessed March 23, 2022, https://www.instagram.com/hingefail/?hl=en.

155 NFL on ESPN, "'Football is an honest game. It's true to life. It's a game about sharing. Football is a team game. So is life.' ~ Joe Namath," Twitter post, October 7, 2014, https://twitter.com/espnnfl/status/519453363419623425.

156 Bruno Manrique, "Steven Adams Doesn't Believe Zaza Pachulia Deserves On-Court Retaliation," Clutch Points, February 26, 2018, https://clutchpoints.com/thunder-news-steven-adams-doesnt-believe-zaza-pachulia-deserves-on-court-retaliation/.

157 "Average Humidity in Ohio," Current Results, accessed March 23, 2022, https://www.currentresults.com/Weather/Ohio/humidity-annual.php.

158 Faze Staff, "An Anvil Was About To Crush This Coyote And You Won't Believe What Happened Next. Truly Heartbreaking," Faze, accessed March 23, 2022, https://faze.ca/anvil-about-to-crush-coyote-you-wont-believe-what-happened/

159 *Pulp Fiction*, directed by Quentin Tarantino (Los Angeles, CA: Miramax Films, 1994).

160 Power of the Pen's website: https://powerofthepen.org/.

161 Eminem, "Stan," featuring Dido, track 3 on *The Marshall Mathers LP*, Interscope, released November 20, 2000.

162 *Encyclopaedia Britannica Online*, s.v. "Supply and Demand," last modified December 22, 2021, https://www.britannica.com/topic/supply-and-demand.

163 Smiljanic Stasha, "17+ Cancer Statistics and Facts," Policy Advice, March 5, 2022, https://policyadvice.net/insurance/insights/cancer-statistics/.

164 "Tradeoffs: The Currency of Decision-Making," Farnam Street, accessed March 23, 2022, https://fs.blog/tradeoffs-decision-making/.

165 "y=mx+b," Cuemath, accessed March 23, 2022, https://www.cuemath.com/geometry/y-mx-b/.

166 *Merriam-Webster*, s.v. "sacrifice," accessed March 23, 2022, https://www.merriam-webster.com/dictionary/sacrifice.

167 *Blue Mountain State*, season 2, episode 11, "Drunk Tank," directed by Jay Chandrasekhar, originally aired January 5, 2011, on Spike, https://pluto.tv/en/on-demand/series/blue-mountain-state/season/2/episode/drunk-tank-2010-2-11.

168 Fun Fact: This is a true story. I had a friend who actually puked so hard he did this once. You can read more about him in Chapter Seven.

169 *Willy Wonka and the Chocolate Factory*, directed by Mel Stuart (Los Angeles, CA: Paramount Pictures, 1971).

170 *Jurassic Park*, directed by Steven Spielberg (Universal City, CA: Universal Pictures, 1993).

171 Lisa Everson and Kim Bainbridge, "How Jeni's Splendid Ice Creams Handled a Listeria Crisis," NBC News, February 26, 2018, https://www.nbcnews.com/business/your-business/how-jeni-s-splendid-ice-creams-handled-listeria-crisis-n851336.

172 u/not_really_black, "Jack and Jill is supposed to be one of the worst movies ever. Has Adam Sandler addressed the reviews for this movie?" Reddit post, December 2, 2011, https://www.reddit.com/r/movies/comments/myeow/jack_and_jill_is_supposed_to_be_one_of_the_worst/.

173 Mark Manson, *Models* (South Carolina: CreateSpace Publishing, 2011), 77–81.

174 *Batman Begins*, directed by Christopher Nolan (Los Angeles, CA: Warner Bros. Pictures, 2005).

175 Douglas Murray, *The Madness of Crowds* (London: Bloomsbury Publishing, 2019), 256.

176 Joey Diaz and Tim Dillon, "#759—Tim Dillon," February 10, 2020, in *The Church of What's Happening Now*, podcast, 1:56:00, https://open.spotify.com/episode/24DQyW5EuuBqVvKVzzbV7s.

177 Chris Gethard and Tim Dillon, "Chris Gethard & Tim Dillon," September 20, 2016, in *Death, Sex & Money*, podcast, 00:36:21, https://www.wnycstudios.org/podcasts/deathsexmoney/episodes/chris-gethard-tim-dillon-death-sex-money.

178 Chris Distefano, Yannis Pappas, and Tim Dillon, "Tim Dillon is WILD!! | ep 169," September 23, 2020, in *History Hyenas*, podcast, 1:12:46, https://www.youtube.com/watch?v=xT039fY_dmQ.

179 Joe Rogan and Tim Dillon, "1457: Tim Dillon," April 13, 2020, in *The Joe Rogan Experience*, podcast, 3:01:00, https://open.spotify.com/episode/1i9rDq65zgW4Y606ry9d7N.

180 Joey Diaz and Tim Dillon, "#759—Tim Dillon," February 10, 2020, in *The Church of What's Happening Now*, podcast, 1:56:00, https://open.spotify.com/episode/24DQyW5EuuBqVvKVzzbV7s.

181 Jeff Dye and Tim Dillon, "Episode 74," September 4, 2019, in *Jeff Dye's Friendship Podcast*, podcast, 1:09:00, https://open.spotify.com/episode/4OEuNcTJ0MiWNXoYpemceu.

182 Joe Rogan and Tim Dillon, "1544: Tim Dillon," October 1, 2020, in *The Joe Rogan Experience*, podcast, 2:24:00, https://open.spotify.com/episode/0DoGgy3H4TVJYAHPJVJo4H.

183 Matthew Love, "10 Comedians You Need to Know," *Rolling Stone*, June 6, 2017, https://www.rollingstone.com/culture/culture-lists/10-comedians-you-need-to-know-199408/.

184 Tim Dillon, "Tim Dillon as Meghan McCain," *The Tim Dillon Show*, November 22, 2019, video, 00:00:54 https://www.youtube.com/watch?v=M4d8jWOOaCI.

185 Tim Dillon, "Interview with the Man Who Stormed the Capitol," January 7, 2021, *The Tim Dillon Show*, video, 00:01:45, https://www.youtube.com/watch?v=npFVkB1rMOc.

186 Tim Dillon, "Jeffrey Epstein's Temple Has Moved To Los Angeles To Find Work," October 31, 2019, *The Tim Dillon Show*, video, 00:02:20, https://www.youtube.com/watch?v=1wkKLEaWnDQ.

187 Megyn Kelly and Tim Dillon, "Tim Dillon on Comedy in the Trump Era, Out of Touch Celebrities, and Alex Jones—Ep. 60," February 5, 2021, in *The Megyn Kelly Show*, podcast, 02:11:00, https://twitter.com/megynkellyshow/status/1357693640764710916.

188 *The Hangover*, directed by Todd Phillips (Los Angeles, CA: Warner Bros. Pictures, 2009).

189 *Superman*, directed by Richard Donner (Los Angeles, CA: Warner Bros., 1978).

190 *The Dirt*, directed by Jeff Tremaine (Los Gatos, CA: Netflix, 2019).

191 *A Beautiful Mind*, directed by Ron Howard (Universal City, CA: Universal Studios, 2001).

192 Aaron Holmes, "Instagram's Following Activity Tab Will Disappear This Week," *Business Insider*, October 7, 2019, https://www.businessinsider.com/instagram-following-activity-tab-removed-report-2019-10.

193 *The Departed*, directed by Martin Scorsese (Los Angeles, CA: Warner Bros. Pictures, 2006).

194 Lauren Goode and David Pierce, "The WIRED Guide to the iPhone," *Wired*, December 7, 2018, https://www.wired.com/story/guide-iphone/.

195 "Facts about Microsoft," Microsoft.com, accessed March 23, 2022, https://news.microsoft.com/facts-about-microsoft/.

196 A compilation of Billy Mays memes: https://knowyourmeme.com/memes/people/billy-mays.

197 Jocko Willink, *Discipline Equals Freedom: Field Manual* (New York: St. Martin's Press, 2017), 2.

198 *Goodfellas*, directed by Martin Scorsese (Los Angeles, CA: Warner Bros., 1990).

199 "How Much Sleep Do I Need?" Centers for Disease Control and Prevention, accessed March 23, 2022, https://www.cdc.gov/sleep/about_sleep/how_much_sleep.html.

200 *The Wolf of Wall Street*, directed by Martin Scorsese (Los Angeles, CA: Paramount Picture, 2013).

201 "Super Saiyan," Dragon Ball Wiki, accessed March 23, 2022, https://dragonball.fandom.com/wiki/Super_Saiyan.

202 *300*, directed by Zack Snyder (Los Angeles, CA: Warner Bros. Pictures, 2007).

203 *Pulp Fiction*, directed by Quentin Tarantino (Los Angeles, CA: Miramax Films, 1994).

204 *The Mandalorian*, season 1, episode 1, "Chapter 1: *The Mandalorian*," directed by Dave Filoni, released November 12, 2019, on Disney+, https://www.disneyplus.com/series/the-mandalorian/3jLIGMDYINqD.

205 "Alexandra Cooper," Boston University Athletics, 2015, https://goterriers.com/sports/womens-soccer/roster/alexandra-cooper/3465.

206 Alexandra Cooper and Sofia Franklyn, "1—Sext Me So I Know It's Real," October 2018, in *Call Her Daddy*, podcast, 00:36:17, https://open.spotify.com/episode/6WeScBow0GCkh4eCN0Uw9f.

207 Caroline Warnock, "Peter Nelson, Sofia Franklyn's Boyfriend: 5 Fast Facts You Need To Know," Heavy, August 10, 2020, https://heavy.com/news/2020/05/peter-nelson-sofia-franklyn/.

208 Dave Portnoy, "81—Daddy Speaks," May 17, 2020, in *Call Her Daddy*, podcast, 00:29:03 https://open.spotify.com/episode/62fPXwVyiBZAEiRZauN4HR

209 Alexandra Cooper, "The Truth about *Call Her Daddy*," *Call Her Daddy*, YouTube video, May 22, 2020, https://www.youtube.com/watch?v=QgYqqSzkvgc.

210 W. Chan Kim and Renee Mauborgne, *Blue Ocean Strategy, Expanded Edition: How to Create Uncontested Market Space and Make the Competition Irrelevant* (Boston: Harvard Business Review Press, 2015).

211 *Casino*, directed by Martin Scorsese (Universal City, CA: Universal Pictures, 1995).

212 Alexandra Cooper and Sofia Franklyn, "3—The Gluck Gluck 9000," October 3, 2018, in *Call Her Daddy*, podcast, 00:29:39, https://open.spotify.com/episode/3hSbq89TaNnENs5BAe3253.

213 Dave Portnoy (@stoolpresidente), ". @scooterbraun has entered the chat," Twitter post, May 25, 2020, https://twitter.com/stoolpresidente/status/1264931229285130246?lang=en.

214 Kirsten Fleming, "Sofia Franklyn: '*Call Her Daddy*' Co-Host Alexandra Cooper Stabbed Me in the Back," *New York Post*, May 19, 2020, https://nypost.com/2020/05/19/call-her-daddy-host-sofia-franklyn-breaks-silence-on-controversy/.

215 Dave Portnoy (@stoolpresidente), "HEY NELSON! DIDN'T ANYONE TELL YOU WHO I AM? I AM THE FUCKING NETWORK!," Twitter post, May 18, 2020, https://twitter.com/stoolpresidente/status/1262472062255468546?lang=en.

216 Ariel Shapiro, "Spotify Mints Alexandra Cooper as Another Top-Earning Podcaster with $60 Million 'Call Her Daddy' Deal," *Forbes*, June 15, 2021, https://www.forbes.com/sites/arielshapiro/2021/06/15/spotify-mints-alexandra-cooper-as-another-top-earning-podcaster-with-60-million-call-her-daddy-deal-barstool-joe-rogan/?sh=2bd8783437f3.

217 Maria Cramer, "Joe Rogan Strikes an Exclusive, Multiyear Deal With Spotify," *The New York Times*, July 1, 2021, https://www.nytimes.com/2020/05/20/business/media/joe-rogan-spotify-contract.html.

218 Sofia Franklyn, "1: SLOOT: A SHORT AUTOBIOGRAPHY," October 9, 2020, in *Sofia With An F*, podcast, 00:36:27, https://open.spotify.com/episode/1csCtQBnbKVYF8TOkdvOhQ.

219 Cheyenne Roundtree, "Podcaster Sofia Franklyn Loses Advertisers after Foul-Mouthed Attack on Disney Star Who Didn't Answer Her DM," *The Daily Beast*, May 26, 2021, https://www.thedailybeast.com/ex-call-her-daddy-podcaster-sofia-franklyn-loses-advertisers-after-foul-mouthed-attack-on-mollee-gray.

220 George Carlin, "Seven Words You Can Never Say on Television," track 9 on *Class Clown*, recorded May 27, 1972, at Santa Monica Civic Auditorium, Atlantic, released September 29, 1972, https://www.youtube.com/watch?v=lqvLTJfYnik.

221 *Shark Tank*, season 3, episode 13, "Episode 313," produced by Mark Burnett, originally aired May 4, 2012, on ABC, https://www.nbc.com/shark-tank/video/313/9000115192.

222 Madeline Stone, "What It Was Like to Hear Jeff Bezos' Amazon Pitch in 1994," *Business Insider*, November 20, 2014, https://www.businessinsider.com/what-it-was-like-to-hear-jeff-bezos-pitch-amazon-in-1994-2014-11.

223 U.S. Securities and Exchange Commission, "Insider Trading," Investor.org, accessed March 23, 2022, https://www.investor.gov/introduction-investing/investing-basics/glossary/insider-trading.

224 U.S. Securities and Exchange Commission, "THERAPEUTICSMD, INC.: 2013 INSIDER TRADING POLICY," accessed March 23, 2022, https://www.sec.gov/Archives/edgar/data/25743/000138713113000737/ex14_02.htm.

225 "KFC and Feits on *Call Her Daddy*, Dave Portnoy, and Peter Nelson—KFC Radio," *KFC Radio*, YouTube video, May 19, 2020, https://www.youtube.com/watch?v=Yz8B6nwev9Y.

226 *Encyclopaedia Britannica Online*, s.v. "Diminishing Returns," last modified December 27, 2017, https://www.britannica.com/topic/diminishing-returns.

227 Ford Motor Company, "Henry Ford Biography,"Ford.com, 2020, https://corporate.ford. com/articles/history/henry-ford-biography.html.

228 Eric Niiler, "How the Second Industrial Revolution Changed Americans' Lives," History.com, January 25, 2019, https://www.history.com/news/ second-industrial-revolution-advances.

229 History.com Editors, "Ford's Assembly Line Starts Rolling," History.com, last modified November 30, 2021, https://www.history.com/this-day-in-history/ fords-assembly-line-starts-rolling.

230 *The Lord of the Rings: The Two Towers*, directed by Peter Jackson (Burbank, CA: New Line Cinema, 2002).

231 Literally any segment with Joel Klatt, usually on Wednesdays. Hilarious.

232 John Misachi, "10 Largest Universities in the United States," World Atlas, October 14, 2021, https://www.worldatlas.com/articles/10-largest-universities-in-the-united-states. html.

233 Jonathan Edwards, "Columbus Ranks Fifth in the World for Quality of Life," NBC4i. com, last modified January 29, 2020, https://www.nbc4i.com/news/local-news/ columbus-ranks-fifth-in-the-world-for-quality-of-life/.

234 "McCoy Center," VYMaps.com, accessed March 23, 2022, https://vymaps.com/US/ Mccoy-Building-703417019678547/.

235 Michaila Hancock, "Pentagon: the World's Largest Office Building—In Infographics," *Architects' Journal*, August 27, 2015, https://www.architectsjournal.co.uk/news/ pentagon-the-worlds-largest-office-building-in-infographics.

236 City of Columbus, "Economic Development: Fortune 1000 Companies,"Columbus. gov, accessed March 23, 2022, https://www.columbus.gov/development/ economic-development/Fortune-1000-Companies/.

237 Lauren Zyber, "The Top Columbus Startups and Tech Companies To Watch in 2021," Purpose Jobs, December 23, 2020, https://www.purpose.jobs/blog/ top-columbus-startups-tech-companies.

238 Nancy Dahlberg, "Kevin O'Leary: Why Business Is War, Sales People Rule and *Shark Tank* Rocks," *Miami Herald*, November 7, 2014, https://miamiherald.typepad.com/the- starting-gate/2014/11/kevin-oleary-aka-mr-wonderful.html.

239 Ed Mylett, "Who is Ed Mylett?" YouTube video, September 29, 2018, https://www. youtube.com/watch?v=_I6E7JuBXIM.

240 Grant Cardone, "*5 Steps to Becoming a Millionaire*—Grant Cardone Trains His Sales Team LIVE," YouTube video June 7, 2018, https://www.youtube.com/ watch?v=Iq4qASI1Fok.

241 U.S. Securities and Exchange Commission, "Pyramid Schemes," Investor.gov, accessed March 23, 2022, https://www.investor.gov/introduction-investing/investing-basics/glossary/pyramid-schemes.

242 *Encyclopaedia Britannica Online*, s.v. "Jonestown," by Alison Eldridge, last modified November 11, 2021, https://www.britannica.com/event/Jonestown.

243 "About LinkedIn," LinkedIn, accessed March 23, 2022, https://about.linkedin.com/.

244 Joe Rogan and Bret Weinstein, and Heather Heying, "Joe Rogan—The Science of Hotness vs. Beauty," YouTube video, February 20, 2018, https://www.youtube.com/watch?v=PvQrFBOyDs0.

245 RallyCap Sports website: https://www.rallycapsports.org/.

246 "Caring For Head, Neck And Spinal Injuries," in *American Red Cross Lifeguarding Guide* (The American National Red Cross, 2016) 342–350, https://highsierrapools.com/wp-content/uploads/2020/04/LG_PM_digital.pdf.

247 "2021 Jeep Wrangler," *IIHS*, accessed March 23, 2022, https://www.iihs.org/ratings/vehicle/jeep/wrangler-4-door-suv/2021.

248 John F. Kennedy, "JFK Moon Speech—Rice Stadium," NASA, September 12, 1962, https://er.jsc.nasa.gov/seh/ricetalk.htm.

249 Geoffrey Wawro, "Everything You Know About How World War I Ended Is Wrong," *Time*, September 26, 2018, https://time.com/5406235/everything-you-know-about-how-world-war-i-ended-is-wrong/ and Victor Davis Hanson, "Why America Was Indispensable to the Allies' Winning World War II," *National Review*, May 14, 2015, https://www.nationalreview.com/2015/05/why-america-was-indispensable-allies-winning-world-war-ii-victor-davis-hanson/.

250 "Olympic Games Records," World Athletics, accessed March 23, 2022, https://www.worldathletics.org/records/by-category/olympic-games-records.

251 Yes, there's literally an entire segment of their website dedicated to this Headassery: https://www.buzzfeed.com/tag/life-hacks.

252 Brittain Ladd, "Ron Johnson Killed JC Penney—But He has Become One of the Brightest Minds in Retail," *Observer*, June 10, 2019, https://observer.com/2019/06/ron-johnscon-jc-penney-retail-guru/.

253 *National Lampoon's Vacation*, directed by Harold Ramis (Los Angeles, CA: Warner Bros., 1983).

254 Denzel Washington, "'Fall Forward'—Denzel Washington's Inspiring Commencement Speeches," Character Action Media, accessed March 23, 2022, https://www.characteractionmedia.com/wp-content/uploads/2019/06/D-Washington-Speech-Transcript.pdf.

255 Jordan Peterson, *12 Rules for Life: An Antidote to Chaos* (Toronto, Random House Canada, 2018), 67–85.

256 Gucci Mane, "My Shadow," Song Search, 2009, https://songsear.ch/song/Gucci-Mane/My-Shadow/1997376.

257 OutKast, *ATLiens*, Arista Records, released August 27, 1996.

258 Ashley Pointer, "Trap Music: Where It Came from and Where It's Going," Berklee Online, accessed March 23, 2022, https://online.berklee.edu/takenote/trap-music-where-it-came-from-and-where-its-going/.

259 Christina Lee, "Trap Kings: How the Hip-Hop Sub-Genre Dominated the Decade," *The Guardian*, August 13, 2015, https://www.theguardian.com/music/2015/aug/13/trap-kings-how-hip-hop-sub-genre-dominated-decade.

260 Gucci Mane and Neil Martinez-Belkin, *The Autobiography of Gucci Mane* (New York: Simon & Schuster Paperbacks, 2017).

261 Yaren İlayda, "All The Beatles Core Albums in Order According to Chart Ranks," Metal Shout, January 21, 2022, https://metalshout.com/all-the-beatles-core-albums-in-order-according-to-chart-ranks/.

262 Gucci Mane, "Freaky Gurl," written by Radric Davis, Rick James, and Alonzo Miller, track 5 on *Hard to Kill*, Big Cat/Atlantic, released September 11, 2007.

263 The price of Microsoft when I did this calculation was $300.99 per share.

264 The price of Apple when I did this calculation was $164.12 per share.

265 Staff, "Elon Musk and Grimes: A Timeline of Their Relationship," *US Magazine*, December 6, 2021, https://www.usmagazine.com/celebrity-news/pictures/elon-musk-and-grimes-relationship-timeline/.

266 Gucci Mane, "Lemonade," written by Radric Davis and Shondrae Crawford, track 6 on *The State vs. Radric Davis*, Warner Bros./Asylum, released December 7, 2009.

267 The price of Tesla when I did this calculation was $959.05 per share.

268 Brene Brown, *Daring Greatly: How the Courage to Be Vulnerable Transforms the Way We Live, Love, Parent, and Lead* (New York: Avery, 2012).

269 Erin Check, "26 Memes For People Who Love The Environment More Than They Love People," Buzzfeed, July 27, 2018, https://www.buzzfeed.com/erinchack/environment-memes.

270 Will Kenton, "Guns-and-Butter Curve," Investopedia, last modified February 28, 2021, https://www.investopedia.com/terms/g/gunsandbutter.asp.

271 *Avengers: Infinity War*, directed by Anthony Russo and Joe Russo (Burbank, CA: Walt Disney Studios Motion Pictures, 2018).

272 *The Terminator*, directed by James Cameron (Los Angeles, CA: Orion Pictures, 1984).

273 Shoutout Theo Von. Gang.

274 *Baby Boy*, directed by John Singleton (Culver City, CA: Sony Pictures Releasing, 2001).

275 Charlotte Alter, "What Does It Mean To 'Break the Internet'?," *Time*, November 12, 2014, https://time.com/3580977/kim-kardashian-break-the-internet-butt/.

276 "Aftermath," Atomic Archive, accessed March 23, 2022, https://www.atomicarchive.com/history/atomic-bombing/nagasaki/page-7.html.

277 Newark, Ohio, municipal home page: http://www.newarkohio.net/.

278 *Ma*, directed by Tate Taylor (Universal City, CA: Universal Studios, 2019).

279 Hillary Mayell, "Genghis Khan a Prolific Lover, DNA Data Implies," *National Geographic*, February 13, 2003, https://www.nationalgeographic.com/culture/article/mongolia-genghis-khan-dna.

280 Patricia Oelze, "How to Eliminate Approach Anxiety," BetterHelp, last modified December 6, 2021, https://www.betterhelp.com/advice/anxiety/how-to-eliminate-approach-anxiety/.

281 *Space Jam*, directed by Joe Pytka (Los Angeles, CA: Warner Bros., 1996).

282 *Fear and Loathing in Las Vegas*, directed by Terry Gilliam (Universal City, CA: Universal Studios, 1998).

283 Urban Dictionary, s.v. "catfished," accessed March 23, 2022, https://www.urbandictionary.com/define.php?term=catfished.

284 Elizabeth Scott, "What Causes the Freshman 15?," VeryWellMind, October 3, 2020, https://www.verywellmind.com/what-causes-the-freshman-15-3145170.

285 *Merriam-Webster*, s.v. "cockblock," accessed March 23, 2022, https://www.merriam-webster.com/dictionary/cockblock.

286 *Breaking Bad* (television show), created by Vince Gilligan, Sony Pictures Television, originally aired on AMC, January 20, 2008–September 29, 2013.

287 *Avengers: Infinity War*, directed by Anthony Russo and Joe Russo (Burbank, CA: Walt Disney Studios Motion Pictures, 2018).

288 Jocelyn Solis-Moreira, "How did we develop a COVID-19 vaccine so quickly?" Medical News Today, November 13, 2021, https://www.medicalnewstoday.com/articles/how-did-we-develop-a-covid-19-vaccine-so-quickly.

289 Jordan Friedman, "Navy SEAL Rob O'Neil Recounts bin Laden's Death," 9/11 Memorial and Museum, accessed March 23, 2022, https://www.911memorial.org/connect/blog/navy-seal-rob-oneill-recounts-bin-ladens-death.

290 Keith Huxen, "The Death of Adolf Hitler," National World War II Museum New Orleans, March 30, 2020, https://www.nationalww2museum.org/death-of-adolf-hitler.

291 *Encyclopaedia Britannica Online*, s.v. "Saddam Hussein," last modified December 26, 2020, https://www.britannica.com/biography/Saddam-Hussein.

292 Jackie Mansky, "The True Story of the Death of Stalin," *Smithsonian Magazine*, October 10, 2017, https://www.smithsonianmag.com/history/true-story-death-stalin-180965119/.

293 Flatbush Zombies, "Bounce," track 2 on *3001: A Laced Odyssey*, Glorious Dead Recordings/ADA, March 11, 2016.

294 This is not an official fact, but I am declaring it one.

295 "Glorious Dead Recordings," Discogs, accessed March 23, 2022, https://www.discogs.com/label/980524-Glorious-Dead-Recordings.

296 Flatbush Zombies, "Trade-Off," track 8 on *3001: A Laced Odyssey*, Glorious Dead Recordings/ADA, March 11, 2016.

297 Arthur M. Okun, *Equality and Efficiency: The Big Trade-Off* (Washington, D.C.: Brookings Institution Press, 2015).

298 Morgan Housel, "The Psychology of *Money*," The Collaborative Fund, June 1, 2018, https://www.collaborativefund.com/blog/the-psychology-of-money/.

299 Morgan Housel, *The Psychology of Money* (Hampshire: Harriman House Ltd, 2020).

300 *Inside Bill's Brain: Decoding Bill Gates*, directed by David Guggenheim (Los Gatos, CA: Netflix, 2019).

301 Erica M. Johnson, "Factbox: Wealth and Philanthropy of Bill and Melinda Gates," *Reuters*, May 3, 2021, https://www.reuters.com/business/retail-consumer/wealth-philanthropy-bill-melinda-gates-2021-05-03/.

302 "The World's Real-Time Billionaires List," *Forbes*, accessed March 23, 2022, https://www.forbes.com/real-time-billionaires/#4338b7aa3d78.

303 Yes, yes they would: https://www.bbc.com/news/52847648.

304 "The World's Real-Time Billionaires List," *Forbes*, accessed March 23, 2022, https://www.forbes.com/real-time-billionaires/#4338b7aa3d78.

305 Hannah Ritchie and Max Roser, "Gender Ratio," Our World in Data, June 2019, https://ourworldindata.org/gender-ratio.

306 Christina Newberry, "38 LinkedIn Statistics Marketers Should Know in 2021," HootSuite blog, January 12, 2021, https://blog.hootsuite.com/linkedin-statistics-business/.

307 Charles Lindemann, "The Wonderous Tale of a Sperm Tail," Oakland University, 2010, https://files.oakland.edu/users/lindeman/web/spermfacts.htm.

308 Will Kenton, "Okun's Law," Investopedia, last modified March 26, 2020, https://www. investopedia.com/terms/o/okunslaw.asp.

309 Zack Cooper and Hal Brands, "America Will Only Beat China When China's Regime Fails," *Foreign Policy*, March 11, 2021, https://foreignpolicy.com/2021/03/11/ america-chinas-regime-fails/.

310 Robin Fall and David Rovella, "Will India Be the Next China?" *Bloomberg*, November 4, 2021, https://www.bloomberg.com/news/articles/2021-11-05/ india-finally-moves-to-challenge-china-its-biggest-economic-rival.

311 "Leadership Actions Needed to Expedite the Administration of COVID-19 Vaccines," American Hospital Association, January 7, 2020, https://www.aha.org/ lettercomment/2021-01-07-leadership-actions-needed-expedite-administration-covid-19-vaccines.

312 David Palmer, "The Cost of The Bomb," Flinders University, accessed March 23, 2022, https://fsi-live.s3.us-west-1.amazonaws.com/s3fs-public/The_Cost_of_the_Bomb.pdf.

313 *Friday Night Lights* (television show), developed by Peter Berg, NBCUniversal Television Distribution, originally aired on NBC, October 3, 2006–February 9, 2011.

314 "NFL Founded in Canton," Pro Football Hall of Fame, January 1, 2005, https://www. profootballhof.com/news/2005/01/news-nfl-founded-in-canton/.

315 Calvin Boaz, "Mount Union: The Best College Football Program in America," *Bleacher Report*, September 11, 2010, https://bleacherreport.com/articles/458967-mount-union -the-best-college-football-program-in-america.

316 *Race*, directed by Stephen Hopkins (Toronto, ON: Entertainment One Films, 2016).

317 *Encyclopaedia Britannica Online*, s.v. "Jess Owens," last modified September 8, 2021, https://www.britannica.com/biography/Jesse-Owens.

318 Deeptesh Sen, "How with 4 Olympic Golds, Jesse Owens Ran Hitler out of His Aryan Supremacy Theory," *The Indian Express*, July 28, 2021, https://indianexpress.com/ article/research/how-with-4-olympics-golds-jesse-owens-ran-hitler-out-of-his-aryan-supremacy-theory-7425918/.

319 "Owens and The Ohio State University," The Ohio State University Library System, accessed March 23, 2022, https://library.osu.edu/site/jesseowens/ohio-state/.

320 Cory Turner, "On Location: Mansfield, Ohio's 'Shawshank' Industry," *NPR*, August 4, 2011, https://www.npr.org/2011/08/04/138986482/ on-location-mansfield-ohios-shawshank-industry.

321 "Football History vs Ohio State University from Nov 28, 1912 - Nov 20, 2021," Michigan Sate Spartan Athletics, https://msuspartans.com/sports/football/ opponent-history/ohio-state-university/145

322 Statistics from 2015 Ohio State–Michigan State game: https://www.espn.com/college-football/matchup/_/gameId/400763573.

323 Lil Wayne, "Blunt Blowin'," written by Carter, Bigram Zayas, and Matthew Arthur DelGiorno, track 2 on *Tha Carter IV*, Universal Republic, released August 29, 2011.

324 Mark Matousek, "Elon Musk Says People Need to Work 80 Hours Per Week to Change the World," *Business Insider*, November 26, 2018, https://www.businessinsider.com/elon-musk-says-80-hours-per-week-needed-change-the-world-2018-11.

325 Tiffany M. Powell-Wiley, Paul Poirier, Lora E. Burke, Jean-Pierre Després, et al., "Obesity and Cardiovascular Disease: A Scientific Statement from the American Heart Association," *Circulation* 143, no. 21 (May 2021): e984–e1010, https://doi.org/10.1161/CIR.0000000000000973.

326 Thananya Saksuriyongse, "Heart Disease and Cancer: The Top 2 Killers in the U.S.," Verisk, March 11, 2019, https://www.air-worldwide.com/blog/posts/2019/3/heart-disease-and-cancer-the-top-2-killers-in-the-u-s/.

327 "Obesity, Race/Ethnicity, and COVID-19," Centers for Disease Control and Prevention, accessed March 23, 2022, https://www.cdc.gov/obesity/data/obesity-and-covid-19.html.

328 *Forrest Gump*, directed by Robert Zemeckis (Los Angeles, CA: The Tisch Company, 1994).

329 Aja Romano, "The Great Clown Panic of 2016 Is a Hoax. But the Terrifying Side of Clowns Is Real," *Vox*, October 12, 2016, https://www.vox.com/culture/2016/10/12/13122196/clown-panic-hoax-history.

330 Yes, there's a video of this too: https://www.youtube.com/watch?v=lHP3aDuR_X0.

331 Nicholas Jasinski, "Why Did Robinhood Stop GameStop Trading? Everything You Need To Know," *Barron's*, January 29, 2021, https://www.barrons.com/articles/why-did-robinhood-stop-gamestop-trading-51611967696.

332 Teach for America home page: https://www.teachforamerica.org/.

333 "Annual Tax Rates," Ohio Department of Taxation, accessed March 23, 2022, https://tax.ohio.gov/wps/portal/gov/tax/individual/resources/annual-tax-rates.

334 I'm 100 percent confident now that he made this up. There's literally nothing I could find on it.

335 Will Kenton, "Reaganomics," Investopedia, last modified May 25, 2021, https://www.investopedia.com/terms/r/reaganomics.asp.

336 *Pinocchio*, directed by Ben Sharpsteen and Hamilton Luske (New York, NY: RKO Radio Pictures, 1940).

337 *Merriam-Webster*, s.v. "clout," accessed March 23, 2022, https://www.merriam-webster.com/dictionary/clout.

338 Urban Dictionary, s.v. "clout," accessed March 23, 2022, https://www.urbandictionary.com/define.php?term=clout.

339 *Encyclopaedia Britannica Online*, s.v. "The French Revolution," last modified September 10, 2020, https://www.britannica.com/event/French-Revolution.

340 History.com Editors, "Napoleon Bonaparte," History.com, last modified September 27, 2019, https://www.history.com/topics/france/napoleon.

341 *Joker*, directed by Todd Phillips (Los Angeles, CA: Warner Bros., 2019).

342 Edward-Isaac Dovere, "How Clinton Lost Michigan—and Blew the Election," *Politico*, December 14, 2016, https://www.politico.com/story/2016/12/michigan-hillary-clinton-trump-232547.

343 Monica Alba, "Hillary Clinton Apologizes to Coal Country Over 'Out of Business' Comments,'" NBC News, May 2, 2016, https://www.nbcnews.com/politics/2016-election/hillary-clinton-apologizes-coal-country-over-out-business-comments-n566451.

344 "Coal," World Wildlife Foundation, accessed March 23, 2022, https://wwf.panda.org/discover/knowledge_hub/teacher_resources/webfieldtrips/climate_change/coal/.

345 Mike *Bloomberg*, "Mike *Bloomberg*: Leadership, Equality in the Workplace & Donald Trump," YouTube video, December 8, 2016, https://www.youtube.com/watch?v=KI1UrUzRvEs.

346 "South Carolina Democratic Debate—CBS News," YouTube video, February 25, 2020, https://www.youtube.com/watch?v=klDbFuxmXrA.

347 "Remember What Joakim Noah Thinks of Cleveland?" CBS Chicago, August 7, 2014, https://chicago.cbslocal.com/2014/08/07/remember-what-joakim-noah-thinks-of-cleveland/.

348 Tyler Carey, "Stephen A. Smith Trolls Cleveland, Reveals He Doesn't Want LeBron James to Stay with the Cavaliers," WKYC Studios, June 29, 2018, https://www.wkyc.com/article/sports/nba/lebron-james/stephen-a-smith-trolls-cleveland-reveals-he-doesnt-want-lebron-james-to-stay-with-cavaliers/95-569332200.

349 Norman Weiss, "Stephen A. Smith, ESPN's Highest-Paid Star, Actually Earns $12 Million a Year," PrimeTimer, July 10, 2021, https://www.primetimer.com/item/Stephen-A-Smith-ESPNs-highest-paid-star-actually-earns-12-million-a-year-MMS3o9.

350 Adam Hayes, "Comparative Advantage," Investopedia, last modified October 26, 2020, https://www.investopedia.com/terms/c/comparativeadvantage.asp.

351 Swag, "hi welcome to chilis vine," YouTube video, January 12, 2018, https://www.youtube.com/watch?v=WEGCAS8nCPU.

352 Yi Wen, "China's Rapid Rise: From Backward Agrarian Society to Industrial Powerhouse in Just 35 Years," Federal Reserve Bank of St. Louis, April 11, 2016, https://www.stlouisfed.org/publications/regional-economist/april-2016/chinas-rapid-rise-from-backward-agrarian-society-to-industrial-powerhouse-in-just-35-years.

353 Ana Swanson, Catie Edmundson, and Edward Wong, "US Effort to Combat Forced Labor Targets Corporate China Ties," *The New York Times*, January 5, 2022, https://www.nytimes.com/2021/12/23/us/politics/china-uyghurs-forced-labor.html.

354 Corey Protin, Matthew Stuart, and Matt Weinberger, "Animated Timeline Shows How Silicon Valley Became a $2.8 Trillion Neighborhood," *Business Insider*, December 18, 2020, https://www.businessinsider.com/silicon-valley-history-technology-industry-animated-timeline-video-2017-5.

355 Ben Casselman, "Startup Boom in the Pandemic Is Growing Stronger," *Boston Globe*, August 19, 2021, https://www.bostonglobe.com/2021/08/19/business/startup-boom-pandemic-is-growing-stronger/.

356 Sydney Johnson, "Computer Science Degrees and Technology's Boom-and-Bust Cycle," EdSurge, April 3, 2018, https://www.edsurge.com/news/2018-04-03-computer-science-degrees-and-technology-s-boom-and-bust-cycle.

357 Marc Chagall, *America Windows*, glass, currently displayed at the Art Institute of Chicago, 1977.

358 Journalism and Media Staff, "Video Length," Pew Research Center, July 16, 2012, https://www.pewresearch.org/journalism/2012/07/16/video-length/.

359 Jordan Peterson, *12 Rules for Life: An Antidote to Chaos* (Toronto, Random House Canada, 2018), 147–161.

360 "Why does DJ Khaled scream his own name in the beginning of every his song?" Quora post, accessed March 23, 2022, https://www.quora.com/Why-does-DJ-Khaled-scream-his-own-name-in-the-beginning-of-every-his-song.

361 "Another day" is right now. Superman is the most trash superhero ever.

362 Joel Ryan, "Farley Funeral: Day the Clowns Cried," E News!, December 23, 1997, https://www.eonline.com/news/35689/farley-funeral-day-the-clowns-cried.

363 "David Spade Explains Why He Didn't Attend Chris Farley's Funeral," TipHero, accessed March 23, 2022, https://tiphero.com/david-spade-and-chris-farley.

364 John Welsh, "Chris Farley's Funeral Depicts Midwest, Hollywood Cultures," *The Journal Times*, December 24, 1997, https://journaltimes.com/news/chris-farleys-funeral-depicts-midwest-hollywood-cultures/article_3d91818c-5d40-507c-9772-3d1c1fa896c3.html.

365 "'Shrek': Chris Farley Recorded Nearly All of His Dialogue as the Original Green Ogre before His Tragic Death,", Showbiz Cheat Sheet, October 9, 2021, https://www.cheatsheet.com/entertainment/shrek-chris-farley-recorded-nearly-all-of-his-dialogue-before-death.html/.

366 Tom Farley Jr. and Tanner Colby, *The Chris Farley Show: A Biography in Three Acts* (New York: Viking, 2008).

367 Brian Boone, "The Tragic Real-Life Story of John Candy," Grunge, December 27, 2021, https://www.grunge.com/231219/the-tragic-real-life-story-of-john-candy/.

368 *I Am Chris Farley*, directed by Brent Hodge and Derik Murray (Canada: Network Entertainment, 2015).

369 *I Am Chris Farley*, directed by Brent Hodge and Derik Murray (Canada: Network Entertainment, 2015).

370 Associated Press, "Auburn Stuns Alabama with 109-Yard Field Goal Return to End It," ESPN, November 30, 2013, https://www.espn.com/college-football/recap/_/gameId/333340002.

371 David Wysong, "How Many National Championships Has Alabama Won in Football?" Sportscasting, January 1, 2021, https://www.sportscasting.com/how-many-national-championships-has-alabama-won-in-football/.

372 "Football Live vs. Dead Ball," Rookie Road, https://www.rookieroad.com/football/101/live-vs-dead-ball/.

373 Jeremy Henderson, "Iron Bowl Earthquake? 'Suspicious' Seismic Activity Registered Saturday as Far Away as Huntsville Correlated to Auburn's Last-Second Iron Bowl Touchdown," *The War Eagle Reader*, December 4, 2013, https://www.thewareaglereader.com/2013/12/iron-bowl-earthquake-suspicious-seismic-activity-registered-saturday-as-far-away-as-huntsville-correlates-to-auburns-last-second-touchdown-to-beat-alabama/.

374 Duane Rankin, "Iron Bowl, Davis 100-Yard TD Return Win ESPYs," *Montgomery Advertiser*, July 17, 2014, https://www.montgomeryadvertiser.com/story/rankinfile/2014/07/17/auburn-iron-bowl-win-davis-100-yard-td-return-win-espys/12774953/

375 "Rivalry Weekend: CBS Tops Overnights with Iron Bowl; ABC's Michigan–Ohio State Up," *Sports Business Journal*, December 2, 2013, https://www.sportsbusinessjournal.com/Daily/Issues/2013/12/02/Media/College-FB-TV.aspx.

376 John DeMarchi, "Is the 2013 Iron Bowl (Alabama vs. Auburn) the Most Dramatic Finish to a Football Game of All-Time?" *The Huffington Post*, December 2, 2013, https://www.huffpost.com/entry/is-the-2013-iron-bowl-ala_b_4372765.

377 Mike Lupica, "End of Auburn vs. Alabama Is One Second in College Football That Will Be Talked about Forever," *New York Daily News*, December 1, 2013, https://www.nydailynews.com/sports/college/lupica-auburn-alabama-talked-article-1.1533789.

378 Mike Vaccaro, "Auburn-Alabama Is Greatest Ending in Sports History," *New York Post*, November 30, 2013, https://nypost.com/2013/11/30/an-ending-well-never-forget/.

379 Brandon Marcello, "CBS Analyst Gary Danielson Compares Auburn's Iron Bowl Victory to Miracle on Ice," *The Birmingham News*, December 3, 2013, https://www.al.com/sports/2013/12/cbs_analyst_gary_danielson_com.html.

380 Garson O'Toole, "They May Forget What You Said, But They Will Never Forget How You Made Them Feel," Quote Investigator, accessed April 7, 2022, https:// quoteinvestigator.com/2014/04/06/they-feel/

381 Think I'm lying?: https://www.instagram.com/p/9FBDc4ivY1/.

382 Katharina Buchholz, "How Much of the Internet Consists of Porn?" Statista, February 11, 2019, https://www.statista.com/chart/16959/share-of-the-internet-that-is-porn/.

383 "How Porn Can Affect the Brain like a Drug," Fight the New Drug, https:// fightthenewdrug.org/how-porn-can-affect-the-brain-like-a-drug/.

384 Andy Conklin, "Pornhub, Parent Company MindGeek, Sued by Child Trafficking Survivors," Fox Business, February 18, 2021, https://www.foxbusiness.com/technology/ child-trafficking-survivors-lawsuit-pornhub-mindgeek.

385 *Breaking Bad*, season 4, episode 7, "Problem Dog," directed by Peter Gould, originally aired August 28, 2011, on AMC, https://www.netflix.com/title/70143836?source=35.

386 *Breaking Bad*, season 3, episode 1, "No Mas," directed by Bryan Cranston, originally aired March 21, 2010, on AMC, https://www.netflix.com/title/70143836?source=35.

387 Robbins, Mel, "How to Stop Screwing Yourself Over," filmed at TEDxSF, June 2011, TED video, https://www.ted.com/talks/mel_robbins_how_to_stop_screwing_yourself _over/up-next?language=en.

388 Scott Barry Kaufman, *Transcend: The New Science of Self-Actualization* (New York: TarcherPerigee, 2021), 59.

389 Dontreadthisblog.com ☺

390 Jordan Peterson, *12 Rules for Life: An Antidote to Chaos* (Toronto, Random House Canada, 2018), 62.

391 Associated Press, "Transcript & Video: President Donald Trump Addresses the Nation On the Coronavirus Pandemic," Colorado Public Radio News, March 11, 2020, https:// www.cpr.org/2020/03/11/transcript-video-president-donald-trump-addresses-the- nation-on-the-coronavirus-pandemic/.

392 Sarah Regen, "Everything to Know about Ego Death—From What It Is to How It Happens," mindbodygreenmindfulness, December 30, 2021, https://www.mindbodygreen. com/articles/ego-death.

393 Eckhart Tolle, *The Power of Now: A Guide to Spiritual Enlightenment*. (Vancouver, BC: Namaste Publishing, 1999).

394 Joseph Campbell, *The Hero with a Thousand Faces* (Navato: New World Library, 2008).

395 Mr. Purrington, "Carl Jung on the 'Loss of Ego,'" Carl Jung Depth Psychology, Children's Dream Seminar, December 30, 2019, https://carljungdepthpsychologysite. blog/2019/12/30/carl-jung-on-the-loss-of-the-ego/#.YexxvBPMIfE.

396 Nick Harwood, "The Flatbush Zombies Consider Themselves Better Off Dead," *Vice*, July 12, 2013, https://www.vice.com/en/article/6x4x76/the-flatbush-zombies-consider-themselves-better-off-dead.

397 For anyone else struggling, a good, cheap blocking technology is called Freedom, and a good community group to join is Fortify. They can both be downloaded in the App Store. For an organization that does a lot of great work on this subject, check out Fight the New Drug.

398 Don't Listen to This Podcast on all major platforms 😊

399 Grant Gordon, "Jon Gruden Resigns as Las Vegas Raiders Head Coach," NFL.com, October 11, 2021, https://www.nfl.com/news/jon-gruden-resigns-as-las-vegas-raiders-head-coach.

400 Nick Selbe, "Report: Jon Gruden Repeatedly Used Mysogynistic, Anti-LGBTQ Comments in Emails," *Sports Illustrated*, October 11, 2021, https://www.si.com/nfl/2021/10/12/jon-gruden-emails-homophobic-misogynistic-slurs-raiders-nfl.

401 Paul Gutierrez, "Carl Nassib of Las Vegas Raiders Announces He Is Gay, Pledges $100,000 to Trevor Project," ESPN, June 21, 2021, https://www.espn.com/nfl/story/_/id/31682318/carl-nassib-las-vegas-raiders-announces-gay.

402 Jim Reineking, "Jeff Fisher Responds to Jon Gruden's Claim Roger Goodell Pressured Rams to Draft Michael Sam," *USA Today*, October 12, 2021, https://www.usatoday.com/story/sports/nfl/2021/10/12/jeff-fisher-rams-didnt-draft-michael-sam-because-roger-goodell/8432575002/.

403 Jason Reid, "Eric Reid, Colin Kaepernick United in Legal Battle against the NFL," Andscape, May 3, 2018, https://theundefeated.com/features/eric-reid-colin-kaepernick-united-in-legal-battle-against-nfl/.

404 "Jon Gruden's Name Officially Removed from Buccaneers' Ring of Honor," Fox 13 News Tampa Bay, October 14, 2021, https://www.fox13news.com/sports/jon-grudens-name-officially-removed-from-buccaneers-ring-of-honor.

405 "Henry Ruggs III Drove 156 Mph Seconds before Fatal Car Crash, Prosecutors Say," ESPN, November 3, 2021, https://www.espn.com/nfl/story/_/id/32543330/henry-ruggs-iii-drove-156-mph-seconds-fatal-car-crash-prosecutors-say.

406 Alicia de Artola, "Derek Carr Reveals Text Message Henry Ruggs Sent Him before Deadly Crash," Fansided, November 2021, https://fansided.com/2021/11/06/derek-carr-text-message-henry-ruggs/.

407 AP, "Coroner: Tina Tintor Burned to Death in Henry Ruggs III Fatal Car Crash," MARCA, December 15, 2021, https://www.marca.com/en/nfl/las-vegas-raiders/2021/12/15/61b974c746163f85208b45a0.html.

408 Des Bieler, "Henry Ruggs III Formally Charged, Could Face At Least 50 Years in Prison," *The Washington Post*, November 10, 2021, https://www.washingtonpost.com/sports/2021/11/10/henry-ruggs-formally-charged-fatal-crash/.

409 Steve Gardner, "Tearful Randy Moss Responds to Jon Gruden's Email: 'National Football League, This Hurts Me,'" *USA Today*, October 10, 2021, https://www.usatoday.com/story/sports/nfl/2021/10/10/randy-moss-tears-up-jon-gruden-email-espns-nfl-countdown/6081266001/.

410 John Breech, "Raiders Reach Undisclosed Contract Settlement with Jon Gruden Just Weeks after Coach's Resignation Over Emails," CBS Sports, October 28, 2021, https://www.cbssports.com/nfl/news/raiders-reach-undisclosed-contract-settlement-with-jon-gruden-just-weeks-after-coachs-resignation-over-emails/.

CPSIA information can be obtained
at www.ICGtesting.com
Printed in the USA
LVHW101312060722
722846LV00006B/115/J